The Women of Hull House

The Women of Hull House

A study in spirituality,
vocation, and
friendship

ELEANOR J. STEBNER

State University
of
New York Press

Photographs of Helen Culver and Mary Keyser are
reprinted courtesy of Jane Addams Hull-House Museum at University
of Illinois at Chicago. Photos of the tea party, Mary Rozet Smith
and child, Jane Addams, Ellen Gates Starr, Alice Hamilton, Julia Lathrop,
Florence Kelley, Louise deKoven Bowen, and Mary Rozet Smith are
reprinted with permission from the Jane Addams Memorial Collection,
Special Collections, The University Library, University of Illinois at
Chicago.

Published by
State University of New York

© 1997 State University of New York

For information, address the State University of New York Press,
State University Plaza, Albany, NY 12246

Marketing by Fran Keneston
Production by Bernadine Dawes

Library of Congress Cataloging-in-Publication Data

Stebner, Eleanor J., 1960–
The women of Hull House : a study in spirituality, vocation, and friendship /
Eleanor J. Stebner.
p.   cm.
Includes bibliographical references and index.
ISBN 0-7914-3487-7 (HC acid-free). — ISBN 0-7914-3488-5 (PB acid-free)
1. Hull House (Chicago, Ill.)—History. 2. Social settlements—
Illinois—Chicago—History. 3. Addams, Jane, 1860–1935. 4. Women
workers—Illinois—Illinois—Chicago—Biography. I. Title.
HV4196.C4S74   1997
361.3′092′277311—dc21
[B]   97-4960
CIP

1 2 3 4 5 6 7 8 9 10

Without the love and support of my grandparents,

Elsie (Adam) Stebner and the late Fred Stebner,

my life would be very different.

As Meister Eckhart said,

the greatest prayer we can utter is

thank you.

Contents

Acknowledgments

THESE PAGES WERE ORIGINALLY WRITTEN as my dissertation proj-
ect for the Ph.D. in religious and theological studies from
Northwestern University and Garrett-Evangelical Theological
Seminary. I am indebted to my former advisor and mentor,
Rosemary Skinner Keller, and the members of my dissertation
committee, Rosemary Radford Ruether, Richard D. Tholin, and
Josef Barton. I owe the staff at the Hammond Library (Chicago
Theological Seminary), the United Library (Garrett-Evangelical
Theological Seminary and Seabury Theological Seminary), and
the Special Collections Library (University of Illinois at Chi-
cago) a great deal of thanks for their wise and detective-like
suggestions.

Many other people contributed to the completion of this
work. Thanks to Weaver Santiniello, Christopher Evans, Koby
Lee-Forman, Carol Allen, and Jeanne Mathews for time shared
in discussion, work, and enjoyment during the years we studied
together. Thanks to Linda Parrish, Administrative Assistant to

the Dean at the Chicago Theological Seminary, and Susan Hogan/Albach, friend and journalist, for their help in preparing the original manuscript. Special thanks to Alice Cudlipp and Mary Ruth Fox for their support and hospitality through the years. A note of deep gratitude to Christiane Kleiner, Annette K. Olsen, Cory L. Kemp, Bianca S. Rauch, Vicki Harder, Martin Forman, and Robert Ford for just being themselves.

Former students and colleagues at the Chicago Theological Seminary and current students and colleagues at the Faculty of Theology, University of Winnipeg, have been extremely supportive. I hope I have been as supportive of their work as they have been of mine.

Introduction

IN 1981, AS AN UNDERGRADUATE student at the University of Alberta, I took a survey course in American History and first heard the name of Jane Addams. My attention was captivated by a few remarks the professor made about her, especially the fact that she was one of the first women to be awarded the Nobel Peace Prize. I wrote my final paper on Addams. Never did I expect that, a decade later, I would be living in Chicago and pursuing a doctorate where Addams had lived and where Hull House was founded.

My interest in Hull House was renewed as I visited the Jane Addams' Hull House Museum on the University of Illinois-Chicago campus, and strolled the streets that now occupy the original social settlement site and neighborhood. Though much had changed in one hundred years, I could still imagine the dirt streets, horse carriages, unpainted wood tenements, and strewn debris that characterized nineteenth-century Chicago. Not everything needed imagination, however, for poverty remains in this area as do the struggles of how to live together socially, politically, and religiously. My curiosity about Hull House was spurred when I realized that its story involved not only Addams but a whole bunch of talented, ambitious, and fascinating women. The women of Hull House became my topic of inquiry.

While many themes could be studied in regard to the women of Hull House, spirituality, vocation, and friendship emerged as my primary foci. These themes emerged in differing degrees for the various Hull House women, reflecting not only different personalities and interests but also available research materials. The themes resonate not only as issues of personal interest. The popularity of Robert Bellah's books, for example, *Habits of the Heart* and *The Good Society*, show these themes as holding contemporary interest for a wide variety of people.[1]

The spirituality of the women of Hull House reflected changes within late-nineteenth-century society related to a dissatisfaction with dominant Protestant evangelicalism and emerging pluralism. The Christian religion in which many of these women were raised did not satisfy either their minds or their hearts. Some of them decided not to speak publicly in religious language, while at least one of them became more religious by converting to Roman Catholicism and becoming a religious sister (nun). Pragmatism has usually been the word used to communicate the spiritual leanings of women like Addams and their desire to transform evangelical Protestantism into a practical source of personal and political power.[2] The social settlement movement of which they were a part has not been studied within the Christian historical tradition (as has the parallel and male-dominated social gospel movement) because their work has been labeled humanistic in its social, economic, and political pursuits. Although these women would not deny being humanists, they also would not deny being religious or spiritual. This characteristic differentiates women reformers of the late nineteenth century from their twentieth-century counterparts.

In this project, spirituality is distinguished from religion. Spirituality refers to a sense of the sacredness and mystery of life, and an openness to the varied experiences of humankind. Religion refers to adherence to historically formed and communally affirmed creedal definitions and practices of mystery.

Intellectual adherence to a particular religious framework—in this case, Christianity—also typically calls for certain practices of devotion, such as church attendance, prayer, tithing, etc. Spirituality, in contrast to religiosity, is much more individualistic and often is based on a personal sense of experience, morals, and ideals. Carol Ochs, a professor of philosophy, defined religion as group consensus into the insights of human experience from which humans can learn to live. In contrast, she defined spirituality as the process of going beyond intellectual knowledge or a conceptualization of reality that puts humans in touch with their emotions, experiences, and life in general.[3]

Spirituality and religion are not mutually exclusive, nor is one way better than the other (although the last assertion would be highly disputed by some individuals). A person can be spiritual and religious, religious but not spiritual, or spiritual but not religious. While the distinctions often overlap, the general differences seem more than apparent. In learning about the women of Hull House, I realized that most of them would have been much more comfortable identifying themselves as spiritual rather than religious. This emphasis, however, does not mean that they were secular or atheist or agnostic; it means that the formal religious life of their day did not provide an overriding and underlying meaning to their experiences and visions that influenced how they spent their time and energy.

A sense of vocation was integral to the spirituality of the women of Hull House. Vocation can simply be defined as the work or the job in which one engages. In this sense, it refers to how people make a living, pay their bills, support themselves and their loved ones. More broadly, however, vocation is an expression of spirituality. It relates to how one regards one's place in the universe, one's specific purpose in life, and one's relations to all living beings. It includes what one perceives to be both duty and delight.

From a Christian religious perspective, vocation has often been defined as including the twin categories of call and service. It has been understood as the way in which a person serves or glorifies God with all of one's life, and in so doing, perhaps serves humankind. Although lip service has been given to the concept of the "priesthood of all believers," Christian vocation has usually been designated or recognized as occurring only within ecclesiastical structures.

The implications of vocation, therefore, have been different for men and for women: Men, desirous of a sense of vocation, have most often assumed roles of monk, priest, pastor, or clergy (and, sometimes, teacher); women, seeking a sense of vocation, have most often assumed roles of nun, wife, or mother. Only recently have women gained official, ordained entry into traditional church vocations—an entry, it must be added, acceptable only within liberal Protestantism and Judaism. Needless to say, even this has not occurred without major battles regarding the nature of women, their ideal role and duty in society, and their overall purpose in living. Vocation, in other words, has most often been gender specific.

The women of Hull House provide an example of the struggle to obtain a sense of vocation within a society that severely limited women's choices. In looking at them, we learn—if we did not know before—that vocation includes more than ecclesiastical service. Those people who stand outside of official church leadership structures and those people who are even critical of orthodox religion and much more willing to talk of spirituality than religion, search for meaning in their lives and a greater, overarching purpose to their activities. The women of Hull House sought the same. They desired to be useful in a time of rapidly changing mores and increasing social problems.[4] Although these women lived and worked one hundred years ago, in many ways their time is not so different from our time.

In addition, vocation has usually been interpreted individualistically. Even in monastic settings, the emphasis has been on individuals uniting in a common, shared life for practical purposes, rather than on the relations shared between individuals for purposes of mutual companionship, support, and love. Friendship, especially exclusive or particular friendship, has most often been curtailed and strictly regulated in monastic settings. Such relationships are viewed as divisive to the whole community and nullifying of one's personal vocational ideals.

For the women of Hull House, vocational goals were innately tied to friendship circles. Mary E. Hunt's definition of friendship refers to "voluntary human relationships that are entered into by people who intend one another's well-being and who intend that their love relationship is part of a justice-seeking community."[5] Friendship occurs even when friends do not agree with each other on political, social, or theological agendas, or when friends differ in race and class. It occurs when friends view society through radically differing lenses of reality. Of course, not all acquaintances become friends, and often friends become estranged. The women of Hull House were human, and their relationships show this reality as well.

For the women of Hull House, much of the connection between vocation and friendship occurred through sharing living space. Hull House was their home. Although men lived there and were part of the community, it was primarily women's space, and women—mostly single women—were its undisputed leaders. Not all the women of Hull House lived there, however. The crucial variable was that they intentionally maintained contact despite busy schedules, business trips, and geographical moves. While it is difficult to determine exactly the kinds of friendships these women shared—after all, most of us do not keep detailed notes of our friends, what we do together, what we debate over coffee or dinner or on the telephone—it is possible to at least point toward the interrelationships shared between these women.

In its own time, Hull House was often thought of as a kind of monastery, and the women of Hull House, as nuns of a "secular" kind. This kind of designation shows the lack of conceptual language available to talk about women living and working together, tying together spiritual, vocational, and friendship ideals. If this kind of definition is needed, perhaps the women of Hull House compare most closely to the Beguines of the twelfth and thirteenth centuries. As a loosely organized movement deemed religious by some and heretical by others, the Beguines involved women who attempted to live independent lives within a society that had little space for women's independence. Beguines did not take vows of celibacy or assume seclusion, but rather, were very much involved in the affairs of their day. While the Beguine movement did involve men—the Beghards—who also lived in communities and were active doing "good works" in their society, it was primarily a female movement.[6]

By focusing on the themes of spirituality, vocation, and friendship, this project offers a different slant to the previous interpretations of Hull House. Questions to be explored include: What were the religious or spiritual understandings of the women of Hull House? How were their vocational desires exemplified? What were their personal ties, and how did their relationships affect their vocations and expressions of spirituality? Because I examine the lives of numerous women who comprised Hull House and not just Jane Addams, one immediate result of this project is to make known the names and life stories of women who have been forgotten during the last century. Many of these women were as well known as Addams during their lifetimes but, for various reasons, have faded into the oblivion.

This project is divided into two parts. Part One provides an overview of the historical setting of Hull House. Part Two examines the lives of some of the women of Hull House. Chapter 1 reviews the secondary literature that has been produced on Hull House, on the women who lived and worked there, and on the theoretical explanations for women's involvement in the social settlement movement. Chapter 2 places Hull House into the context of the social settlement movement and in so doing compares it to the more overt religious movements of the nineteenth century such as the social gospel, the social mission, and the institutional churches. Chapter 3 provides a historical sketch of the city of Chicago. Chicago not only has a fascinating history, but it is a microcosm of the changing society of the United States in the late nineteenth century.

Chapters 4, 5, and 6 comprise Part Two, and are the heart of the project. The content of these chapters is selective. Only a handful of women can be discussed even though Hull House attracted a myriad of talented people. Chapter 4 discusses the co-founders of Hull House, Jane Addams and Ellen Gates Starr, as well as Mary Keyser, the housekeeper they initially hired to move into Hull House with them. Because Addams and Starr provide such a major contrast in how they lived their spiritual lives, spirituality and religion is emphasized in this chapter. Chapter 5 focuses on the residential aspects of Hull House and on three particular women who found their vocational niches through Hull House and went on to become leading figures in social reform within U.S. society: Julia Lathrop, Florence Kelley, and Alice Hamilton. Questions of vocation are specifically discussed in relation to the lives of Lathrop, Kelley, and Hamilton. Chapter 6 focuses on the institutional aspects of Hull House and discusses three elite and wealthy women who became Hull House trustees: Helen Culver, Mary Rozet Smith, and Louise deKoven Bowen. While these last women may simply be considered examples of nineteenth-century philanthropists, the insights they give—especially when connected with the lives of the other Hull House women—regarding the importance of friendships within communities that seek social change are most fascinating.

Among all the women discussed, attention is given to their religious or spiritual motivations, to their vocational strivings and social reform work, and to their interactions as colleagues and friends. As with some recent feminist scholarship, I argue that for women in particular, these themes go hand in hand. While the women of Hull House exhibited a remarkable range of spiritual and religious motives, Hull House provided the space for them to develop their vocational niches and the personal relations necessary to sustain their lives and their work. This study suggests that individual actions for social change must be grounded in a shared sense of spirituality involving personal and communal aspects. A level of uniting vision is necessary, as is space for diverse actions and varied viewpoints.

This research could be categorized as a group biography.[7] Conventional biographies study in depth the life of one person; group biographies focus on numerous individuals. Conventional biographies often assume a Great Man (literally) approach to history, whereas group biographies assume that transformation occurs through more than individual efforts. A group biography assumes a community system wherein individuals are both influenced by and influential of one another. Their personal characteristics may be similar and/or contrasting, but it is their relations that make the group. By its very definition, group biography provides a window into historical periods that focuses on individuals connecting as social beings rather than on individuals acting as solitary figures. It attempts to delineate the complexity of human life and social change.

While the term, group biography, is contradictory, its contrariety is helpful in pointing out the tension existent in traditional methods of historical interpretation as well as the tension existent in the lives of many contemporary people.

I explore this topic from the position of my own particularities. I am a white woman raised within evangelical Protestantism. I am ordained to speak in religious language and to officially act within Protestant Christian communities, yet like many Christians before me and with me, I am dissatisfied with only this kind of discourse or action. I am especially perturbed about elitist claims made by many religious people (whatever their theological bent) and the difficulty many people of faith have connecting their theological beliefs with issues of economic, social, and environmental justice. I am a product of late-nineteenth-century European immigration to the North American continent and am one generation removed from the farming communities of Western Canada. While in my early twenties, I moved to the United States and have lived in various cities within this nation state. Through the years, I have become more North American in outlook than either Canadian or American, and more urban in lifestyle than rural. My own spiritual and vocational journey is intimately tied to my interpersonal relationships with women and men. I am educated in Western-style thought and knowledge (as some of my Asian students have very kindly pointed out to me), and am privileged in my access to educational and professional opportunities. I am economically self-supportive but have never had either ample money or leisure time.

These personal characteristics influence and impact my general perceptions of the world and my specific interpretations of the women of Hull House. Each reader will bring her or his own particularities to the interpretation of the data, and for this, I am thankful. The institution of Hull House, its location in the social world of the late nineteenth century and the emerging modernism of the twentieth century, and the lives of the people who were involved in it, are worth much more contemplation and interpretation than I alone can give in this project.

Part One

The Context of Hull House

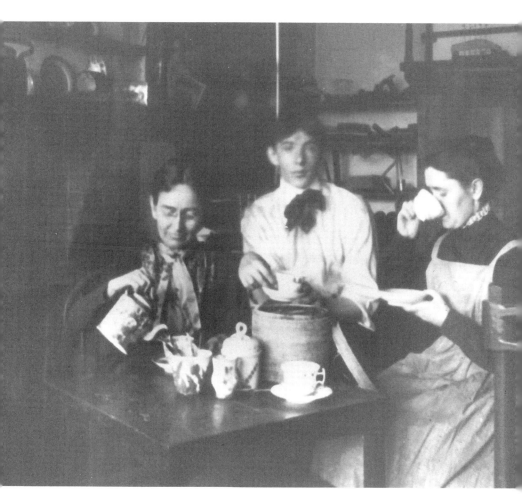

Ellen Gates Starr pouring tea, Jane Addams sipping, unidentified woman in the middle

1

Review of Literature

Hull House was founded on the near west side of Chicago in 1889 and became the most famous social settlement house in the United States, if not the entire world. Only twenty years after opening, it mushroomed from a second-floor rental space in an old dilapidated house to a well-planned, multi-purpose building complex encompassing a city block.[1] By its very size, Hull House stood apart from its community.[2]

Thousands of people—neighbors as they were called in settlement lingo—passed through its doors on a weekly basis to participate in a myriad of social, educational, and political activities.[3] These activities ranged from the mundane to the radical. There were clubs for girls, boys, women, and men; classes on art, music, literature, drama, and philosophy; lectures on socialism, Christianity, and suffrage; basketball games in the gymnasium, which also housed public bath facilities; groups organizing picnics and groups picketing unfair labor practices; clinics caring for baby health and teaching nutrition to young mothers; and meetings on improving sanitation and garbage collection. Hull House even had a coffee shop that provided reasonably priced hot lunches for working people, as well as breakfast and dinner for its staff.

Its activities intersected with and impacted the lives of many neighborhood people.[4] They were not the only ones, however, attracted to Hull House. A "salon in the slum" is how one historian described the magnetism of Hull House.[5] As a salon in the slum, Hull House became the place for budding reformers, esoteric intellectuals, foreign princes, and idealistic journalists to gather. At the least, such people would visit, have dinner, and engage in stimulating conversation. British journalist William Stead spent his evenings relaxing and talking with the folks at the house while researching his book, *If Christ Came to Chicago.*[6]

The regular work of Hull House relied on people other than visiting dignitaries and obscure revolutionaries. In order to maintain its multi-faceted programs, Hull House needed workers and leaders. People from the middle- and upper-middle classes filled these roles. These people, both women and men, led the clubs and classes, planned the picnics and parties, protested the neglect and corruption of government or business, and managed the calendars and balanced the budgets of this growing institution.

Many of the people who volunteered their time and energy did so on a sporadic or temporary basis. As a result, they remain as anonymous to us as the thousands of neighbors who used the Hull House facilities. At most, their involvement may be recorded by their unidentified presence in a black and white snapshot or by a brief reference in a *Hull-House Bulletin.*[7]

Other workers were involved in Hull House over longer periods of time, as popular club leaders or wealthy patrons. Louise deKoven Bowen, for example, who lived most of her life in a mansion on Astor Street in a wealthy section of Chicago, was present at Hull House almost daily for more than forty years.[8] She served in a number of different roles, as Woman's Club President, Hull House Trustee, and Treasurer. She was also benefactor *extraordinaire,* providing the funds to build Bowen Hall (which housed the Boy's Club) and donating seventy-two acres of land in Waukegan, a community forty miles north of

Chicago on Lake Michigan, to establish a Hull House Country Club in memory of her late husband.[9]

The social settlement concept, however, centered on the role of resident. Residents were workers who lived at the house (or in its compound). They usually paid their own room and board through outside work and volunteered their time and skills to the life of the house. The presence of residents made social settlements different from other organizations in the late nineteenth century, such as mission agencies or institutional churches.[10] Indeed, the idea of individuals moving into a neighborhood—settling in as neighbors—gave the movement its very name. The settlement movement was a conscious attempt of middle- and upper-middle-class folks to cross boundaries of class and ethnicity, and to connect with others usually identified as different from themselves on a human, everyday basis.

Hull House has been the focus of many studies through the years. Most of these studies originated from within the broad disciplines of history and sociology. As a way to summarize the multitudinous research on Hull House, I have categorized the materials into four parts: (1) those works focusing on specific people, namely, on Jane Addams or one of the other Hull House workers; (2) those studies analyzing the involvement of women in the social settlement movement, and the variables of home, profession, and ideals of Victorian womanhood; (3) those works alluding to or evaluating the religious underpinnings of settlement workers; and (4) the most contemporary critiques of Hull House which center on issues of race and class.

Addams and Cohorts

In its early decades, Hull House comprised an amazing group of residents. Long-term residents included not only co-founders Jane Addams and Ellen Gates Starr, but also Mary Keyser, Julia Lathrop, Florence Kelley, Alzina Stevens, and Alice Hamilton. Many books and articles have been written about Jane Addams, some of which are solid academic works and others which reflect an idealized, mythical, and saintly Addams.[11]

Historian Jill Conway suggested that Addams came to be seen as a sage or prophetess and is remembered and studied because she epitomized the nineteenth-century "stereotype of the female temperament."[12] Conway said women such as Addams were celebrated and uplifted because their wisdom was designated as coming from innate femininity. The role of sage contrasts with the category of expert. Women experts or scientists such as Florence Kelley, Julia Lathrop, and Alice Hamilton, were not celebrated or remembered because they did not fulfill nineteenth-century feminine ideals.

Another historian, Gerda Lerner, said women's history generally has been done on two levels—compensatory history and contribution history. Scholars focused on Addams because of the perception that she was exceptional in comparison to other, more ordinary women. Lerner referred to this interpretation as compensatory history. At the same time that attention was granted to Addams in this compensatory manner, she was not granted innovative interpretations. Rather, she was perceived as supporting the traditional male historical framework of the progressive movement, and interpreted only in terms of how she contributed to predetermined historical frameworks. Emphasis on Addams' contribution to progressive politics misfocused her significance. Lerner concluded:

> [Therefore], Jane Addams' enormous contribution in creating a supporting female network and new structures for living are subordinated to her role as a Progressive, or to an interpretation which regards her as merely representative of a group of frustrated college-trained women with no place to go. In other words, a deviant from male-defined norms.[13]

The interpretations offered by Conway and Lerner help explain twentieth-century North American historiography. Addams came to be solely identified with Hull House and Hull House with Addams. Historians generally overlooked or forgot the fact that other very capable, talented, and spirited reformers—who were Addams' friends and companions—lived and worked at Hull House. This occurred despite the fact that the first biography of Addams written after her death by her nephew, James Weber Linn, contained a chapter devoted to six other women of Hull House: Ellen Gates Starr, Julia Lathrop, Florence Kelley, Louise deKoven Bowen, Alice Hamilton, and Mary Rozet Smith. Linn wrote: "A biography of Jane Addams that did not include special mention of this group would be absurd."[14]

Few scholars have focused on these other women of Hull House. Indeed, in comparison to the sources available on Addams, the research is deficient. Just before her death in 1935, Jane Addams wrote a biography of Julia Lathrop which remains the only major source on Lathrop's life.[15] The life of Alice Hamilton, with a focus on her medical research work, was examined in a 1967 biography by Madeleine P. Grant.[16] A collection of her personal letters with helpful commentary by Barbara Sicherman has added a fuller dimension to Hamilton's long life, family, friends, and work.[17] No major biographical work has been published on Ellen Gates Starr, who was a key figure in the Hull House group. Still, most of the women of Hull House were given brief sketches in *Notable American Women: A Biographical Dictionary, 1607–1950.*[18]

Other than Addams, the most research on a Hull House woman has been on Florence Kelley. Josephine Goldmark, a friend and younger colleague of Florence Kelley, wrote a rather idealized yet very personal book about Kelley in 1953. Dorothy Rose Blumberg later wrote a biography focusing on Kelley's social action.[19] Kathryn Kish Sklar edited the autobiography of Kelley, which was a reprint of articles originally published in various issues of *The Survey Graphic.* More significantly, Sklar has spent the last ten years researching and writing a biography of Kelley which examines her tremendous influence within women's political culture in the United States.[20]

Most of the biographical work to date on Hull House women, including that on Addams and Kelley, has emphasized their political actions and agendas. Relatively little attention has been directed toward other aspects of their lives, from their interpersonal relationships to their religious motivations. Rebecca L. Sherrick examined the public persona of Hull House women in light of their personal lives in her 1980 dissertation on the women of Hull House. She discovered that several key Hull House women shared similar childhoods and college experiences. Sherrick argued that Hull House provided women with the opportunity to utilize their abilities in progressive politics and society while at the same time fulfilling nineteenth-century ideals regarding women's home roles.[21]

Only three other studies examine the group of women in the context of Hull House. Kathryn Kish Sklar examined the women of Hull House during the decade of the 1890s. She discussed the women's friendships and support for one another as well as revealing connections the women of Hull House had with other reformers, who were almost always men. Sklar argued that the social power of the women of Hull House came from both their internal (i.e., Hull House group) and external (i.e., extra-Hull House ties) support networks.[22]

The work of Sklar was validated and extended in a 1991 study by Robyn Muncy. Muncy focused on the political and social reforms the women of Hull House undertook and argued that their success was due less to their connections with one another than to the interconnections they established with more powerful male reformers. The metaphor of a political dominion was used by Muncy to analyze both the independence and the dependence of the women of Hull House.[23]

In regard to this specific project, a 1986 article by Virginia Kemp Fish was most useful.[24] Fish discussed what she called the Hull House circle, the groups of women that lived and worked at Hull House during different time periods. Writing from a sociological perspective and utilizing biography and history, she examined the friendship networks that resulted in successful reform work and the overlapping of personal and public activities. Fish argued that Jane Addams and Hull House became the lifelong leitmotif of the inner circle of Hull House women: "Friendships begun there endured, were strengthened and reinforced by the same and overlapping interests, organizational memberships, and social reform efforts."[25] Fish identified two circles of Hull House women. The first circle comprised Julia Lathrop, Florence Kelley, and Alice Hamilton, who came to live and work at Hull House between 1890 and 1897. A later circle developed in the first decade of the twentieth century and included Grace and Edith Abbott and Sophonisba Breckinridge. This project expands upon the first circle of Hull House women as identified by Fish.[26]

Overall, previous research on individuals connected to Hull House has focused on Addams, with some work done on Kelley and Hamilton. Regardless, the few works that explore the interconnections between the Hull House women are significant. Research such as that provided by Fish has been foundational for this project, especially in its identification of the key women of Hull House and its focus on friendship ties.

Women's Space

Hull House was primarily a women's community, although it was one of the first settlements to provide housing for women and men as well as for married couples and families. The fact that it was women's space is not surprising since between the years 1889 and 1914, three-fifths of all social settlement residents were women.[27] Most of these women were single, white, and college educated.[28]

Women embarked on settlement residency for many different reasons. Some joined because of curiosity, wanting to know how the poorer classes lived, or desirous of adventure, wanting to expand their personal life experiences. Some joined because of a sense of idealism, wanting to personally address the social problems of the late nineteenth century. Some joined because as the first generation of college educated women, they had nothing else to do short of domestic duty (marriage and motherhood), grade school teaching, or missionary service.

Psychological interpretations have often been used to explain the attraction of late-nineteenth-century women to the social settlement movement. Probably the most significant biographer of Addams, Allen F. Davis, said in 1967: "[A]mong the many influences that combined to create the settlement impulse, anxiety, alienation, and guilt were important."[29] A contemporary of Davis, Daniel Levine, suggested that the social settlement movement provided a public outlet for essentially internal feelings:

Restlessness and unhappiness in turn drove many strong-willed and capable women into social reform or social service of some sort. The temperance, settlement house, and suffrage movements all benefitted from the leadership of this sort of woman.[30]

Gerda Lerner would argue that to wholeheartedly accept the interpretations of these scholars would be to engage in writing history by placing women in a "male-defined world." The interpretations of Davis and Levine negated the experience of white, middle-class women during the last decade of the last century. Social historian and theorist Christopher Lasch provided a more positive framework than either Davis or Levine for the reality of restlessness which afflicted well-educated, elite women in the late nineteenth century. He contended that restlessness was existent because such women had no place to focus either their abilities or their energies.[31] Jane Addams used the term "family claim" versus "social claim" to summarize what many nineteenth-century women attempted in stepping out of their prescribed female roles of domesticity into public roles of reform.[32]

Some scholars have suggested that the women who chose social settlement life were attempting to replicate college dormitory living or, at the least, expand the concept of home into the larger society.[33] For example, Judith Ann Trolander wrote that one of the important factors regarding social settlements was that they provided not only an occupation but also a home. In so doing, social settlements provided a legitimate option to privileged women seeking alternatives to traditional roles:

> [Women] sought not only an occupation but a substitute for traditional family life. . . . Residence in the settlement house was a lot like [the college dormitory]. Furthermore, since the stated purpose was to help the poor, young women who eschewed family obligations to be settlement residents could hardly be accused of selfishness. The semi-protected environment of the settlement house was respectable, and the camaraderie among the residents provided an alternative to family life.[34]

Historian Carl N. Degler also argued that the social settlement, and later, social work, was an acceptable occupation for nineteenth-century women because it simply extended the boundaries of the home into the larger society:

The settlement house, in short, was the extension of women's traditional role into the tenement and the slum. It enlisted all the sympathy, understanding, warmth, and emotion which were ascribed to women by the principle of separate spheres. Although settlement-house work was literally outside the home, and a profession that not infrequently deflected women from marriage and motherhood, it nevertheless was easily accommodated to the idea of separate spheres. It did not contradict the popular view that women and men were different and properly engaged in different spheres of work. At the same time, however, settlement work clearly offered a career and useful service to educated women.[35]

Other scholars have pointed out how settlement work initiated and supported the emerging social science fields. Early research conducted through Hull House and other social settlements provided a wealth of data for the nascent discipline of sociology.[36] In fact, in 1895 the Hull House residents published *Hull-House Maps and Papers*, a book which Mary Jo Deegan said started the Chicago school of sociology.[37] Deegan also argued that the significance of the work of Hull House residents was not fully recognized because it was done mostly by women outside an affiliation with an educational institution such as the University of Chicago.

This kind of research indicates a crucial link between the need for occupational opportunities as well as alternatives to traditional home life. In this way, the need for women's space existed on a multidimensional plane. Women were not restless simply due to internal psychological problems, but were restless because their choices were limited in both private and public arenas. Women needed both public and private (or personal) space within nineteenth-century society, space that would allow them to use and develop their skills, and space to live as independent adults. Both goals were interrelated.

Religious/Spiritual Ideals

Few scholars have pointed out the religious motives for settlement women. Of those who do, some argue that such religious motivations emerged from late-nineteenth-century liberal Christianity. Historian Clarke Chambers, for example, wrote that many social settlement leaders used Christian rhetoric to express ideals of nineteenth-century humanitarianism:

> Steeped in nineteenth-century humanitarianism, many settlement leaders expressed their motives in words and tones familiar to a Bible-reading and Bible-believing generation. They echoed the cries for social justice of Old Testament prophecy, and took seriously the redemptive power that Christ released in the New [Testament]. . . . They sought not "righteousness" for a "scattered few," but "a more abundant life for all."[38]

The religious motivation of settlement women has usually been interpreted as humanitarian or humanist. This is especially apparent when compared to the religious motives of women who got involved in more traditional evangelical work such as city or foreign missions.[39] Unlike these latter women, religious proselytizing was not the goal or vision of settlement women. Rather, they wanted to engage in service to humanity based on principles all people—Protestants and Roman Catholics, for example—could affirm. The women of Hull House sought to be religious in the broader understanding of the word, meaning that their motivations were spiritual rather than religious. They advocated a "religion of humanity," as Mina Carson argued in a book on settlement folk.[40] Put differently, the women of Hull House did not seek the religious conversion of others, but attempted to draw upon common religious principles shared by a variety of people and to engage in service to humanity.

Scholars have debated the question of how social settlement women received their religious ideals of service to humanity. The ideal of service may have emerged out of patterns of self-sacrifice prescribed for Victorian women. In this regard, ideals of Victorian womanhood, with the corresponding principles of mothering altruism and inherent female moral characteristics may explain the desire to engage in service embodied by the Hull House women.[41]

Jane Addams perhaps best expressed the religious foundation and service ideal of the social settlement movement in an early article called "The Subjective Necessity for Social Settlements." She saw involvement in the social settlement as an attempt to humanize Christianity and, at the same time, make religion less sectarian. Addams wrote that the early Christians "believed in love as a cosmic force. . . . They identified themselves with slaves. . . . They longed to share the common lot." She identified young people in the nineteenth century as seeking this aspect of Christ's message:

> They resent the assumption that Christianity is a set of ideas which belong to the religious consciousness, whatever that may be, that it is a thing to be proclaimed and instituted apart from the social life of the community. . . . The Settlement movement is only one manifestation of that wider humanitarian movement which . . . is endeavoring to embody itself, not in a sect, but in society itself.[42]

She concluded by arguing that the social settlement reflected the "renaissance of the early Christian humanitarianism." It was occurring, she said, without much writing, philosophizing, or talking, but "with a bent to express in social service, in terms of action, the spirit of Christ."[43]

Jean Bethke Elshtain, a political ethicist, reviewed the life and action of Addams and wrote that scholars must come to understand Addams as a social theorist whose basis was Christianity:

> Addams viewed her world through the prism of Christian symbols and injunctions, purposes and meanings. These gave her world its shape . . . [and] conviction that the moral life consists in "the imitation of Christ," not in abstract obedience to a formal model of moral conduct.[44]

The aim of Hull House, Elshtain said, was to "meet the needs of Addams and others like her to put their beliefs into practice, to lead lives of action . . . . To serve but in serving to reveal oneself." According to Elshtain, late-nineteenth-century society, though "[p]aternalistic, hypocritical, and stifling," especially toward its women, instilled in its young people through Christian religious principles a final conviction that a "*human* life is one lived with purpose, dignity, and honor."[45]

Stephen Kalberg, a scholar in the field of social work, reviewed the lives of selected people involved in the settlement movement. He discovered settlement leaders were not raised in environments of liberal Christianity, an assumption often made by historians. They were raised in homes that upheld staunch religious principles as well as participation in political action. Kalberg argued that both these factors were necessary in directing individuals into settlement work:

> If either traditional religious or political perspectives had been taught to them exclusively, the career reformers might have become leaders in the churches or joined one of the many political movements of their day. . . . In effect, they sought a synthesis of the two socialization orientations—the religious and the political—dominant in their homes.[46]

If Kalberg's thesis is correct, it is possible to view the women of Hull House as combining both religious and reform ideals. In so doing, they expanded the definition of religion and anchored reform in spiritual principles. Acknowledging and using the prescribed Victorian roles in society, the women of Hull House redefined ideals regarding their responsibility as guardians of the home and of true religion. Much to their surprise, they became reformers within the larger social context, as Robyn Muncy noted:

> Settlement workers did not set out to become reformers. They were rather women trying to fulfill existing social expectations for self-sacrificing female service while at the same time satisfying their need for public recogni-

tion, authority, and independence. In the process of attempting to weave together a life of service and professional accomplishment, they became reformers as the
wider world defined them.[47]

The kinds of activities offered by social settlements were replaced in later years by community or neighborhood centers,
and the leadership switched from being primarily female to
being almost exclusively male.[48] The leadership transition resulted in the emergence of social workers, people who were both
specifically trained and salaried.[49] Concomitantly, the religious
underpinnings of social work lessened. Clarke Chambers found
that latter generations of social workers were embarrassed by the
religious idealism of the initial social settlement workers:

[A]lthough the official and private statements alike of
settlement leaders continued to proclaim spiritual motives and goals, the religiosity of the pioneer generation began to pale in the 1920's and the younger
generation tended to build other, though often related,
rationales [for their work]. The younger generation, entering settlement work during the interwar years,
tended to be embarrassed at times and sometimes impatient with the unashamed piety of their elders.[50]

The fact is that the social settlement movement in the nineteenth century was very much a spiritual and—to a certain extent—a religious movement. The women of Hull House were
motivated in their work by the ideals—and the shortcomings—
of the Judeo-Christian tradition. Kathryn Kish Sklar, in a paper
presented at the 100th anniversary of the founding of Hull
House, argued that it was only after 1920 that women's political
culture in the United States lost its anchoring in religious and
moral authority. The factors that explain why this is the case
need further study. While the scope of this project does not
allow for a detailed analysis of the early twentieth century, some
of the factors contributing to the loss of religious and spiritual
ideals become clearer by looking at the experiences the women
of Hull House had with dominant Christianity in their day.

Race and Class

Recent scholarship has identified class and race issues inherent in the settlement movement generally and in Hull House specifically. Thomas Lee Philpott raised concerns regarding the allocation of leadership roles within Hull House to white, middle-class people rather than to the neighbors who were to benefit from the many programs.[51] This paternalism of Hull House workers resulted in their inadvertently engaging in the regulation of the lifestyles of the poor. As a consequence of this paternalism, negative outcomes resulted from good intentions. For example, Hull House has often been praised for establishing the first public playground in the city of Chicago. Philpott pointed out, however, what is usually not noted, which is that a block of tenements had to be destroyed to establish the playground. The "dispossessed tenants . . . mourned their loss of homes" and, quite understandably, came to regard the Hull House workers as callous.[52]

From late-twentieth-century perspectives and understandings of mutuality and multiculturalism, the lack of shared decision-making power and direct involvement of the neighbors is problematic. Reflective of a Victorian mind set, the worker/neighbor division shows the presence of strict class, ethnic, and race divisions within nineteenth-century society. Historian Rivka Shpak Lissak said that Hull House workers wanted to eliminate these divisions by simply assimilating ethnic working-class neighbors into middle-class, white Anglo-Saxon Protestant culture. Only unintentionally did Hull House work lead to the growth of pluralistic ideals within the larger society.[53] Other scholars have also studied the settlement house and its role in immigrant assimilation, acculturation, and Americanization.[54]

Another historian, Gwendolyn Mink, similarly argued that the formation of the welfare state was based on class and race assumptions; namely, that white, Northern European, middle- and upper-middle-class Protestant women needed to uplift the poor, working, African American, Central or Southern European Catholic or Jewish immigrants, and instill, especially in mothers, values suitable for future U.S. citizens.[55] Mink suggested that these desired reforms were not based on white supremacy but on the desire for race improvement (a common nineteenth-century term used to refer to the human race). But Thomas Philpott suggested that Jane Addams and the workers of Hull House simply showed no understanding of the difference between economic and racial injustice.[56]

Issues of race and class need to be acknowledged when examining the women who comprised Hull House. By and large, they were privileged women and had luxuries not available to other women of the nineteenth century. Their ideals regarding class and race were reflective of the dominant white, middle- and upper-middle-class Protestant culture of their time. Today, we easily identify inherent classism and racism in some of their thoughts and actions. These characteristics cannot be ignored in doing a historical study. Still, it is inappropriate to apply late-twentieth-century standards to nineteenth-century persons. People must be understood in relation to their own time and historical judgments need to be historically grounded. This does not mean, however, that contemporary critiques are unnecessary or irrelevant. Acknowledging limitations and past injustices is crucial, and provides insight for our present culture and our attempts to create a more just society.

Summary and Aims

Previous research on Hull House women and the settlement movement can be summarized as follows: (1) Addams has been remembered and uplifted because she embodied acceptable and exceptional conceptions of nineteenth-century womanhood, which her cohorts, who have been largely ignored, did not symbolize. (2) White Protestant women of the middle- and upper-middle classes, especially those who were college educated, pushed the boundaries allotted to them regarding their place within the larger society and how they were to live their personal lives. (3) Religious ideals, perhaps more accurately labelled as spiritual ideals, were a significant basis for the involvement of settlement workers and motivation for their vocational ideals and life. (4) Hull House women generally perpetuated attitudes of classism and racism because of their own social location and their general ignorance of the consequences of their well-intentioned behaviors.

This project is a new contribution to the historical and sociological works that have already been done on Hull House. By engaging in a study based on a group rather than on an individual, the multifarious nature of Hull House becomes clear. Yet the problem of source materials then arises. Because so many of the women are not not well known, autobiographies and biographies, combined with scant other primary and secondary sources, become the basis for interpretation. Despite this limitation, a wide range of experiences and visions of some of the Hull House women seep through to the present time. These women were all talented and skilled. Addams, the leader of their house, was not any more exceptional than many of her friends and associates. These women show not only the significance of higher education for women and the ensuring possibilities for female professionalization, but the centrality of claiming vocational dreams and the essentiality of a solid friendship base and shared community. They show the importance of seeking an ultimate sense of meaning that encompasses all that we are, do, and say, even if this means breaking down, ignoring, or redefining certain societal understandings of gender distinctions, private and public divisions, and orthodox religious assumptions. In this way, the women of Hull House provide not only a window into the past, but a reflection back into the present. We learn about ourselves and our society as we explore the world of the women of Hull House.

2

The Social Settlement Movement
and Christianity

Love of God and love of neighbour hang together.
—Samuel Barnett, *The Service of God* [1897]

DURING THE HEYDAY OF THE social settlement movement, much discussion and debate occurred as to its religious underpinnings and dimensions. Contemporary historians do not fully discuss the connections between the social settlement movement and Christianity, or, if they do, they claim that the religious motivations were non-apparent or non-existent. Martin Marty, church historian at the University of Chicago Divinity School, for example, wrote of the social reformers in the progressive era:

Whatever their personal religion, if any was obvious, they intended to help provide syntheses and programs that were ready for democratic and pluralist America. Thus their philosophy had to be non-Jewish and non-Christian, in no way reliant on synagogue or church. They were moderns who must find new forms of dealing with the modernity they were all somehow ready to encounter.[1]

27

The fact is, however, that strong connections existed between the social settlement movement and various forms of nineteenth-century Christianity. Rather than embodying a so-called secular or modern movement, the social settlement movement was ultimately religious or spiritual in its underpinnings. This chapter focuses on the roots of the social settlement movement and the connections between the social settlement movement and Christianity.

Beginnings

The social settlement movement started in 1884 when Samuel Barnett opened Toynbee Hall in a slum in East London.[2] Barnett, a Canon in the Anglican Church, was influenced by the philosophy of John Ruskin. He understood Toynbee Hall as a place for college men to address problems of class separation and economic poverty in nineteenth-century England. Toynbee Hall was more than a place, however; it represented a particular understanding of society and a method to improve society. Barnett believed class misunderstandings and suspicions would be lessened if classes within society would mingle with each other. Toynbee Hall was opened, then, on the premise that all people in society comprised a whole society, and that people of different classes needed to recognize their interdependence and learn from each other.

Toynbee Hall was not opened to provide charity or even to directly address issues of social injustice. Barnett believed charity perpetuated class divisions by making the lower classes dependent on the higher classes. The roots of social injustice could best be addressed by the mutual interaction of people of all classes. Upper-class men, by simply moving into poorer areas and living as neighbors, would bridge the class worlds of nineteenth-century London.

Leo Jacobs, an early-twentieth-century sociologist, wrote of the pattern Toynbee Hall set for social settlements:

Its idea is that the solidarity of human kind is manifested by the reciprocal functioning of its parts; that the settlers gain from their neighborhood as much as their neigh-

borhood gains from them. The Settlement stands for
fellowship despite the differences that exist among men
in regard to nationality, religion and race.[3]

Toynbee Hall, and the social settlement movement that followed, developed as a consequence of a number of different
attitudes and occurrences converging in the nineteenth century. Not least of these attitudes regarded understandings of
cities in general. Barnett, for example, unlike many of his contemporaries, understood the city not as a place in need of elimination, but rather, as a place in need of reform.[4] Allen F. Davis
wrote that Toynbee Hall and the settlement movement resulted
from a number of different causes: "[It was a] culmination of
diverse movements, closely allied with Romanticism, that sought
to preserve humanistic and spiritual values in an age dominated
by materialism and urban industrialism."[5]
    Leo Jacobs placed the social settlement movement into the
broader social ethical movement of the nineteenth century.[6] He
said that both the social ethical and the religious ethical movements shared the same ultimate goal—of making society more
humane—but they differed in method and in word. He wrote:
"[T]he Social Ethical Movement endeavors to universalize culture and comforts in the interests of human solidarity," while
"the Religious Ethical Movement endeavors to Christianize our
industrial and economic life."[7]

The Context of the United States

In the United States, the social settlement movement is usually
placed within the broad framework of the progressive era, a
time roughly defined as occurring between the end of the Civil
War and the end of the First World War. During this time period, 1865 to 1920, especially during the first decades of the
twentieth century, the United States was "swept by a reforming
wave such as it had not felt since the 1840's."[8]
    The progressive era was marked by much change within the
social, cultural, and economic fabric of the United States. The
nation experienced remarkable industrial growth, as well as
staggering population growth, the latter occurrence due mostly

to the influx of immigrants.[9] Accompanying economic and population growth was the development of industrial cities, new centers for the concentration of both capital and people, and focal points in the growing transportation web tying the country together.

Consequently, the reform movements that arose during the first decades of the twentieth century must be understood as responses to, or reactions against, these changes in the basic fabric of the nation. No longer was the nation primarily rural-based. No longer did it appear that people were living in relatively stable, unchanging communities. Rather, there was conspicuous movement from country to city and from farm to factory. Middle- and upper-middle-class women began to be admitted into institutions of higher education. Working women, African-American women, and immigrant women pushed the limits of Victorian concepts of womanhood by their very presence in the marketplace and their often-exploited labor in the industrial economy. These years were exciting for those people who dreamed of amassing large personal fortunes. But they were also overwhelming to those people who viewed the consequences of expansion, mobility, urbanization, and ever-increasing manufacturing and commerce. Poverty had never before been so apparent. Political corruption had never before been so blatant. Cultural differences had never before been so obvious.

In this milieu, reforms were attempted from many fields and disciplines. Martin Marty said of this era: "The word 'social' acquired new social power at the turn of the century. Sociology, social settlement, social service, a Social Gospel, social philosophy were all invented."[10]

Religion, more precisely Christianity, was affected by these many changes in U.S. society. Between the years 1860 and 1926, for example, the proportion of white people belonging to Protestant denominations of British heritage dropped from almost seventy percent to less than fifty percent. Emerging on the religious scene during these years were larger numbers of Roman Catholics, Black Baptists and Methodists, Lutherans, Jews, and Eastern Orthodox adherents.[11] The Protestant hegemony, if it ever truly existed, began to disintegrate among increasingly noticeable religious differences.[12] The World's Parliament of Religions, held in Chicago in 1893, not only highlighted the differences within Christianity but gave new prominence to the religions of Islam and Judaism, and initiated knowledge of Eastern religions such as Buddhism and Hinduism among middle-class European Americans.

Although many Christian leaders had a growing awareness of the religious differences and disunity between them during this time period, there was also a concerted effort to unite in joint or ecumenical undertakings. Widespread social needs seemed to stimulate this new work among Christian denominations and organizations. The worldwide Christian student movements, nondenominational missionary organizations, and federated church councils are but major examples of the emerging desire on the part of some Christian leaders to move beyond theological or sectarian differences to a shared work and a united purpose.

Other Christians began to voice their concern with the dehumanization of poverty and suffering resulting from unchecked industrialization and laissez-faire economics. These persons argued that nineteenth-century Christianity needed to include economic and social concerns as well as doctrinal and faith matters. The social gospel movement—primarily white, male, and Protestant—reflected the concern that religion address the current times by preaching social salvation in addition to personal salvation. Richard Ely, one of the most significant social gospel proponents in the late nineteenth century, summarized the social gospel perspective: "The gospel of Christ is both individual and social. It proclaims individual and social regeneration, individual and social salvation."[13] To solve urban problems, social gospel advocates said a revival of Christianity was needed in the churches. Ely and others proclaimed that a religious awakening that transformed individuals (and their characters) was needed to solve the problems of nineteenth-century society: "The city needs religion, and without religion the salvation of the city is impossible."[14]

From its beginnings in England, then, the social settlement movement became an important part of the progressive atmosphere which spread quickly throughout the United States. In August 1886, Stanton Coit opened the Neighborhood Guild (later renamed the University Settlement) in New York City, after he visited Toynbee Hall. Shortly afterward, Vida Scudder, an instructor at Wellesley College, and some of her friends concerned with social problems formed the College Settlement Association. On September 1st, 1889, they opened the College Settlement in New York City. Two weeks later, Jane Addams and Ellen Gates Starr opened Hull House (as it came to be called), making it the third settlement house in the United States. Although it was not the first social settlement in the United States, Hull House became foremost in reputation and popularity.

From these minor beginnings in the later part of the nineteenth century, the social settlement movement gathered momentum and snowballed into the twentieth century. Statistics show that there were 6 settlements in the United States in 1891; 74 in 1897; 103 in 1900; 204 in 1905; and more than 400 in 1910.[15] Most of these settlements were founded in large urban and industrial areas such as New York, Boston, and Chicago. They were also scattered throughout the United States and in various parts of Canada and Europe.[16] Not until after World War I did the movement decline, slowly being replaced by a social welfare system and community centers largely initiated by the settlement movement itself.

The Purpose of Social Settlements

Julia Lathrop, in an article entitled "What the Settlement Work Stands For," wrote that the major characteristics uniting the social settlement movement were its name and its reliance on residents.[17] Lathrop pointed out the diversity within the movement and how settlement houses differed immensely from place to place. While Toynbee Hall provided the prototype for social settlements in general, settlements developed based on local needs, interests, and the skills of residential staff.

Openness to differences was one of the purposes of the movement. Settlement houses were to be places where people could freely express their opinions. Lathrop wrote, "The settlement stands for a free platform. It offers its best hospitality to every man's honest thought."[18] As a platform for the expression of various ideas, the settlement movement defined itself as a vehicle of social democracy. As Lathrop observed in the above-noted article, social settlement work was a "humble but sincere effort toward a realization of that ideal of social democracy."

Jane Addams spoke and wrote prolifically on the ideals of social democracy. She understood the purpose of social settlements as "an attempt to express the meaning of life in terms of life itself."[19] She believed, like many other progressives, that democracy would flourish if it was reformed to include not only political aspects, represented by the franchise, but also social aspects, represented by a shared common culture. Democracy was a way of life to Addams, and much more than a political system. The purpose of social settlements was to extend democracy within society. Like Barnett, she did not believe that class divisions would be eliminated in a true democracy, but hoped that classes would not exist in isolation or antagonism if mutual exchanges of knowledge and experience were shared by all people.[20]

William Cole, an early-twentieth-century professor of sociology, Congregational minister, and settlement resident at the South End House in Boston, stated their purpose slightly differently than Addams. He said all social settlements shared the spirit of friendship and the purpose of service.[21] This was the lowest common denominator of social settlements, according to Cole: "All that is really essential to it is a personal relation involving service through sharing in the spirit of friendship."[22]

Due to the emphasis on openness and social democracy, particular social settlements came to have particular slants or specializations. In London, for example, Toynbee Hall became primarily an educational institution, Oxford House focused on social elements, Bermondsey Settlement became empathically evangelistic, and Mansfield House focused on Christian Socialism.[23]

A similar pattern unfolded in the United States. Jane Addams identified social settlements in Illinois that were primarily educational in emphasis (e.g., Northwestern University), social in emphasis (e.g., Maxwell Street), and evangelically Protestant in emphasis (e.g., Chicago Commons).[24] Because Hull House was in a league of its own, its emphasis is difficult to classify.

Size and scope made it unlike other social settlements, which were usually much smaller both in number of residents and in programs offered. Unlike most other settlements, Hull House had the resources and the geographical locality to successfully engage in multiple emphases.

Regardless of how social settlements manifested themselves, most leaders involved in them recognized religion as their underlying value. Religion was not defined according to creed or institution, but in terms of exploring the totality of life itself. Mary K. Simkhovitch, who became the head resident at Greenwich House in New York City, stated this view:

> The settlement is not a mission, not a school, not a charity, but a group of persons living a common life, learning the meaning of life by which they are surrounded, interpreting this life to others and acting on what they have learned. And religion in our common thought of it means the framework of life—the outline by which we measure events, that which makes proportion possible, our thought of the whole of things. That which commands the best and the most of us is religion for us.[25]

Addams, when stating the underlying religious value of social settlements, asserted that social settlements uphold "one of the tenets of all the great ethnic religions," namely, "the permanent dignity and value of human life."[26] In the centrality of affirming life, Addams connected her ideals of social democracy with her understanding of religious goals. Not surprisingly, it was a connection not all nineteenth-century Christians considered valid.

Conflicts Between Christianity and Social Settlements

In the early years, social settlements were often criticized because they were not Christian enough. George Hodges, an early-twentieth-century theologian who was dean of the Episcopal Theological School and president of the South End House in Boston, wrote that most of the settlement workers were Christian in their personal beliefs. But as a movement dedicated to social democracy and religion in the broadest sense of the word, their houses were not overtly Christian, like churches or missions. He said that to expect settlements to be like churches was unfair:

[To] complain of the settlement that it has no sermons and no prayer-meetings, and makes no public confession of religion, is like complaining of the physician that he does not wear a surplice, and that he carries a medicine-case instead of a Bible.[27]

Richard Ely also identified the conflict social settlements caused among Christian churches and authorities, specifically in the criticism of Hull House:

It is doubtless known . . . that there is opposition to Hull-House on the part of a few narrow-minded people because it does not float any sectarian flag. One would suppose that while the churches are talking so much about Christian unity they would be delighted to rally about an undenominational institution.[28]

The criticism of social settlements based on their apparent lack of religiosity was mingled with social and political criticisms. Charles Richmond Henderson, an ordained Baptist minister who was head of practical sociology at the University of Chicago in the early twentieth century, identified such connections made by conservatives toward social settlements:

Many conservative persons stand aloof from [social settlements] or regard them with suspicion because they manifest an appreciation for trade unions and socialists, because they do not conduct revivals and Sunday schools, because they do not attempt to make proselytes to Protestant churches, because the residents often become quite radical themselves, because free discussion is tolerated and encouraged. Thorough acquaintance with the surroundings of the settlements in the crowded quarters of immigrant populations would at least teach critics patience and kindly understanding of the residents. It is very easy, cheap, and unprofitable to find fault; it is much more difficult and more useful to do constructive and educative work. Before condemning the settlements let the class of men try to do some of this work themselves.[29]

Henderson's major critique of nineteenth-century Protestant churches was that they did not exist within immigrant and working class communities. Therefore, many lacked an adequate understanding of the social issues of the day:

> The Protestant churches are very generally a long distance from the colonies and districts of immigrants and laborers, and therefore our pastors, teachers, and members have a very dim notion of the hopes, fears, anxieties, ambitions, tastes, beliefs, sufferings, prejudices, sacrifices, and character of the multitudes who come from other lands, bringing their customs and faiths with them.[30]

He also argued that social settlements could function as a mediating agency between newly arrived immigrants and established societal institutions, including the Protestant churches:

> A Protestant church in a colony of Catholics or Jews is hated; a "mission" is despised; the form of service is repulsive; the crude music of the Salvation Army jars on the nerves of the Italians. With the kindest intentions our church methods often collide with the feelings of people we would win, because we do not know them. They do not understand us nor our language; our creed is heresy to them; all attempts to proselyte are regarded as devilish enticements to disloyalty to ancestral faith.[31]

In the above quote, Henderson alluded to another critique of social settlements, this one coming not from conservative Protestants but from the Roman Catholic religious leadership. Many Roman Catholics believed settlements were engaging in Protestant proselytizing. The fact that many settlements were located in communities comprised of at least nominally Roman Catholic immigrants gave grounding to this critique. John Patrick Walsh, in a dissertation analyzing the work of the Catholic Church in Chicago during the late nineteenth and early twentieth centuries, wrote of Jane Addams and Hull House:

> This famous settlement house in the heart of the Italian district of the city was held in deep suspicion among Catholic authorities. The Italian people were probably the most vulnerable elements in the Catholic Church in Chicago to proselytism. This was true for a variety of reasons, including an inadequate number of Catholic churches, Italian priests, and Italian parochial school. . . . Catholic authorities were well aware of this vulnerability. . . . It was their conviction that Jane Addams and Hull House were stealthily engaged in proselyting among the Italians, although this was denied by Miss Addams and her supporters.[32]

Catholic authorities also feared, like their Protestant conservative counterparts, that Hull House was too radical, politically and socially. Walsh quoted from the *New World*, the official publication of the Archdiocese, regarding settlements such as Hull House:

> [Settlements seemed to be] roosting places for frowsy anarchists, fierce-eyed socialists, professed anticlericals and a coterie of long-haired sociologists intent upon probing the moonshine with palefingers.[33]

Roman Catholic leaders, however, recognized as good and necessary the work Hull House did in uplifting and relieving the poor. As a way to offset the predominantly Protestant involvement in social settlements, Roman Catholics began to engage in such work themselves. In Chicago, the Catholic Women's National League developed and supported the work of three Catholic settlements, St. Anne's, St. Elizabeth's, and All Saints, located in the West, North, and South areas of the city, respectively.[34]

The general uneasiness or fear of conservative Protestants and Roman Catholics regarding social settlements was not illusionary, but based on fact. Herman Hegner described the social settlement as a "social clearing house, where rich and poor, learned and ignorant, Catholic and Protestant, capitalist and la-borer, can meet on common ground and find that they are all brothers after all."[35] In this sense, social settlements were breaking down previously accepted societal and religious divisions—an unwelcome and perhaps scary possibility to many people.

While it is clear that Addams and Hull House did not intentionally or consciously participate in proselytism of Catholic immigrants, most leaders within social settlements were Protestant in their personal religious backgrounds. Settlement women like Ellen Gates Starr, who eventually became Roman Catholic, and Lillian Wald, a Jewish woman and founder of the Henry Street Settlement in New York City, were especially important when put in this overwhelmingly Protestant context.[36]

Addams attempted to explain why young people had entered social settlement work rather than official church work during the last decade of the nineteenth century. She held that churches had lost touch with the social realities of the times:

> The religious educator lost hundreds of young men and women who by training and temperament should have gone into the ministry or the missionary field, simply because his statements appeared to them as magnificent pieces of self-assertion totally unrelated to the world.[37]

In another article, Addams related an example of a young women who went into social settlement work only after she realized that the Christian Church was either unwilling or unable to use her skills:

> Of the dozens of young women who have begged me to make a connection for them between their dreams of social usefulness and their actual living, I recall one of the many who I had sent back to her clergyman, returning with this remark: "His only suggestion was that I should be responsible every Sunday for fresh flowers

upon the altar. I did that when I was fifteen and liked it then, but when you come back from college and are twenty-two years old, it doesn't seem to quite fit in with the vigorous efforts you have been told are necessary in order to make our social relations more Christian."[38]

Shailer Mathews, a prominent professor at the University of Chicago Divinity School from the last decade of the nineteenth century until his retirement in 1933, observed that the relationship between churches and settlements was one of "mutual ignorance and distrust." His critique, however, mostly regarded the work of the churches and not of the settlements. He believed churches needed to be involved in what he called dynamic religion, rather than in what he called regulative religion. Churches in particular, and Christianity in general, needed to "appeal to and stand for life, not philosophy."[39]

Conflicts between social settlements and Christianity, therefore, occurred on various fronts. Some Christians held that settlements were not religious enough, while others held that they were religious and engaged in select proselytism. Some Christians viewed settlements as dangerous because of their political and social atmosphere. Settlement defenders countered that churches were out of touch with urban and industrial communities, their theology did not relate to life or reality, and they lost the potential leadership of young people who entered the more relevant social movements of their day.

Social Settlements, Missions, and Institutional Churches

Debate not only occurred regarding social settlements and Christianity, but more specific discussions took place about the differences between social settlements and Christian missions. Social settlement leaders often assumed defensive stances in their attempt to explain why they were different from missions and how their work was legitimate even though it was not overtly Christian. Samuel Barnett observed that many people saw the social settlement as a kind of mission, "another form of the proselytising spirit, a rival of other converting agencies to be approved or condemned as something either better or worse."[40]

He disagreed with this view, and stated that missions—not settlements—exist to proselytize: "There will be Missions as long
as believers in what seems good desire that others should share
that belief." Settlements and missions, he argued, have completely different goals:

> A Mission has for its object conversion.
> A Settlement has for its object mutual knowledge.
> A Mission creates organisations, institutions, and
>   machinery.
> A Settlement uses personal influence and tends to
>   human contact.[41]

Jane Addams, like Barnett, also clearly distinguished between missions and settlements. But she went beyond Barnett
by suggesting that missions may stand for a higher good than
social settlements:

> They are really two distinct things, and harm is done to
> both movements, from this mental confusion . . .
> [Canon Barnett] says a mission is a group of people who
> are committed to one point of view, a religious point of
> view . . . . They go into a neighborhood, and try to per-
> suade the people who live there to believe as they be-
> lieve, and to this end, in order to increase their
> acquaintance, they have classes, clubs, and many of the
> things a settlement has, but it is all secondary as it were,
> for they hope in the end that they may promote their
> propaganda. I am ready to say a mission is a much finer
> thing than the settlement.[42]

Addams stated that the purpose of settlements was not to "dis-
turb the people in their religious beliefs," but to help people
unite on the "manifest needs of the community." She added:
"To reproach a settlement because it does not give religious
instruction as a mission does, or to reproach a mission for not
being a settlement, is equally absurd."[43] Addams identified certain settlements in Chicago that would better be classified as
missions, including the Central Settlement, the Frances Willard
Settlement, and the Marcy Home.[44]

Graham Taylor, Professor of Christian Sociology at the Chicago Theological Seminary and founder of the Chicago Commons Settlement, also clearly distinguished between the work of the settlement and the work of the church:

> Respectful toward the distinct prerogatives and functions of the church and the synagogue, the settlement never claims to substitute anything for them, much less to fulfill the function of either. Even across the frontier in the rear where the churches are conspicuous for their absence or their feebleness, the settlement disavows being in any sense a substitute or a rival of the church or the mission.[45]

Taylor stated further that a settlement cannot show preference toward any particular denomination or religion. If it did, "it would forfeit its own prerogative of being common ground, the clearinghouse, the cooperative center of the whole community, for the fellowship and work of those of all faiths or no faith."[46] However Taylor attempted to distinguish religion from settlement, he also claimed that settlements were ultimately religious, for they combined both the social and religious spirit: "As much, if not more, than any other influence, the settlement spirit has humanized religion and thus made it all the more divine."[47] Unlike Hull House, the Chicago Commons was closely tied to a congregation, the Tabernacle Church, which was pastored by Taylor himself and met within the Chicago Commons' building. The work done by the Commons and the church, however, was kept separate, which reflected Taylor's understandings of the methodological differences between settlement work and religious work.[48]

Taylor identified the influence social settlements had on Christian churches by pointing toward the changes some churches made in their adoption of social methods. In this way, he tied together the social settlement movement with the growth of so-called institutional or open churches. Institutional churches attempted to minister not only to the spiritual needs of their people but also to recognize the social needs of their people. As Charles Henderson stated, they ministered to the "whole complex nature of human beings."[49]

Like social settlements, institutional churches—and neighborhood houses, which developed in the twentieth century—offered programs relating to the totality of people's lives: clubs, societies, classes, etc.[50] As a new movement, institutional churches represented an attempt to make Christianity both more applicable and more integrated with the everyday life of its members and potential members. They represented an understanding that religion could apply to the whole of people's lives.[51]

The institutional church movement can be interpreted in a number of different ways. It can be understood as a reactionary response to the social settlement movement. Historian Nathan Irvin Huggins offered this opinion, claiming that institutional churches developed because social settlements "proved more successful in reaching the unchurched poor."[52] Edwin Oscar Berreth, while a seminary student, studied the ideas settlements could give to churches. He stated the relationship between the two movements this way: "What is it that the settlements have that the churches do not, which makes people going to the settlements more enthusiastic about being there than those going to the church?"[53] A pastor with the Methodist Episcopal Church, Dr. Frank Crane, addressed a group of Methodist ministers meeting at Hull House. He said that the settlement movement was "supplanting the church" mostly because churches failed to address issues of urban poverty:

> When a congregation gets rich . . . it moves away from the poor and puts them in missions. [The church's] ideals are of wealth. Our little tin god is the rich man. As soon as we get anything we get away from the publicans and sinners. Not on paper, of course, but really, you know. A few of the more harebrained live in settlements, but most of us move over to the boulevards. The great powers of the church are doing nothing for the poor.[54]

On the other hand, Samuel C. Kinceloe, a professor of sociology at the Chicago Theological Seminary, argued that institutional churches did not simply follow settlement patterns. As an example, he cited the formation of industrial schools, which developed out of the Sunday School movement.[55] Kinceloe understood the final purpose of institutional churches to be providing service rather than attempting proselytization: "Much of the work and cost of the institutional church and the neighborhood house must be charged up to 'doing good' or 'pure service work' as against the 'building of fellowships' in the sense of securing church members."[56]

Cause and effect explanations for the relationship between institutional churches and social settlements are not the best way to understand their connection. Both movements can be better understood as resulting from the need to adapt and to engage in necessary change within a rapidly changing social context. The social settlement movement likely contributed to the formation of institutional churches, at least in terms of providing a model for possible ministry within urban environments. At the same time, the theology of the social gospel movement provided a theological basis for this new type of church ministry. In this way, the social gospel and social settlement movements were connected.[57]

Like social settlements, institutional churches were also targets of criticism; not all Christians saw them as positive. Institutional churches and neighborhood houses were viewed by some Christians as "represent[ing] the secularization of the church." Church workers involved in institutional churches responded to this accusation in much the same way social settlers responded to the accusations against them; namely, by saying they were "socializing the message of the gospel."[58]

The movements of reform as seen in the social settlement, social gospel, and institutional church must be understood as innovative responses to nineteenth-century society. As Walter Rauschenbusch, a social gospel contemporary of Ely, stated regarding the institutional church: "The institutional church is a necessary evil. The people ought to be able to provide for themselves what the churches are trying to provide for them."[59] The idea that social settlements were "necessary evils" could also be said.

Religious versus Spiritual

The attempt of Barnett and Addams to distinguish between settlements and missions did not prevent another kind of reasoning regarding the social settlement movement, namely, that it was a movement ultimately spiritual in its goals and methods. Many social settlement leaders believed that their movement added a fuller aspect to conventional religion. Charles Richmond Henderson wrote that the social settlement movement started as a religious movement, and religion was its ultimate ideal. But religion, in this case, was not to be defined by sectarian institutions or doctrines but by individual norms of spirituality:

> [U]p to this day religion is regarded as the crown and blossom of the toil. Laymen have put a stamp upon the institution which ecclesiastics do not always recognize from the outside; but if religion be genuine, confidence in the essential good at the heart of the world, yearning for unity of life, hope of universal reconciliation on the high plane of righteousness, then religion is present and potent. The individual is left to choose for himself the particular symbol which most fitly and sincerely expresses his personal creed. All are tolerant and all are free. All is positive and creative, rather than destructive and polemical.[60]

Ellen Gates Starr, the most explicitly and theologically Christian of the Hull House women, wrote about the religious basis of the social settlement movement:

> One of the beliefs at the root of the impulse which expressed itself in the Settlement movement was the belief that the Holy Ghost is not conditioned by stations in life. We were taught this by the Annunciation and Incarnation, but we have often forgotten it. Indeed, in practice, it is seldom remembered, even in the Christian Church.[61]

Starr continued to reflect on the differences and connections between social settlements and churches. She said that for her-

self, it was a hard decision to decide whether to be more involved in the settlement or the church. Yet she recognized that
in the context she lived, she could do more in the settlement
than she could in the church:

> To some of us, I am sure, it has not been an easy ques-
> tion to settle whether our efforts ought not to bear the
> stamp of the religion which inspires them rather than
> to be classified with purely secular undertakings. The
> choice, I fear, is between two sacrifices. In the one case
> we must give up, together with her help, something of
> what might accrue to the repute of the Church from
> any recognized good results of our energies, and her
> increased power consequent upon that; in the other
> case, alas, it seems clear that we must sacrifice largely
> the desired end itself; I mean to say that the social re-
> sults for which we are working in settlement can not,
> at this day, be achieved within the Church so well as
> without.[62]

While the first generation of settlement workers understood
their work as religious, they were often forced into positions of
defending their work and themselves because they neither operated within ecclesiastical structures nor advocated particular
religious viewpoints. Yet many insisted that the settlement was
an ultimately religious or spiritual movement. Dean George
Hodges wrote that the religion of the settlement could be seen
in the work that it did:

> Its faith is made evident by its works. We may know
> whether it is really religious or not by looking at it. If to
> labor to change the city of destruction into the city of
> God be religious; if to teach the word of God as it is
> written in the great world be religious; and if it be reli-
> gious not to be ministered unto, but to minister,—we
> need not be greatly troubled about the settlement, for
> beneath its roof the blind begin to see and the lame
> begin to walk, and they who have been palsied take on
> strength, and the poor hear the good news of the gos-

pel, that blessed gospel of the love of God which is interpreted by the service of man.[63]

Both the institutional church movement and the social gospel movement, therefore, represented the attempt of individual Christians and particular churches to become integrated with the totality of life and, in so doing, lessen the emphasis placed on orthodox or particular belief systems. In the 1940s, seminarian David W. Barry, explored the relationship between social settlements and the social gospel movement. He wrote that while causal links were difficult to identify, the two movements were most strongly connected by their advocating a new definition of religion:

> [The settlements and the social gospel] both had a new concept of religion itself. They believed it to be something applicable to the whole of life, not to be separated from any part of life or put into a compartment off by itself. Religion was a "way of life" and not a creed, a belief, a book, a ritual, or a form of church organization. If religion stopped at the church door or was confined to the personal religious life, then it was not true religion. And it was for this reason that the settlement has never considered it necessary to have religious services and the social gospel has contributed to the breaking down of denominational barriers.[64]

To advocate a broader definition of religion was the goal of the social settlement, social gospel, and institutional church movements of the nineteenth century. Religion, according to these movements, was more than an intellectual adherence to a theological tradition. It was the underlying motive of all service and participation within society—to love one's neighbor and to love God. These goals ultimately broadened the definition of religion in the late nineteenth century. Religion began to be defined not by ecclesiastical membership or particular creedal affirmations, but by an overriding and underlying sense of the sacredness of how one lived one's life and tolerated varying belief systems. It was a movement perhaps best defined as spiritual rather than religious.

The growth of the social settlement movement and its relation to Christianity was always influenced by particular geographic and civic milieus. In the next chapter, the setting of Chicago is explored. Chicago was the home to many churches, missions, and social settlements. It became a crucial locale in the development of nineteenth-century industrialism and culture. Hull House was established and became famous in Chicago; it was in Chicago that the women of Hull House converged and from there established their spiritual outlooks, vocational niches, and friendship ties. Specifying the context of Chicago, therefore, is necessary to ground the cultural and religious debates of the progressive era, and to outline the environment in which the women of Hull House lived and labored.

3

Chicago in the Late Nineteenth Century

Hog Butcher for the World!
Tool Maker, Stacker of Wheat,
Player with Railroads and the Nations Freight Handler;
Stormy, husky, brawling,
City of the Big Shoulders.
                              —Carl Sandburg, "Chicago"

THE WORDS OF THE POET and journalist Carl Sandburg vividly describe Chicago as a vital and vibrant economic center in the late nineteenth century. Situated at the base of Lake Michigan on the portage between the Mississippi Valley basin and the Great Lakes, Chicago was incorporated as a town in 1833. This occurred only thirty years after the first offical settlement in the area, Fort Dearborn, had been established along the Chicago River.[1] At the fin de siècle, then, it was still a young city.

Chicago had encountered and survived its share of calamities in its short history, from the so-called massacre at Fort Dearborn in 1812 to the Black Hawk wars of 1832, from droughts and economic recessions to periodic epidemic outbreaks of cholera, diphtheria, typhoid, even malaria. European-American settlers swarmed to and through Chicago from the mid-nineteenth century onward, successfully defeating and excising the Native American population early in the city's history.[2] The great fire of 1871 rendered one-third of the population homeless and about five hundred people dead or missing. Much to the surprise of many national observers, the fire did not indefinitely diminish Chicago's growth; a new Chicago swiftly emerged from the swampy ashes, taller and bigger than before. In some ways, post-fire Chicago became the epitome of hardiness, success, and unlimited possibility in the late nineteenth century's perceptions of continuous expansion and survival of the fittest.

Between the years 1880 and 1890, Chicago's population more than doubled. Its geographical area grew from thirty-five square miles to a sprawling 178 square miles.[3] The crown of glory for many wealthy and business-minded Chicagoans was preparing for and hosting the World Columbian Exposition of 1893. This event was to depict the triumph of technology and the endurance of the human spirit in controlling and shaping the material world.[4] In conjunction with the fair, a number of important assemblies were held, including the World's Parliament of Religions and the Woman's Congress.[5] Before the festive exposition concluded, its intended glory became tarnished by the assassination of Mayor Carter Harrison and Chicago's most serious economic depression.

The "white city" depicted in the architectural design of the World's Fair was a facade to the real Chicago, a city brewing with social, economic, and political tensions.[6] Two major uprisings seethed to the surface: the Haymarket riot of 1886 and the Pullman strike of 1894. In part, both events showed the chasm between the laborers and the wealthy. The wealthy included the likes of George Pullman, Marshall Field, Philip Armour, Cyrus McCormick, and Potter Palmer, all millionaire magnates who exemplified the self-made man.[7] The working class included recently arrived immigrants, many of whom were said to be socialist in politics and anarchists in practice. In 1890, Chicago had an immigrant population (strictly defined as people born outside the United States) of nearly forty-one percent.[8] Many of these European immigrants lacked adequate housing, employment, and access to health and educational services.[9]

In this urban context, Jane Addams and Ellen Gates Starr opened their social settlement house. Hull House was in Chicago's nineteenth ward, which was an immigrant neighborhood comprised mostly of Italians and Germans. During the last decade of the nineteenth century new immigrants, mostly Jews from central Europe and Greeks from southern Europe, arrived, changing the ethnic makeup but not the impoverishment of the area.[10] Inadequate tenements and garbage collection, the prominence of saloons and gambling dens, unemployment, and abuses related to the sweatshop system and child labor predominated in this neighborhood, which was far removed from the mansions of the Chicago elite. Indeed, the saying that Chicago was not only a city but a city of cities, adequately summarized the economic and social divisions that existed in late-nineteenth-century Chicago.[11]

Carl Sandburg further described the underside of life and economic development in the Chicago he experienced:

> They tell me you are wicked and I believe them, for I
>   have seen your painted women under the gas lamps
>   luring the farm boys.
> And they tell me you are crooked and I answer: Yes, it is
>   true I have seen the gunman kill and go free to kill
>   again.
> And they tell me you are brutal and my reply is: On the
>   faces of the women and children I have seen the
>   marks of wanton hunger.

Despite the violence, hunger, and corruption Sandburg identified, he spoke of Chicago with an overwhelming sense of optimism and pride. He believed Chicago would overcome the odds against it.

> And having answered so I turn once more to those who
>   sneer at this my city, and I give them back the sneer
>   and say to them:
> Come and show me another city with lifted head singing
>   so proud to be alive and coarse and strong and
>   cunning.
> Flinging magnetic curses amid the toil of piling job on
>   job, here is a tall bold slugger set vivid against the
>   little soft cities;
> Fierce as a dog with tongue lapping for action, cunning
>   as a savage pitted against the wilderness,

Bareheaded,
Shoveling,
Wrecking,
Planning,
Building, breaking, rebuilding,
Under the smoke, dust all over his mouth, laughing with
white teeth,
Under the terrible burden of destiny laughing as a young
man laughs,
Laughing even as an ignorant fighter laughs who has
never lost a battle,
Bragging and laughing that under his wrist is the pulse,
and under his ribs the heart of the people,
Laughing!
Laughing the stormy, husky, brawling laughter of Youth,
half-naked, sweating, proud to be Hog Butcher, Tool
Maker, Stacker of Wheat, Player with Railroads and
Freight Handler to the Nation.

This was the Chicago Sandburg depicted: Contrasts between
haves and have nots, between corseted women of high society
and painted women of the street, between naive farm boys and
polished politicians, all coexisting with the determination of the
entrepreneurs to build and rebuild against all odds, flouting
fate and ignoring the smaller consequences of human suffering.
It was a city not unlike other U.S. cities during this time period
when industrialization and immigration spurred urbanization
and excused abusive labor practices, although the extremes may
have been more apparent in Chicago.

Contrary to conventional depictions, Chicago was not all
business and production, crime and violence. It was not devoid
of social and religious institutions or of generous philanthropists who earnestly desired to alleviate the suffering of the less
fortunate and bring beauty to an otherwise stark environment.
The pride of nineteenth-century Chicagoans was largely related
to the cultural amenities they perceived in their city. A late-nineteenth-century French visitor observed that the city was a
"strange combination of pork and Plato."[12] The city was, indeed,
a strange combination of industry and so-called higher culture.

Religious Presence

Not surprisingly, Christian churches were among the first public institutions founded, paralleling the settlement and development of Chicago itself. Father Jacques Marquette, a Jesuit missionary, travelled the Mississippi River and the waterways of the Great Lakes. In 1673, he became the first white European to pass through what was to become the Chicago area.[13]

More missionaries, representing various denominations and religious traditions, came to the area over the next centuries. The Reverend Isaac McCoy, a Baptist clergyman, is said to have been the first Protestant missionary. He preached in English to a predominantly Native American audience in 1825. The Methodist presence was exerted next, when the Reverend Jesse Walker arrived in Chicago from Peoria in 1826. The Methodists, primarily because of their ability to follow the westward frontier and their method of establishing and supporting scattered groups through a circuit riding leadership, established the first permanent religious presence in the area. Regular Methodist worship services were held in "Father Walker's log-cabin" from 1832. Shortly after, in 1833, three other permanent religious organizations were officially formed representing the Roman Catholic, Presbyterian, and Baptist traditions. The first Methodist Church was officially incorporated in 1834.[14]

By the end of the nineteenth century, Chicago contained the diversity of religious perspectives found throughout the United States. Catholic and Methodist Episcopal parishes, along with Lutheran parishes—indicative of the immigrant waves from Central and Northern Europe settling in the middle lands of the North American continent—were the largest traditions in the city. Catholics had 134 congregations with a membership in the Chicago archdiocese of about 1 million; Methodist Episcopals had 138 congregations with a membership of 27,500; and Lutherans had 97 congregations with an estimated membership of 38,500. Baptist (20,976 members), Congregational (14,625 members), Episcopal (7,800 members), and Presbyterian (16,505 members) denominations all had a strong presence in Chicago. Religious denominations or *sects* (as they were often called in the nineteenth century), such as the Adventist, German Union Evangelical, Christian Science, Unitarian, and Universalist had a secure albeit smaller presence in the Chicago religious community. Although the environs of Chicago was overwhelmingly Christian, a Jewish presence was represented, with twenty-seven synagogues.[15] Between the years 1890 and 1906, church membership in Chicago rose from thirty-five percent to nearly forty percent of the total population.[16]

In the nineteenth century, the differences between religious groups were perceived to be immense, even by lay people. Nineteenth-century Lutherans and Methodists, for example, were markedly different in language and ethnic makeup, as well as in worship and theological points. The chasm between Protestantism and Catholicism was even greater. Many Protestants held Catholics to be non-Christian. Catholic doctrine held that all other expressions of Christianity (e.g., Lutheran, Reformed, Anglican) were defiant of the only true, Catholic Church, and needed to repent and be reunited with it. Given the Protestant hegemony of dominant U.S. society, strident anti-popish and anti-Romish sentiments were most commonly hurled about in public circles.

Differing moral values, politics, and ethnic makeup account for much of the anti-Catholic rhetoric of the nineteenth century. The essence of nativism was reflected in the formation of the Native American Party—commonly called the Know-Nothings—in the mid-nineteenth-century. While the World's Parliament of Religions managed to bring many Christian denominations into association and invited the participation of representatives from other world religions, much debate and conflict occurred over Catholic participation from both within and outside the Catholic community. The question for Catholics, as for other religious groups to a lesser extent, was how they were to function in a society that was at least theoretically based on principles of religious pluralism.[17] In part, many Catholics feared that participation in the Parliament would convey the idea that they no longer thought of themselves as the only true Christian Church.

Hannah Soloman, a prominent nineteenth-century Jewish Chicagoan, wrote of the disagreements between Protestants and Catholics, Christians and Jews, and how these religious ties affected social mingling in the city:

The rift between Christian sects was wide, though the points at issue were based largely upon some specific detail, rather than fundamental religious tenets. As the study of biblical criticism and of comparative religions became more general, however, a new understanding emerged. . . . Respect and appreciation, though by no means universal, slowly replaced many prejudices. Nevertheless . . . Catholic and Protestant groups mingled but little and the Jews, with few exceptions, formed their associations among their own people.[18]

Soloman herself reflected the attempt by some late-nineteenth-century liberal Chicagoans, influenced by the romantic cultural movement of the day, to bridge the gap between religious groups. She wrote:

Most of us today maintain that not any one sect, or creed, or book holds all truth. Many Jews and Christians now share a common point of view, considering religion as interpretation of life; believing in the singleness of humanity as it strives toward the perfecting of a human race in harmony with itself.[19]

Nondenominational and non-parish based religious movements, groups, and organizations also were present in late-nineteenth-century Chicago. Chicago experienced the excitement of urban revivalism in 1876, when Dwight L. Moody planned and executed a major three-and-one-half month revival which was largely financed by wealthy Chicago businessmen. In 1893, he returned to Chicago to conduct another revival that paralleled the World's Fair.[20]

The Illinois Woman's Christian Temperance Union had chapters throughout Cook County. The Temperance movement united mostly white women from various denominations in pursuing the goals of alcoholic abstinence and legal prohibition, and in encouraging women to enter any work "to which the Lord may call."[21] Both Catholics and Protestants came to support temperance as one of the most important reform movements of the nineteenth century, indicative of a prevailing

Christian focus on individual codes of morality. Jay P. Dolan, a prominant Roman Catholic historian, suggests that temperance was to nineteenth-century Catholics what anti-contraception was to mid-twentieth-century Catholics; it was a cause deemed essential to Catholic salvation, yet temperance was controversial among the faithful.[22]

A number of evangelical organizations originally established in England spread to the United States and were active in Chicago, including the Young Men's and Women's Christian Associations and the Salvation Army. The Salvation Army was an especially effective military-modelled organization working in charity and relief.[23] An association of Congregational Churches, the Chicago City Missionary Society, was formed in 1882. The City Missionary Society reflected the late-nineteenth-century synthesis of religious principles and moral values. The Society held that city dwellers were in particular need of propagandization, and urban neighborhoods were in great need of Christianization. Its charter read:

> To promote religion and morality in Chicago and vicinity by the employment of missionaries, the establishment and support of churches, Sabbath schools, mission stations and chapels for the preaching of the gospel of Jesus Christ, and for the diffusion of evangelical knowledge.[24]

Chicago was generally perceived by the religious communities of the late nineteenth century as a city ripe for the message of religion. Religious groups, regardless of their specific tradition, viewed individual morals as in a state of great decline and as therefore in need of great conversion. While religious leaders were concerned about the overall social ills of their day, they generally believed that the way to make society better was to make the individuals who comprised society better.

Charles M. Sheldon's best-selling book, *In His Steps*, exemplified the popular social gospel literature of his day. Sheldon urged individuals to ask themselves at every moment of decision and action, "What would Jesus do?" In doing this, they would experience conversion and would also respond to the pressing problems of society.[25] Despite the religious emphasis on individuals, almost all religious organizations were active in works of charity, specifically in the operation of hospitals, schools, and orphanages. For example, the Sisters of Mercy, who arrived in Chicago in the 1840s, founded Catholic grade schools, orphan asylums, and Mercy Hospital.[26] Through these privately funded hospitals, schools, and asylums, the religious community of Chicago was a crucial and integral element within the social and cultural life of the city.

Culture and Charity

Organizations without explicit religious agendas were also present in late-nineteenth-century Chicago. Many such groups emphasized cultural and educational concerns. The Chicago Academy of Design, for example, was formed in 1869, a school that was re-conceptualized in 1889 to form the Art Institute of Chicago. Numerous libraries were funded and opened in the nineteenth century, such as the Chicago Public Library in 1873, the Newberry Library in 1887, the John Crerar Library in 1894.[27] One of the earliest cultural formations was the Chicago Historical Society, formed in 1856. In general, these kinds of cultural organizations were initiated by the wealthy men of Chicago in an attempt to keep their city from becoming a "town of mere traders and moneygetters; rude, unlettered, hard, sharp, and grasping."[28]

Women's organizations flourished in postbellum Chicago. The prestigious Fortnightly Club was formed in 1873 and the Chicago Woman's Club was formed in 1876. These two clubs were elitist in membership and represented the female brass of Chicago society, but they were not the only women's groups in town.[29] At the turn of the century, sociologist Thomas Riley estimated approximately 110 women's clubs in the city of Chicago. The membership and activities of these clubs varied. The Council of Jewish Women, for example, had 1,100 active members, the Bohemian Woman's Club, fifty members, and the Ida B. Wells Woman's Club had thirty four members. Some groups, such as the Fortnightly Club, were purely social and cultural in design, emphasizing the arts and literature. Other groups supported civic services, such as vocation and domestic science schools, children's homes, hospital work, and legal aid societies. The Chicago Woman's Club fell into this latter category and was called the "mother of woman's public work" in the city. Like the religious communities of the day, it was very active in extending charity. Members were involved in various efforts, including attempts to reform the poorhouse and the situation of women and children prisoners under the Chicago Police system.[30]

Education was important to many leaders in nineteenth-century society who believed that society would be improved and culture maintained (or controlled) through the learning process. Major educational centers catering to the middle and upper-middle classes and initially for men only were opened during this time period. These included: Northwestern University in 1855, St. Ignatius College (later renamed Loyola University) in 1870, and St. Vincent College (later renamed DePaul University) in 1898. The University of Chicago, opened in 1892, was different from the other educational institutions in that it was coeducational from the start. Various Protestant theological seminaries, founded principally to prepare men for the ordained ministry, also were opened. The Chicago Theological Seminary (Congregationalist), Garrett Biblical Institute (Methodist), and McCormick Theological Seminary (Presbyterian) all began in the 1850s.

Certain educational organizations were designed specifically for women, including the Illinois Training School for Nurses (ITN), and the Chicago Training School for City, Home, and Foreign Missions (CTS). ITN, one of the first professional nursing schools in the United States, was founded in 1880. Its founders believed that nursing ought to be a skilled career, intended for "educated and Christian women."[31] CTS was founded in 1885 by a Methodist, Lucy Rider Meyer. Offering a two-year program, it provided training in what came to be called social work, and gave impetus to the deaconess movement in the United States.[32]

Educational institutions intended for working classes, such as manual training schools, also opened. The Armour Institute of Technology, founded in 1893 by meat packer Philip D. Armour, with the encouragement of his minister friend, Reverend Frank W. Gunsaulus, provides an excellent example of the success of such schools in Chicago. It started as a simple mission providing technical courses for men and domestic courses for women. After Armour heard Gunsaulus preach a sermon entitled, "What I Would Do If I Had a Million Dollars," he began to think a school such as his could do more. He and Gunsaulus decided to tour some eastern schools, including the Massachusetts Institute of Technology and the Pratt Institute. Upon their return to Chicago they decided to open the Armour Institute. Gunsaulus was its first president. The Armour Institute offered a range of courses, all of which were deemed practical rather than theoretical. Although the school was intended for the working classes, at one point Gunsaulus observed that they were admitting more "rich people's sons and daughters" than they had intended.[33]

A system of free public schools for children was authorized by the state of Illinois in 1855. The city of Chicago complied with this legislation, although throughout much of the nineteenth century student attendance was non-compulsory, facilities often wretchedly inadequate, and teachers' salaries minimal.[34] The problems related to the public school system were especially apparent in immigrant neighborhoods, where children often needed to work for wages rather than sit in classrooms. Campaigns against truancy were conducted by middle-class reformers, including the women of Hull House. It soon became clear to them, however, that school absenteeism was innately connected to larger societal issues such as child labor and lack of daycare facilities for younger children, not to mention the lack of English language programs for newly arrived immigrants.[35]

In addition to the cultural and educational impetus, charity began to be centrally organized in the latter part of the nineteenth century. While the ideal lingered that charity ought to be disbursed by religious and civic groups, and supported by various women's organizations and wealthy individuals, specific charitable groups gradually formed in the attempt to meet the needs of poorer Chicagoans.

Three significant charity organizations included the Chicago

Orphan Asylum (COA), formed in 1849, the Chicago Relief and Aid Society (CRAS), formed in 1857, and the Chicago Bureau of Charities (CBC), formed in 1894. The COA was particularly necessary during the mid-part of the nineteenth century, when it was estimated that hundreds of children were roaming Chicago streets without proper familial supervision and care. The CRAS was an especially significant group, and was responsible for distributing aid after the Chicago fire of 1871. The CBC functioned as an umbrella organization to oversee all charity work in the city, the first such coordinated and centralized effort in this regard.

Nineteenth-century charitable values generally distinguished between the worthy poor and the unworthy poor, or between the godly poor and the ungodly poor.[36] Poverty was understood as reflecting a person's moral fiber or character. The systemic roots of poverty were virtually unknown. The values underlying attitudes toward poverty as well as religion were generally individualistically conceptualized in nineteenth-century society.

Late-nineteenth-century Chicago was a city rumbling with manufacturing and industry, as well as a city resonating with various religious, cultural, and charitable impulses. But the needs of many people were not being met by the existing structures of religion, education, or charity. The reforms of progressivism, the rhetoric of the social gospel, and the philosophy of the social settlement movement attempted to address the unmet issues encompassed in a city like Chicago, a microcosm of late-nineteenth-century urban life and society.

Richard Hofstadter, in his 1955 groundbreaking analysis of progressivism in the United States, argued that middle-class people got involved in these movements of social change because they themselves were feeling displaced and powerless in their rapidly changing society. Even if this were the case—and it does seem to be true in regard to white, middle-class women—it does not detract from attempts to address such concerns.[37] Middle- and upper-middle-class people could no longer ignore the facts around them: poverty existed, violence was escalating, civic government was corrupt at worst or ineffectual at best. The ineluctable conclusion to those concerned was that the social, cultural, and religious organizations designed to hold society together as a well-functioning whole were not working. Something needed to done. The progressive era emerged in this context.

The Women of Hull House in the City

Chicago was a city the women of Hull House knew very well. Some of them, such as Mary Rozet Smith and Louise deKoven Bowen, were born and raised in wealthy Chicago families. Others moved to the city as adults, including Jane Addams, Ellen Gates Starr, Helen Culver, Julia Lathrop, Florence Kelley, and Alice Hamilton.

Most of the women of Hull House had privileged economic, social, and educational backgrounds. Only a few of the women had working-class roots: both Alzina Stevens and Mary Kenney O'Sullivan found themselves moving to Chicago for the simple necessity of attaining employment. In addition, Dr. Harriet Rice was the only African-American woman associated with Hull House in its first decade. For various reasons, her association was limited.

The women of Hull House in many ways represented the elite of Chicago. Due to their privileged social location, they were able to connect with cultured Chicagoans, who supported them and their ideas of progressive reform. Mary Wilmarth was an honored member of the Fortnightly Club, yet instrumental in forming the Chicago Woman's Club. In suggesting the agenda of the new club, Wilmarth related a challenge she received from an unnamed Chicago businessman who said to her: "[Perhaps the women should form] some kind of Club to fight our civic evils; we men have tried it and failed; perhaps you women can do something."[38]

Jane Addams, a newcomer to Chicago in 1889, and Ellen Gates Starr, a resident of Chicago since 1879, spoke to women's clubs, visited local churches, and attended cultural gatherings for the purpose of promoting their idea of a social settlement house even before they opened the doors of Hull House. Starr wrote of the support she and Addams received from the Reverend Gunsaulus:

Dr. Gunsaulus is the most popular minister in the city with the exception of Professor Swing, and he is fast rivaling him, and Dr. Gunsaulus is unqualified and enthusiastic in his adherence. We had a charming conversation with him in his study. He is a brilliant man and he simply pointed out one bright thing after another. He was very clever in the way he went to work to find out what our idea was and not to help us to one, or give his color to it.[39]

Jane Addams wrote that the Reverend David Swing, then pastor of the Central Church, supported the idea of Hull House and even penned a column in the *Evening Journal* saying so. Addams also met in the home of Mary Wilmarth to discuss the idea of Hull House with her and other invited guests.[40]

In the 1890s, all of the women of Hull House found themselves involved in differing ways within the city of Chicago. Julia Lathrop, who focused on inadequate relief for the needy and the restructuring of hospital and penal systems, received an official appointment to the Illinois Board of Charities in 1893. Florence Kelley and Alzina Stevens addressed labor issues, especially as related to women and child workers and the abuses they experienced in factories and piecework. Ellen Gates Starr became the first president of the Chicago Public School Art Society in 1894 and used her interests in art and labor to transform individual existence and social inequalities. Jane Addams became the garbage inspector of the nineteenth ward and literally forced the city to clean up its neighborhoods.[41] Dr. Alice Hamilton, who arrived at Hull House in the late 1890s, brought an interest in health and eventually became a major advocate for factory safety and industrial medicine. Other women of Hull House, such as Louise deKoven Bowen and Mary Rozet Smith, though active in various civic clubs and groups, remained essentially philanthropists.

Overall, the women of Hull House were involved in various ways in the life of the city. In keeping with the true definition of social settlements, they attempted to know their neighbors and bridge gaps between the powerful and the powerless, as well as between religious institutions and the poor.[42] They cre-

ated for themselves their life work or vocation, as well as a collection of friends with whom they would associate for the remainder of their lives.

Like many of their social contemporaries, the women of
Hull House were proud of the city. Yet, through their connections and their multifaceted work among immigrants, laborers,
child delinquents, and tired mothers, the Chicago of the hungry and the homeless was as real to them as the Chicago of the
proud and the ambitious.

In Part One, we have reviewed the literature related to Hull
House, discussed the relationship between the social settlement movement and Christianity, and provided an overview of
the context of Chicago. In Part Two, we examine the lives of
some of the Hull House women themselves. As mentioned earlier, the women discussed in this project were not the only
women involved in Hull House. Many others were involved for
long periods of time and made substantial contributions. Unfortunately, due to a lack of data on many of these other
women as well as the limited scope of a written project, only a
select number of women can be discussed. Some men, too,
were involved in Hull House. While brief mention will be made
of some of them, because Hull House was founded and fundamentally operated by women the focus is on the women of Hull
House.

The women discussed in the next chapters can be viewed
as "a galaxy of stars." The phrase, "a galaxy of stars," was used
in various nineteenth-century articles to depict the women who
lived at or worked from Hull House.[43] The expression commu-
nicates the sentiment that Hull House included a variety of
women who all contributed, each in her own way, to the work
of the house. Not all the women were reformers in the strict
sense of the word, but they all struggled to find their sense of
vocation, identity, and spirituality within a rapidly changing social ethos. The displacement and powerlessness experienced by
many of these women related to their emerging individual and
collective identity. But these women—the stars of Hull House—
were not perfect, saintly, or unaffected by late-nineteenth-century class and race biases. They were white women, generally

privileged in economic stability and educational opportunities. They have a "double identity," as theologian Sharon D. Welch wrote regarding herself; they were both oppressors and oppressed.[44] To study these women enlarges the scope of North American history and more accurately acknowledges the contributions of largely unremembered women to the religious, social, and political life of North America.

Part Two

Constellations of Hull House
—"A Galaxy of Stars"

Mary Rozet Smith and child from Hull House neighborhood

4

Constellation One
—Initial Stars

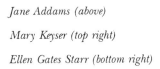

Jane Addams (above)

Mary Keyser (top right)

Ellen Gates Starr (bottom right)

THREE WOMEN SLEPT AT HULL HOUSE when its doors opened in September 1889. From the beginning, these women were connected with Hull House in differing ways. Jane Addams, who provided the original idea and much of the initial money for the enterprise, quickly became its undisputed leader. Ellen Gates Starr provided many of the early contacts with Chicago society and focused on making the house a center of culture and art in the neighborhood. She gradually became more religious and more politically radical. Mary Keyser was the housekeeper hired by Addams and Starr who became an integral part of the house and a crucial connection between it and the neighborhood before her premature death in 1897.

Because the life history and published works of Jane Addams are relatively well known, discussion in this chapter emphasizes an aspect of her personhood least analyzed, namely, her religious experience and her spiritual outlook as a mature adult. Addams was not agnostic or secular, a classification historians have usually designated to her. She embodied a liberal Christian tradition that emerged within a growing pluralistic society. She and Starr, however, provide a major contrast between how nineteenth-century women responded to the religious and spiritual yearnings of their day.

Taken together, Addams, Starr, and Keyser represent the nascent diversity of interests and talents associated with Hull House. They form the initial grouping of the Hull House constellation, and studying them provides insight into white, middle-class, nineteenth-century Americana.

Jane Addams

Born in 1860 in Cedarville, Illinois, Jane Addams became one of the most loved, respected, and famous women in the United States. This does not suggest that Addams never had opponents or detractors. During World War I she was severely criticized and ostracized by politicians, journalists, and religious leaders for her unpopular and unyielding pacifist position. Yet, after the war, Addams' popularity returned. In 1931 she was awarded the Nobel Peace prize, becoming the first American woman honored in such a way, and in 1933 she was voted one of the most influential women of the past one hundred years by the *Ladies' Home Journal* and *The Christian Science Monitor.*[1]

Addams' notability may have reached even greater heights after her death in 1935. In a book on Chicago published in 1964, for example, the author called Jane Addams "[t]he [g]reatest Chicagoan of [a]ll," because she combined the characteristics of artist, scientist, and religionist.[2] In some ways, Addams' name assumed grandiose, even mythical qualities. Martin Marty called Addams a "secular saint."[3] An interesting consequence of Addams' ascendant stardom was that her philosophical and theoretical thought was submerged until the 1960s, when scholars such as Christopher Lasch and John Farrell seriously reexamined, demystified, and reinterpreted her intellectual work.[4]

The childhood years of Addams provide no indication that she would become such a recognized person. In her autobiography, *Twenty Years at Hull-House*, Addams discussed her years before Hull House. Born into a relatively well-to-do family, Addams came to greatly admire, respect, and idealize her father, John. This may have been in part due to the death of her mother, Sarah, when Addams was only two years old. Nevertheless, the great influence shaping Addams' life was her father.

John and Sarah (Weber) Addams were pioneers when they migrated from Pennsylvania to the north-central part of Illinois in 1844. John was a miller by trade, but became a banker and a politician. He was a friend and colleague of Abraham Lincoln and, like Lincoln, an abolitionist. A Quaker by background, John Addams never joined a church, nor was he particularly devoted to church activities. (As a leader in his small community, however, he occasionally taught Sunday School.) Jane Addams' faith position was molded by her father's philosophy or theology, which upheld universal mystery and personal morals over particular dogmas or creeds.

In *Twenty Years at Hull-House*, Addams recounted a conversation she had with her father about foreordination (predestination), a subject she had difficulty understanding even though an unnamed childhood friend "understood it perfectly." Addams asked her father to explain this theological perspective to her:

To [Jane's] delighted surprise . . . he [her father] said
that he feared that he and I did not have the kind of
mind that would ever understand foreordination very
well and advised me not to give too much time to it; but
he then proceeded to say other things of which the final
impression left upon my mind was that it did not matter
much whether one understood foreordination or not,
but that it was very important not to pretend to understand what you didn't understand and that you must
always be honest with yourself inside, whatever happened.

Addams completed this vignette with an adult interpretation:
"Perhaps on the whole as valuable a lesson as the shorter catechism itself contains."[5]

Addams' life was relatively uneventful for her first twenty-
nine years. Her father remarried when she was seven. She never
developed a close emotional tie with her stepmother, Anna
Haldeman, although they always stayed in contact with one another. Anna was different from Jane and her husband, John.
She was fun-loving, interested in decorating the house, hosting
social gatherings, and developing an appreciation for music and
literature. Overall, Anna had a reverse effect on Jane who rejected the life Anna upheld, enjoyed, and deemed appropriate
for women.

In 1877, on the insistence of Addams' father and against
her own desire to attend Smith College, Addams enrolled at
the Rockford Female Seminary, a finishing school previously
attended by her two older sisters. Rockford Seminary had been
founded in 1849 by Anna P. Sill. Sill believed the seminary to
be her "missionary" work. "It was her constant prayer that [her
students] would come to hope in Christ."[6] Addams did not
fulfill Sill's prayers nor succumb to the evangelical pressure of
Rockford Seminary. She was "unresponsive to the evangelical
appeal." In short, Addams did not have a conversion experience
or decide to enter the missionary field, despite the pressure put
on her and the other "unconverted" women at the school: "We
were the subject of prayer at the daily chapel exercise and the
weekly prayer meeting, attendance upon which was obligatory."[7]

Addams did not express disdain for such conversion attempts in her autobiography. Rather, she concluded, "curiously enough, the actual activities of a missionary school are not unlike many that are carried on in a Settlement."[8]

Addams may not have been converted to late-nineteenth-century evangelical Christianity during her four-year stay at Rockford Seminary, but she was influenced in other ways. For example, in studying medieval history, she was fascinated by what she called an "ideal of mingled learning, piety, and physical labor."[9] She also was influenced by the philosophy of Thomas Carlyle and John Ruskin. Perhaps more importantly than the academic stimulation Addams received at Rockford Seminary was the popularity she experienced with students and teachers. This popularity surprised her because she viewed herself as a serious person, rather quiet and withdrawn. She also considered herself unattractive. Yet other women found her attractive and charismatic, and desired to be in her company.

As a sign of her popularity, Addams was chosen to give her class's commencement address in 1881. Entitled "Cassandra," the address spoke of the unique role women could play in helping others if they would use their intuition and "make themselves heard" in the world. She concluded by stating her belief that if women would "bring this force to bear throughout morals and justice, then she must take the active, busy world as a test for the genuineness of her intuition."[10]

Upon completing her course work and stint at Rockford Seminary, Addams decided to continue her education by studying medicine. The sudden death of her father in the summer of 1881, and a bout with back problems that eventually resulted in surgery, contributed to her withdrawal from the Woman's Medical College of Pennsylvania.

For the next seven years, Addams struggled to find her voice and a way to take an active part in the world she encountered. She took two trips to Europe, the first in 1883 and the second in 1887. (Travelling abroad was a common practice utilized by middle- and upper-middle-class families as a way to complete or finish the education of their daughters.) Between these major trips abroad, she stayed with her stepmother in Cedarville and her stepbrother, George Haldeman, in Baltimore. With her

stepmother's encouragement (or insistence), Addams participated in the social niceties expected of a single, white, middle-
class woman of her day. She did not particularly enjoy having
tea, engaging in polite conversation, or hosting social gatherings because she found such a life fundamentally futile.

During this hiatus, Addams maintained an intense letter-
writing relationship with Ellen Gates Starr, her former classmate
at Rockford Seminary. In these letters, Addams and Starr wrote
of their love for each other and lamented as to what they were
going to do with their lives. They discussed faith and theology.
They questioned such doctrines as the incarnation and divinity
of Christ. As with many young people, they were searching for
a plausible God.[11]

In 1885, in the middle of this personal sifting period, Addams joined the Presbyterian Church in Cedarville, Illinois. Addams wrote she did not join because of external influence:

At this time there was certainly no outside pressure
pushing me toward such a decision, and at twenty-five
one does not ordinarily take a step from a mere desire
to conform. While I was not conscious of any emotional
"conversion," I took upon myself the outward expressions of the religious life with all humility and sincerity.[12]

She expounded further that the "young clergyman" at the Presbyterian Church did not enforce upon her as a common lay
person "assent to dogma or miracle," but upheld a simple Christianity. In joining the church, Addams said she longed to belong
to an "outward symbol of fellowship, some bond of peace, some
blessed spot where unity of spirit might claim right of way over
all differences." She also acknowledged her increasing attraction to the ideals of democracy and connected these ideals to
the early Christian movement, when the "faith of the fisherman
and the slave had been boldly opposed to the accepted moral
belief that the well-being of a privileged few might justly be built
upon the ignorance and sacrifice of the many."[13]

Religious issues were not the only concerns Addams had
during her twenties. Like other privileged white women in the
nineteenth century, Addams suffered from what she called nervous

exhaustion or nervous depression as well as bouts of sciatic rheumatism.[14] Periods of literal invalidism enforced Addams' sense that there was nothing for her to do in life, that society itself had disallowed her and other women like her any options for making their lives useful. Society was now willing to educate women, Addams repeated time and time again, but then disallowed them to apply their knowledge and skills beyond their immediate family. Women themselves, Addams later argued, needed to understand that their role had been extended outside of the home due to society itself becoming more complex.[15] Addams eventually interpreted the dilemma and the depression she experienced as a consequence of the maladjustment of society to women desiring to be active in public life.[16]

During the years between 1881 and 1889—between completing formal education at Rockford and moving into Hull House—Addams did not engage in theorization about her general state of aimlessness, listlessness, melancholy, and illness. Rather, she simply attempted to keep going and create for herself a place and a role. She struggled against the dominant perceptions of womanhood iterated and enforced by her society. Historian Jill Conway argued that because Addams was a woman of privilege, she may have felt guilty about her inherited wealth and obligated to use it in constructive ways. Psychological interpretations around guilt may or may not be accurate. It is the case, however, that despite her class Addams was a woman severely imprisoned by the gender restrictions of her culture.[17]

Much of the struggle Addams encountered during this time period was internal. She was not entirely self-dependent or withdrawn in her struggles, however, for she drew heavily upon the support and strength of her friend Ellen Gates Starr.[18] Indeed, throughout her life, her emotional—and possibly her spiritual—strength came from her circle of close companions and friends. Even joining the Presbyterian Church in Cedarville was an attempt to find community, not a profession of theological convictions. Her decision to join the church reflected her early attempts to utilize friendship networks to gain a sense of spiritual community in the uplifting of certain common ideals.

Addams' solution to her spiritual and social dilemmas crystallized during her second trip to Europe. Historian Anne Firor

Scott wrote of the trip taken with Ellen Gates Starr and Addams' former teacher and friend, Sarah Anderson:

> Though their journey was superficially the usual pursuit of art and culture, for Jane Addams it was still a search for the answer to the fundamental question: What is good? Upon this would depend what she was to do with life.[19]

While viewing a bullfight in Madrid, Addams realized her fascination with an event so bloody and violent, and related that insight to the self-centeredness of her concerns:

> Nothing less than the moral reaction following the experience at a bullfight had been able to reveal to me that so far from following in the wake of a chariot of philanthropic fire, I had been tied to the tail of the veriest ox-cart of self-seeking.[20]

Scott interpreted the insight Addams received after the bullfight as her conversion experience: "After this experience in Madrid Jane Addams was not a different person, but her seeking, searching, and self-doubt gave way to purpose, drive, conviction, and inner poise."[21]

Addams finally verbalized to Ellen Gates Starr a notion she had about going to live among the poor. The notion was a vague dream, but it showed her intense desire to do something useful with her life. Much to Addams' relief, Starr was excited about the possibility of implementing the idea. As a practical gesture and to gain insight into "whatever perplexities and discouragement concerning the life of the poor," Addams visited Toynbee Hall before returning to the United States.[22] In January 1889, Addams moved to Chicago. She and Starr looked for a place to settle and began to make contacts with the religious and civic leaders of the city. As two white and privileged women who knew how to make the social and cultural rounds of clubs and churches, they rather quickly gained support for what they called their "scheme."

Addams, of course, found her life vocation in Hull House.

It became her spiritual community and her launching pad for activity within the larger realms of society. Hull House was Addams' home from age 29 until her death at age 74. She remained the inspiration behind its work, whether or not she was actually physically present. Addams spent significant portions of time away from the house—resting in the Chicago home of her friend and companion, Mary Rozet Smith, or the summer house she and Smith bought in Maine, or travelling to give lectures or to participate in and preside at meetings.

Addams spent the 1890s addressing mostly local concerns, such as the need for garbage collection and the elimination of corruption in local politics. From the power base of Hull House, she engaged in a life of reform within larger and larger contexts. She formed liaisons with national and international social reformers, and asserted her leadership in various ways. In 1909, she became an executive member of the National Association for the Advancement of Colored People; in 1911, she became vice-president of the National American Woman Suffrage Association; In 1915, she became the first Chair of the Woman's Peace Party; and in 1919 and 1920, she helped to found the Women's International League for Peace and Freedom and the American Civil Liberties Union.

Her life at Hull House and the relationships she shared with strong women residents, co-workers, and friends enabled her to reach beyond the immediacy of the nineteenth ward. Through Hull House, Addams fulfilled her personal desire for social usefulness and was empowered to address the many pressing societal issues of her day.[23] She had found her voice in activity.

Twelve years after she and Starr had embarked on their scheme, Addams reflected that her initial decision to move to Chicago and open a social settlement house was one of "absolute recklessness." Practicality emerged from her retrospection, however, as she stated that "[if] one is to die, one may as well die doing what she likes."[24]

Historians recorded a change in Addams' religious qualities as she moved out of her searching years into her active Hull House years. Some acknowledged that she began her enterprise with religious underpinnings, often talking and writing, for instance, about the humanization and renaissance of Christianity.

But they found a movement away from explicit religious expressions. Historians do not address whether she was a church member or active in a religious community during her Hull House years. Only one historian asserted that when Addams moved to Chicago she transferred her church membership from the Cedarville Presbyterian Church to the prestigious Fourth Presbyterian Church.[25] The problem, of course, was that Addams herself, in *Twenty Years at Hull-House* and in lesser-known writings, did not discuss her church involvement after joining Cedarville Presbyterian Church. This void contributed to the overall disregard of the issue by most scholars. It is a central issue for this project, however.

Records show that Addams transferred her church membership from the Presbyterian Church in Cedarville to the Ewing Street Church in Chicago, a Congregational parish. A church membership survey dated February 1895 lists the members of Ewing Street Church. The pastor recorded Addams as a charter member and as a regular attendant. The following notation was made next to Addams' name: "First resident at Hull House. Desires to have the work of the church more closely cooperative with Hull House."[26]

The Ewing Street Church was organized in 1891, less than two years after Hull House opened and was "a union of three missionary enterprises—Clinton Street Church, Harrison Street Mission and the 12th Street Mission."[27] More significantly, it was an outreach congregation sponsored by the Chicago City Missionary Society. Located down the street from Hull House, it served the same populace. Church literature describing its neighborhood and that of Hull House is interchangeable with one key exception: Ewing Street Church is explicitly and evangelically Protestant.

> This is in large part a district of factories closely surrounded by thousands of tenements of the poorest sort into which are crowded nearly 25,000 Italians, 11,000 or more Greeks, large numbers of Jews, Poles and Bohemians. . . . As the only representative of English-speaking Protestant Christianity in a district over a mile square stands this church and house. . . . The Church

stands as a beacon in Chicago's most congested ward. It purposes, through the earnest preaching of the Gospel, to uphold Christ as the Light of the World and to point out the way of righteousness.[28]

At least some of Addams' contemporaries knew she was a member of the Ewing Street Church. Helen Campbell wrote that Addams kept in touch with all the Hull House activities "no less than with the life of the little Congregational Church around the corner, where she is a faithful and well-beloved attendant and member." The Reverend Theodore Crowl, in an 1894 article on Hull House, described Addams and Starr as "[t]wo Christian women, the one a Congregationalist, the other an Episcopalian."[29] Other Hull House residents attended this same church, including Mary Keyser. One of the male residents of Hull House, Clifford W. Barnes, even served as interim pastor from June to November of 1893.[30] Addams was actively involved at Ewing Street Church at least through the mid-1920s.[31]

Evidence indicates, then, that Addams belonged to and was active in an evangelical, Protestant Church. It is unlikely her church membership changed through the years, although it's equally apparent her public religious behavior did change. Edward L. Burchard, the first male resident at Hull House, in a letter written to Ellen Gates Starr in 1938, reflected on the early years he spent at Hull House:

> It seems like yesterday and the jolly evenings around the parlor table when Miss Addams and you, and Julia Lathrop and Florence Kelley and Mary MacDowell ate apples and bananas that I stocked up from Halsted Street, while you all told unforgettable incidents of the day's work, or when Miss Addams led in evening Bible and prayer with every one on their knees. No perhaps that was before Florence Kelley came.[32]

Burchard's recollection of Addams leading evening prayer "with every one on their knees" may be rather surprising given the later non-religious, even secular, image of Addams and Hull House. Yet this practice is not unbelievable behavior given Addams encounters with evangelical Christianity at Rockford Seminary and her membership in a congregation sponsored by the Chicago City Missionary Society.

Whatever her personal beliefs, Addams was determined to keep Hull House free of "sectarian religion." Hull House, therefore, never sponsored religious services, although in its early years, residents gathered for informal worship and prayer. The minutes from a resident meeting held on November 25, 1893, record this practice, noting Addams' announcement that "devotions would be held as usual at 9 o'clock on Sunday evening, and that attendance would not be obligatory."[33] These informal gatherings were dropped once it was realized that residents did not share similar theologies. In the attempt to include and be respectful of differing religious traditions, the religious gatherings of Hull House residents turned into another reading and discussion group, an extra event quickly deemed replicatious of other house programs.

The topic of religion was not ignored at Hull House, however. Madame Blanc, a visitor to Hull House during the 1893 World's Fair, noted that "Miss" Starr announced an upcoming lecture to be given by a preacher. Blanc wrote that Starr said all people would be allowed to express their doubts and personal ideas, although she hoped that respect would be present.[34] In a single month in 1896, Washington Gladden, John Dewey, Charles O. Boring, and William D. MacKenzie all spoke at Hull House on the general topic of the Social Gospel, or applied Christianity, as it was often called.[35]

Through Hull House, Addams attempted to create an environment where religion would not be a divisive force, but where it could be discussed in relatively open and respectful ways. Since Hull House was not a mission or a church, its intent was not to convert anyone to particular doctrines or dogmas. At the same time, religious topics were not avoided. Religion was addressed and acknowledged in much the same way as were other complexities and problems of nineteenth-century society. The personal beliefs of residents, however, were not to interfere with work in furthering conversation and understanding between people of differing religious perspectives.

From the twentieth century on, Addams hardly made public

her personal beliefs. It is questionable whether her closest work associates knew of her religious affiliation.[36] In part, nondisclosure of her personal or private religious practices and views was probably an attempt not to become a barrier to other people's religious search and beliefs. Yet in the study of U.S. religious history, this veil has served not to enhance religious matters but to silence them. Historians, noting Addams' lack of discussion regarding religion, concluded she became agnostic; they interpreted Addams' silence as another example of the secularization of twentieth-century society, rather than probing deeper for likely reasons regarding her silence.

Addams' silence about her personal religious perspectives was directly related to her sense of spirituality and implementation of vocation. From memories regarding her early childhood and her father's insights into foreordination through her experience of the evangelical pressure of Rockford Seminary and her questing letters to Starr, Addams came to believe that particular religious beliefs were secondary to how one lived one's life. "The Christian faith is a life and not a doctrine," were words repeated by Addams.[37] She refused to state in fact what she did not know in experience, and came to have a profound appreciation of the mysteries of life.

Addams attempted to publicly clarify her spirituality in her second to last published book, *The Excellent Becomes the Permanent*, a book generally neglected by historians. On one level, the book was simply a collection of the addresses, speeches, and sermons given by Addams at the memorial services of some of her most cherished friends and associates. On another level, the book enabled Addams to reply to two questions asked her, "What do you believe?" and "What is your attitude toward the future life?"[38] Not surprisingly, Addams did not answer these two questions doctrinally. She did not quote the Bible and used Christian metaphor only generally. Death, to Addams, was the great equalizer of all people; as to what happens after death, she affirmed as mystery. Her focus was on living life well and having the wisdom, courage, and faith to do so. For example, speaking at the funeral of Jenny Dow Harvey, the first kindergarten teacher at Hull House, Addams stated:

And yet we know, now that death has set his seal upon her, that too, in time, must seem gracious and right. We will remember at last the paramount interest of life, all that makes it lofty and worthy, all that lifts it above the commonplace, lies in the sense of mystery that constantly surrounds it, in the consciousness that each day as it dawns may bring the end either to ourselves or to our best beloved. . . .[T]he consciousness of the unknown is all that can give life a meaning and make it in any sense worth living.[39]

From a pastoral and personal perspective, Addams encouraged people to grieve, to remember the love and the work of the deceased and, in this way, to carry on their work and make it a permanent part of the world. From a theological and ideological perspective, Addams did not provide platitudes in the face of death and its mystery. Rather, she told people to embrace it as an experience shared by all human beings and something that may one day be understood.

In 1960, theologian Georgia Harkness offered an important interpretation of Addams' religious framework. Harkness first asked, "What of Her Religion?", in probable response to the commonly held belief that Addams was irreligious. Harkness stated that she "long had an unsatisfied curiosity" about Addams' "attitude toward the Christian faith." Harkness—like everyone else—affirmed the humanitarianism of Addams, but stated—like everyone else—that Hull House had no religious services and that Addams' own church affiliation "was so minimized that [she] had not heard of it." After reading Addams' works, Harkness was persuaded of her spirituality and located it at the liberal end of the Christian spectrum:

A diligent search of [Addams'] writings now convinces me that Miss Addams was a theist and a liberal Christian whose motivation came primarily from the ethical teachings of Jesus; her depths of religious insight, while not ecclesiastical or fully evangelical, were nevertheless real and powerful. In short, her religion did not have in it

the full gamut of Pauline Christian thought, but what
she drew from the Gospels motivated her both to a faith
in God and to works of love far in excess of those of the
many who looked on Hull House as an irreligious institution.[40]

Harkness's interpretation, offered more than thirty years ago,
needs to be reaffirmed and restated. Given the religious context
of Addams' life and the radical disagreements between religious
bodies in the nineteenth century, Addams attempted to live her
faith in a way not yet fully understood or accepted. She desired
to be authentic to her experience and participate in a religious
community. She also desired to live a life of love and service
based on what she perceived to be the early teachings of Jesus.
But she found abhorrent the idea of dictating her perceptions
to others.

Furthermore, as Harkness acknowledged, Addams lived in
a religiously pluralistic neighborhood and worked with people
of differing beliefs or none. Harkness stated that Addams
"might have instituted some voluntary, nonsectarian services of
worship, but until we have come closer to the solution of this
problem it is surely inappropriate to condemn her for not doing
so."[41] Indeed, the problem of religious pluralism remains to this
day. Self-defining contemporary ecumenical communities con-
tinually struggle with how to share common worship and work
in the midst of real differences. In our late-twentieth-century
context, when we are beginning to realize the complexities and
illusiveness of nonsectarianism, the solution Addams embraced
one hundred years ago seems reasonable. Addams pointed to
a common spiritual plane where all people stood as mortal in
the presence of mystery and where life itself was to be the
affirmative chorus—the "Amen"—of all people.

Addams was not a theologian yet she was explicit about her
belief system, which was based on spiritual rather than religious
principles and ideals. Although a member of an evangelical congregation, the assertion of shared doctrinal or dogmatic tenets
did not motivate her life. Rather, what motivated her was the
action of loving one's neighbor and learning to live together in
recognition of the humanity of all. A skilled and practiced peace-

maker and conciliator in matters of political and social reform, Addams brought the same characteristics to her understandings of late-nineteenth- and early-twentieth-century Christianity. Her arbitrations and opinions in political and social matters, however, were far better received and understood—though certainly not consistently liked or appreciated—than her attempts to bridge the entrenched and deepening chasms within Christianity.

Ellen Gates Starr

The life and faith embraced by Ellen Gates Starr, Addams' dear college friend and partner in the initial Hull House enterprise, took her in a very different direction than Addams. Starr lived at Hull House for more than thirty years. Like Addams, she was absent only when work and studies took her away for select time periods. But, unlike Addams, Starr's presence and leadership at Hull House faded over time. While she remained active in Hull House until 1920, and added to it an energetic and radical edge, Hull House did not provide the all-encompassing vocational and spiritual outlet for her that it provided for Addams. While Starr used Hull House as a base and home in much the same way as did Addams and the other women of Hull House, she turned to other institutions in her vocational and religious search. Unlike Addams, Starr did not become an admired woman but died in relative obscurity and poverty. Starr, therefore, provides a profoundly different picture of the choices and fates of women in the late-nineteenth and early-twentieth centuries.

Starr was born in Laona, Illinois, in 1859. Her family migrated from Connecticut to rural Illinois a few years before her birth. Starr's early education was received in a one-room schoolhouse. Her father, Caleb, was a sailor on the East Coast who became a farmer and a businessman in Illinois. Her mother, Susan Gates, had three other children and managed to save enough money to send Starr to Rockford Seminary for one year. Starr and Addams met there during the academic year of 1877-78.

After Rockford, Starr taught in a country school in Mt. Morris, Illinois. After one year as a rural teacher, she received a new job—and a much better one—teaching at Miss Kirkland's

School for Girls in Chicago.[42] While at Kirkland's School, Starr increased her knowledge of art and intensified her religious explorations, two interests that would remain her moorings throughout her eighty years of life.

Starr wrote of her spiritual journey in an autobiographical work called *A Bypath Into the Great Roadway.*[43] Starr's ancestors, when they arrived in the New England colonies in the seventeenth century, were Puritans in faith and practice. Her immediate family, however, was Unitarian because her grandparents were converted by the early-nineteenth-century preaching of William Ellery Channing and Theodore Parker. Despite this rich religious background, Starr stated that her parents gave her virtually no religious instruction:

> I was never urged to read the Bible, and when I began to do so of my own motion, my father seemed a good deal amused by my comments. I recall his saying that he had always felt a curiosity as to how the Scriptures would impress a quite unbiased mind; and he seemed to feel that the opportunity for gratification was at hand.

In continuing her reflections on her early religious influences, Starr noted her inability to connect with the evangelical religion she encountered in the social environment around her:

> [R]eligion occupied my thoughts very little as a young girl. And the very Protestant and evangelical form of religion which was first urged upon me at school, never really engaged my interest or attention. It was quite alien ground, regarded not wholly without condescension, and remained indifferent to me, except for a temporary interest aroused by the personality of a Protestant minister under whose influence and instruction in literature I came for a time at the age of eighteen or nineteen. But after that episode, as before it, evangelical religion made no appeal to my interest.[44]

After Starr moved to Chicago she began to explore religious alternatives. She attended the Church of the Unity, pastored by

Dr. Robert Collyer, saying, "Going to church on Sunday appealed to my New England sense of decorum, and no further demand was made upon me by it than an ethical one." She also attended Central Music Hall to hear the preaching of Dr. David Swing. While enjoying the intellectual stimulation of Swing's sermons, she felt the "lack or rarity of any devotional atmosphere."[45] During this phase of Starr's life, she noted a "spiritual craving" within her as she "browsed in different pastures, seeking." It is during these years that Starr and Addams exchanged their many letters containing their religious and theological questions. Finally, in 1884, at age twenty-five, Starr was baptized and confirmed in the Episcopal Church. She noted of this decision: "I came in at the 'low' end, entirely 'Protestant-Episcopal'; indeed, protesting actively, receiving the minimum of dogma, and putting the freest and vaguest interpretation on that."[46]

Like Addams, then, Starr joined a religious institution not on the basis of doctrine but as a way to enable and enhance her search for spiritual community. Neither Starr nor Addams found evangelical Protestantism spiritually appealing even though both were exposed to it, especially in their Rockford Seminary days. Starr and Addams were not antagonistic about Protestant evangelical religious expressions; it simply did not interest them or connect with them. Ultimately, there was nothing in it that could motivate them in their life journeys. The individual conversion experiences upheld by nineteenth-century Protestant evangelicalism, the emphasis on personal moral codes and individual salvation, as well as credence to specific doctrines, would have narrowed—not enlarged—the life choices of women like Starr and Addams.

After Starr's reception into the Episcopal Church and while teaching at Miss Kirkland's school in Chicago, she and Addams took their life-altering trip to Europe. Starr could not have afforded to go if Addams had not paid for half of the travel expenses.[47] The import of the European trip has already been noted in regard to Addams; while there she vocalized her dream of Hull House, receiving support and acceptance of it from Starr. What has not been previously noted, however, is that Starr, too, had a conversion experience on this European tour. This was a turning point in Starr's life, and may have been the determinative factor in Starr's decision to lend her hand to Addams' social settlement idea.

While Starr and Addams were in London in 1889, a major dock strike was occurring. Starr followed the events in the newspapers with great interest. She then heard for the first time a priest who was to become her spiritual leader. Starr said of her initial introduction to Father James Otis Huntington:

> It was his deep concern for justice to the workers which first drew me to Father Huntington. Later he aroused my interest in the welfare of my own soul. . . . My "first conversion" did not occur at the time of my baptism and confirmation in the Episcopal Church, but after I came under the influence of Father Huntington. It was the beginning of my interest in Catholic truth.[48]

Huntington was an Episcopalian priest who, in 1881, founded a monastic order called the Order of the Holy Cross. The order emphasized liturgical renewal and ritual (especially the centrality of the Mass), prayer, and confession. In other words, it advocated a return to the Catholic roots of Anglicanism, which was a reflection of the Oxford movement in England and the Anglo-Catholic movement in the United States. In addition to the spiritual concerns of Huntington was an equal concern with the social problems of the nineteenth century. Huntington himself lived in urban poverty—in the slums of Manhattan—and later founded the Church Association for the Advancement of the Interests of Labor.[49] Virgil George Michel, a priest in the Order of St. Benedict, popularized Huntington's theology in the United States and influenced not only Starr but also Dorothy Day.[50]

Starr's conversion to a new spirituality and social justice occurred virtually simultaneously. From this point on, Starr was unable to separate her religious convictions and spiritual devotion from her work in the neighborhood of Hull House or in specific issues of labor. Starr became very critical of the Christian Church in general and its typical responses to poverty: "What people like to call 'charity' is far more popular than the cardinal virtue of justice."[51] She interpreted the lack of organized efforts on the part of the church to the overwhelming social problems of her day, and said, "The cause of the Church's weakness in dealing with social needs seems to be found on the one hand in lack of imagination and on the other in worldliness."[52]

Starr did not lack either imagination or spiritual devotion. During the early years of Hull House, her interests in art, religion, and labor were synthesized under the general rubric of spiritual justice. She brought to Hull House replications of the classical works of art, and hung them on the walls for all people to see, even the children in the kindergarten room. She held to the tenet that "art must be of the people if it is to be at all."[53] She believed that beauty needed to be present even in places of poverty or, better stated, art was especially needed in dark, dirty, and dingy neighborhoods. Starr believed that art was a medium of communication. More importantly, it was a method by which people could work toward a fuller and more just way of life. She came to understand art as theology, and as part of the process of human redemption. With her influence, Butler Gallery, the first of thirteen building projects of Hull House, was constructed in 1891. She also became founder of the Chicago Public School Art Society and served as president between 1894 and 1897.[54]

In 1896, Starr explained the emphasis she placed on art in her work for social justice and in her understanding of the work of the church. She wrote: "We shall have art again when life is artistic. Art must come back to life through the channel of its daily occupations. All life must be redeemed."[55] For Starr, then, art connected the mundane of life with the miracle of new life. It was not a passive medium but was a powerful political, social, and spiritual expression of people's experiences and hopes.

Starr gave many lectures and speeches during her years at Hull House. Most of her presentations focused on this trinity of art, religion, and economic justice. At the Hinsdale Woman's Club, for example, she spoke on "The Teachings of Christ on Industrial Orders, Work, Wages, House and the Common Welfare."[56] At the Chautauqua Institution in New York state, a fashionable adult summer school founded in 1878, she lectured on the history of art.[57] At Hull House, she not only taught art appreciation, English literature, and Bible, but also became involved in the labor movement of her day. She eventually joined the Socialist Party, and ran as an aldermanic candidate in the 1916 Chicago civic election. As a woman and as a socialist, Starr knew that winning the election was unlikely. Still, she ran to raise people's awareness of the issues of the day.[58]

Starr linked her progressively radical politics to her increasing religious devotion. She stated that while William Morris became a socialist because he was an artist, she "became a Socialist because [she] was a Christian." Starr explained this connection further:

> The Christian religion teaches that all men are to be regarded as brothers, that no one should wish to profit by the loss or disadvantage of others. . . . "Civilized" life is in grotesque contrast to all this. And the individual, acting individualistically, is helpless to modify it very much. . . . Many Christians who would otherwise be Socialists are frightened because many Socialists are materialists. Socialism does not make a materialist of me; nor does even the capitalistic system; but I can easily understand how the latter drives many to it. . . . Socialism only, so far as I could find out, offered any effectual method to put down the mighty from their seats and to exalt the humble and the meek.[59]

Two episodes from Starr's life illuminate how she combined her ideological stances with a desire for social justice. In 1897, Starr went to Hammersmith, London, to study bookbinding at the Dove's bindery. Her goal was to learn this vanishing art and bring it back to the people of Chicago. Upon returning, Starr realized that the craft she learned was not useful to poor, laboring people because they could not afford to buy such beautiful books. Starr did not want to make books only the rich could buy.[60] While this occurrence disappointed Starr, it reinforced to her how art was a product controlled by the wealthy. Through this incident Starr became more invested in fostering art for the well-being of the common people.

Providing another insight into Starr and her vocational and

spiritual convictions were her numerous arrests in Chicago labor strikes. Mary Anderson, a Swedish immigrant and shoe factory worker who got involved in the labor movement through Hull House, described the role Starr played in the restaurant workers' strike of 1914.

> The police were very tough; they yanked the arm of one girl out of its socket and another girl had her arm broken. Ellen Gates Starr . . . came down to me one morning and said, "What can I do to help?" I said, "I wish you would go to the picket line and see that the girls get better treatment. I'll be along later."
>
> She went off and when I arrived a little later, I could not get through the crowd. Some of the newspapermen were taking pictures from the lamp posts. I elbowed my way through and there stood little Miss Starr with a big policeman holding her arm. I asked what was the matter and the policeman said, "If you don't shut up, I'll arrest you too."
>
> When they were arrested, the girls would not walk over to the police station. The police had to get the patrol wagon. Then when the girls were put into the wagon they would make speeches from the back.
>
> Miss Starr was bailed out immediately. She had said that she had a right to walk on that sidewalk as an American citizen. We knew there had to be a test case for illegal arrest in this situation and we decided that Miss Starr was a good person to make it.[61]

Due in part to Starr's small stature (she weighed less than one hundred pounds), her close association with some of the elite of Chicago, and her politeness during arrests, Starr's actions were successful in drawing public sympathy to the side of the workers. Her solidarity with striking workers and her method of behavior during and after an arrest is noted in one of her obituaries:

> [Starr] made a practice of approaching a policeman who was placing a striker under arrest and saying, "As

an American citizen, I protest against the arrest of this person, who is doing nothing against the law."

The story is told that because a policeman in court once testified that she had said, "Leave them girls be," she was released and the case against her dismissed, the lawyer representing her having emphasized that the grammar could not possibly be Miss Starr's.[62]

After her arrest during one of the garment workers' strikes, Starr called on the help of her longtime friend and Hull House associate, Mary Wilmarth. Wilmarth, a Chicago socialite, came to the Des Plaines Police Station to bail out Starr and her five arrested comrades. Bail was set at $400 per person. In lieu of cash, Wilmarth offered as collateral the land upon which the Congress Hotel was built. The police clerk refused to believe Wilmarth's ownership of such prime property. Wilmarth then located Judge McGoorty, an old friend, convinced him to go to the police station with her and vouch for her financial security. As Anderson put it, "[t]he clerk was finally convinced [of Wilmarth's identity] and accepted the collateral, and the girls were liberated."[63]

Starr's spiritual commitment continued during all these political and social activities. She maintained involvement in the Episcopal Church and in the Order of the Holy Cross, but increased her participation in Catholic liturgy. She began to use the Roman Breviary for her own personal devotions.[64] While she believed that "the ultimate miracle can only be written by the mystic and the poet," she also became convinced that the Roman Catholic Church was the spiritual community where she most authentically belonged.[65]

Starr mulled over her decision to join the Catholic Church for many years. She made a list of reasons for and against joining the church.[66] Under contra, Starr noted the inertia of the church, its tendency to "remain, if possible, where one is, without disturbing the sense of stability," and the "vulgarity and apparent unspirituality of many Roman Catholic priests one meets." She noted the difficulties she had with making full profession of faith, stating she had not read the decisions of the Council of Trent and did not "detest the sects." She noted the positive changes happening in the Episcopal Church, especially those regarding educating for social justice and democracy. Her greatest obstacle to joining the Roman Catholic Church, not surprisingly, was its "reactionary attitude. . . in matters of social and political progress, [and its] organized and authoritative opposition to socialism." In this final objection, Starr's religious and political leanings clashed with no apparent compromise available.

On the pro side, Starr first noted her great appreciation of the "Catholicity in the Roman Church," the sense of oneness, universality, and historic connection that it provided. In contrast, the Episcopal Church seemed impermanent and lacking in uniformity. She was especially troubled by the fact that some Episcopal churches no longer heard private confessions. Engaging in this search for spiritual community as a woman nearly sixty years of age, Starr related that she was "longing for peace for the last of [her] life," and desired to "cease pulling against the stream and to go with [her] impulses and inclination." On another level, she noted her "increasing sense of and belief in the communion of the saints and their interest in us." Most importantly, Starr found the Mass of the Catholic Church a central source of life, energy, and mystery. Starr's "increasing devotion to Our Lord in the Blessed Sacrament" swung her decision to officially convert to Catholicism; it outweighed even her greatest concern regarding its anti-socialist stance.

In 1919, Starr gave the Episcopalians one last try by attending the General Convention of the Protestant Episcopal Church in Detroit. The heated debate concerning whether the Episcopal Church was Protestant or Catholic, and the resulting decision that it was indeed Protestant and that the "Catholic Church was the proper place for Catholics" affirmed Starr's decision that she could no longer think of herself as an Anglican Catholic but must join the Roman Catholic Church. She returned to Chicago and began spiritual direction with a Paulist father. In February 1920, she visited St. Joseph's Benedictine Monastery in Louisiana, a community of nuns. She joined the church on March 2, received her First Holy Communion on March 3, and was confirmed in Chicago's Holy Name Cathedral on May 23.[67] She then moved out of Hull House and into the convent (priory), where she was later accepted as a member. She occasionally visited Hull House from 1920 onward.

Starr's journey into increasing religious devotion and political activity negatively affected her standing at Hull House. Many of the other residents came to think of her as too outspoken and opinionated. She was perceived as fanatical by some residents, especially the younger ones. She was thought to be rather moody and was believed to unnecessarily "act up." Alice Hamilton, for example, wrote in 1904 that she would have a visitor stay in Starr's flat but she was not sure "Miss Starr would be nice to her" since the visitor was not a High Church Episcopalian, a member of the Holy Cross, an ardent confessor and devoted rosary user. Ten years later, Alice Hamilton wrote that during one of the restaurant strikes "Miss Starr [was] picketing and passionately longing to be arrested." Hamilton continued, "I do hope it [the strike] will be over . . . Miss Starr is so difficult when she is striking."[68] When Hamilton first came to Hull House, she was slightly afraid of Starr, but in time grew tolerant of her and even learned to like and respect her.

The friendship between Starr and Addams lessened during the first decade of Hull House, especially as Addams found personal support from Mary Rozet Smith, another Hull House woman. Yet, in the early years of Hull House, their interests and skills were greatly complimentary:

> [Addams and Starr] made a wonderful team. Jane Addams with her warm sympathy and her strong sense of the immediacies of her environment, and Ellen with her wit and wisdom—for she had it even as a girl—of the ultimate relation of all good things, including good works, to God in whom the giving of her "all" was but reasonable service . . . their respective lines of service were clear. Jane was to keep Ellen's attention from wandering away from the woes of man toward a frank enjoyment of whatever was delightful about him . . . and Ellen's task was never to lose sight, nor if possible ever to let others lose sight of the holy purpose of their service, which was, in her view, simply to please God.[69]

Addams admired Starr's "aesthetic qualities."[70] To Addams' credit and consistent with her professed ideal of tolerance, she never seemed to curtail Starr's radicalness or publicly express displeasure of Starr's activities. While Addams was out of Chicago during the restaurant workers' strike, and Starr was being criticized by the public and conservative Hull House followers for her involvement in it, Starr stated: "I shall not stop. If Miss Addams were in town, I am sure she would not ask me to. Miss Addams is not autocratic; she does not dictate [to] members of her household."[71]

Starr and Addams operated from Hull House in very different ways. Starr did not have inherited wealth as did Addams, and therefore needed to find financial support to enable her vocation of art and protest. Mary Wilmarth financially backed Starr by paying for her room, board, and furnishings at Hull House; she even financially supported Starr's 1916 campaign. Indeed, Wilmarth was devoted to Starr and the work in which Starr engaged. She encouraged Starr to not give away the little money she had to more needy people, but keep it for herself and her own needs.[72]

Despite Starr's reputation as a difficult personality, especially in her relations with other residents, she, like other Hull House women, made significant contacts with neighborhood folks. Starr received an inheritance of $6000 from Hull House "regular" Mr. Dodge, who considered Starr a good friend and appreciated her "kindness in finding him chess adversaries."[73] She also was remembered by some Hull House folks as a "beloved friend and teacher." Jane Reoch, a Chicago woman who attended Starr's reading classes at Hull House, wrote to Starr:

My life would look bare indeed if the memory of those evenings spent with you were taken out of it. Sometimes if I am inclined to be lazy or not do a thing as it ought to be done, I say to myself, "I would be ashamed to have Miss Starr know that." So I pull myself together and try to be better. There is no telling how many lives you have touched in just the same way.[74]

Although some of the Hull House residents were uneasy with

the intensity of Starr's religious convictions, Starr seemed able to get along with people who were not religiously devoted. Victor Yarros who, along with his wife, Rachelle, was a longtime Hull House resident, wrote Starr on the occasion of her eightieth birthday: "You and I have. . . much in common. It is not religion, to be sure, since I remain an incurable Agnostic. But we have the same humanistic point of view, and we believe in fighting wrong and injustice."[75]

While Starr's work from the early days of Hull House centered on art, politics, and religion, some of her friends and acquaintances interpreted her life as involving varying emphases through the years. Alice Hamilton, for example, wrote that when she first met Starr, she thought of her as an artist; then she thought of her as a "socialist in pickets." Finally, she thought of her as a person with "deeper needs." She meant religious needs.[76]

These vocational identities may indeed have been Starr's public persona, as she attempted to live her life with authenticity and in response to the needs she perceived around her. While being fanatical was against social settlement principles of tolerance and acceptance—and was probably one reason why Starr encountered some difficulties at Hull House and why her position of authority lessened as the years went by—she probably would not object to such a label. Starr wholeheartedly believed in what she did. Whether she was promoting art within public schools or walking the picket lines; whether she was arguing the merits of socialism over capitalism or agonizing about the fallenness of the Christian Church, she did it all without reservation or hesitation. She did not mince words. She did not succumb to playing the role of a nice, meek, and gentle Victorian lady, but astutely used her influence and social standing to advance the causes in which she believed. Unlike Addams, Starr blatantly communicated the connectedness of her religious and political convictions. There was no room for compromise within Starr's character or theology, and this may have made her life at Hull House a rather lonely existence. Underlying all her words and actions was an unyielding sense that she was living as God desired. Indeed, Starr wrote that the "Christian vocation demands everything that we can possibly be called upon by our personal or social conscience to do."[77]

In stark contrast to Starr's years of vigorous activities, her last years of life were spent as an invalid. In 1929, she had a spinal operation which left her paralyzed from the waist down. In 1930, she found a convent in New York state, the Holy Child in Suffern, which agreed to accept her for a nominal fee. In 1935, she became an Oblate of the Third Order of St. Benedict. During her last years, she corresponded with a diverse variety of friends and painted. She died February 10, 1940, which was St. Monica's Day. She had outlived not only Addams, but many of the other Hull House women, and was buried in the convent cemetery.

Mary Keyser

The third original resident of Hull House was Mary Keyser. Keyser and her family had been friends of Addams and her family from their Cedarville days.[78] Other than this, nothing is known of Keyser's life before Hull House. Unlike Addams or Starr, Keyser was not a writer and left no recording of her life. Nor was she a reformer in the strict definition of the word. In addition, she perhaps died too young to make a real impact on the history of Hull House. A discussion of her presence, however, provides a fuller picture of the early years of Hull House and the variety of vocations necessary to keep it going.

Addams devoted one sentence to Keyser in *Twenty Years at Hull-House:*

> On the 18th of September, 1889, Miss Starr and I moved into it [Hull House], with Miss Mary Keyser, who began by performing the housework, but who quickly developed into a very important factor in the life of the vicinity as well as in that of the neighborhood, and whose death five years later was most sincerely mourned by hundreds of our neighbors.[79]

Keyser enjoyed telling the story of the first night she, Addams, and Starr spent at Hull House. The three of them, a little leery of their new neighborhood, very carefully and intentionally locked the front door before going to bed. The next morning they woke to find that not only had they left the back door unlocked, but wide open. "[Keyser] always declared that any notion of 'a dangerous neighborhood' was forever laid to rest by that peaceful experience."[80]

Keyser was responsible for purchasing food, doing house-keeping tasks, and otherwise maintaining the practical aspects of life, which Florence Kelley interpreted as a "full-time professional job."[81] These duties led her into immediate contact with the Hull House neighborhood. Winifred E. Wise, a Hull House visitor, wrote that Keyser came to the house to do the housework and "ended up caring for half the neighbor children." Wise said that when Keyser went to the market, she "invited the wives of the butcher, the baker, and the saloon keeper for tea, and they came, first out of curiosity and again out of liking."[82] Despite the poetic and stereotypical language, the idea conveyed is of how Keyser very rapidly became part of the everyday life of the nineteenth ward.

Keyser established an almost immediate rapport with her neighbors; she became known to them through simple and nonflamboyant works of kindness. The children of the neighborhood called her "Miss Mary," while they called Addams and Starr "Miss Addams" and "Miss Starr." Though responsible for the household tasks of Hull House, Keyser apparently found time and energy to be an "intimate friend and counselor of the poor neighbors. . . . Hers was the neighborly work, the visiting of the sick, the daily ministrations to the needy and heartsick and the despairing."[83] She became responsible for the Labor Bureau for Women which operated out of Hull House, and attempted to help women secure appropriate work and child care.[84]

Keyser had received some training at the Illinois Training School for Nurses, but found she was not physically strong enough to "carry on nursing as a profession."[85] This did not prevent her from offering informal care, however. She cared for sick neighbors and Addams' ill sister, which enabled Addams to carry on with her Hull House work rather than totally succumbing to the responsibility of the "family claim." In the Ewing Street Church Membership Survey, the pastor noted of Keyser, an attendant and member of the church: "Miss Keyser was for most of the summer at Storm Lake taking care of Miss Addams' eldest sister who was very ill through all the summer and died during the last of July."[86] Whether Keyser cared for Addams' sister as a hired nurse or as an uncompensated and willing friend is unknown, although either would be likely. Keyser's mother and brother were attendants, though not members of the Ewing Street Church. It is possible then, that when Keyser moved to Hull House, her family moved to the neighborhood as well.

It is unfortunate that no specific data exists on Keyser's background or on why she came to be hired by Addams and Starr as their housekeeper. Like Starr, Keyser was not financially independent and came to receive monthly fellowships for her work at Hull House.[87] Through her association with Hull House, Keyser became known and respected throughout the Chicago settlement network. When she died unexpectedly (following an unnamed brief illness) on January 9, 1897, the date her thirty-sixth birthday, the *Chicago Commons* newsletter wrote of her death:

> [N]ot only was [it] an event of great sadness and bereavement to her family and to her devoted friends in the Hull House circle, but was keenly felt by those in the Chicago settlements who knew her as one of the most faithful and devoted of workers.[88]

The *Chicago Commons* went on to note that it was in large part due to Keyser's "faithfulness and good management" that Hull House ran so smoothly, and that she was a "power and a well-loved sister." Her power, however, was very different than that wielded by either Addams or Starr. Keyser relied on the personal relations of care she established with individuals in need and the fulfilling of household duties to give her vocational purpose. Only indirectly—through such acts of service—was her reputation fortified. In this way, she provides a much more traditional insight into the experience of women in the late nineteenth century. Although competent, able, and interested in issues of reform, she was not a leader in the way that Addams or Starr exemplified. She was a more ordinary woman, who performed household duties, attended church, and impacted the immediate lives of people with whom she came in contact. Unlike Starr and Addams, she does not appear to have been driven by great ideals of social justice or political reform. Yet she provided a vital humanizing presence within Hull House and its neighborhood.

Keyser's funeral was held the day after her death at the Ewing Street Church, with an evening memorial at Hull House. Both events were led by the Rev. B. C. Baumgartner, pastor of Ewing Street Church, who spoke "tenderly to the goodness and usefulness of the life that had been ended in human service."[89]

Keyser's life, work, and death provide a glimpse into the situation of women at the turn of the century. She needed to work to support herself. The work she found was traditionally female. Through this work, she participated in extending the values of nurturing and caring, apparently thriving on such activities and becoming known and loved for her kind heart. Although she played a supportive, behind-the-scenes role to Addams and Starr, she seemed to have carved out a satisfactory vocational niche for herself. Why she died, however, is unexplained and raises questions: Did she tire herself out from all the Hull House activities and management tasks? Is she an example of nineteenth-century ideals of women's self-sacrifice, giving too much to others and not taking care of her own physical needs? Was her body simply unhealthy and, if so, why were so many young women physically sick during this time period? The questions could go on and, to a large extent, specific answers are unobtainable. As is the fate of most of humanity, only passing reference can be made to Keyser's life. While she appears to have lived well even within the constraints of her society and to have greatly contributed to the formative years of Hull House, her life was too short and too obscure to be fully recorded in the annals of history.

Discussion

The lives of Jane Addams, Ellen Gates Starr, and Mary Keyser provide ample material for contrast and comparison. All three women searched for something to do with their lives. They desired active lives of meaning to themselves and of service to their larger society. In their own ways, they all pushed at the dominant perceptions of nineteenth-century womanhood. At the same time, they had particular gifts and talents that they utilized, and their vocational searches took them in very different directions.

Addams was the charismatic and undisputed leader around whom the people of Hull House flocked. It is interesting that many residents found Addams impersonal in her direct interactions with them, since she was the inspiration and the uniting force within Hull House. She made people generally and Hull House residents specifically feel important, as though they were contributing to a great cause. Although Addams downplayed her own administrative skills in her autobiography, she was very talented at organizing and motivating people. Indeed, much of her time and energy went into the necessary and never-ending task of fundraising to keep the doors of Hull House open. While doing this, she constantly explained and re-explained the vision of a social settlement like Hull House. She saw its purpose as to serve as a place of gathering within neighborhoods and cities. It was a place where people could begin to work together to alleviate some of the most pressing social problems of her day, but also a place where people could simply engage in stimulating conversation free of ideological and theological constraints. Her leadership role was that of a gatherer.

Unlike many charismatic leaders, Addams did not claim unique authority or wisdom in her role as Hull House leader. People within the Hull House community were devoted to her, however, because she inspired social and spiritual vision. Amanda Porterfield, in her book on feminine spirituality in the United States, wrote that Addams presided over Hull House as a "matron of moral virtue."[90] Perhaps in her older years she was viewed as such, but not in her younger years. In the first decade of Hull House, Addams was a refreshing oddity within late-nineteenth-century America. She was a woman who came to know what she wanted to do and she had the courage to use her life to impact change. Hull House was certainly her home, yet the world became her concern. She did not claim values that were innately feminine or specifically religious but values she believed to be innately human and spiritual: goodness, truth, love, care, justice. And she believed that women, most especially, needed to use the qualities within them to impact their world. Perhaps most significant about Addams' leadership was that she had the sensitivity and capacity to elicit the dreams of a wide variety of people and facilitate diverse methods toward the common goal of social betterment.

Addams' personality and leadership style were very different from those of Ellen Gates Starr. Starr was acknowledged to be a committed reformer, highly talented artist, and critical thinker, but was not universally admired at Hull House. She was perceived by many people as strident, a quality Addams was never accused of embodying. Due to her passion for social justice and all-demanding religious devotion, Starr was not a uniting figure. As co-founder of Hull House with Addams, she was an insider, but she also was an outsider in her own vocational and spiritual pursuits. Yet Starr had a dedicated following. Through the years, she had more personal impact than Addams on many neighborhood people who appreciated her acts of caring and capable teaching abilities. An energetic, determined, and intelligent person, she was a seeker who found eventual vocational fulfilment in conforming to disciplines of spiritual direction and submitting to Roman Catholic authority by becoming a religious sister. This decision was gradual. In it, Starr, like many religious before her, realized her path of life and power within this traditionally religious activity where one receives what one has given up. Unlike Addams, Starr found the religion of Christianity to be all-encompassing and all-sufficient to ground her life and vision for the world—but only if she was totally dedicated to it.

Keyser did not have the kind of strong personality exhibited by either Addams or Starr, yet she made a difference through her position as housekeeper and the many everyday interactions she had with other residents and neighbors. From taking care that the Hull House floors were polished to ordering enough food, Keyser's role enabled Addams and Starr to carry on with their more publicly acclaimed work. Keyser did not seem to resent this division of labor, but rather appeared to thrive on her responsibilities and roles within the house.

The personal relationships forged by these women were significant. Hull House, after all, was a home. Addams and Starr had conceived of it as such from its very beginning. All drew personal support from individuals at Hull House. In the early years, Addams and Starr were close friends. As time went by, their friendship waned, though they kept in touch all their lives. Addams began to find personal support from other select women at Hull House, including Julia Lathrop and Florence Kelley in the early years. She drew particular support from her relationship with Mary Rozet Smith. Starr found her personal friendships not with the regular Hull House residents, but with more radical visitors and like-minded people within the city of Chicago and religious organizations like the Order of the Holy Cross.[91] Whereas Starr polarized people—she was the kind of person people either liked or disliked—Keyser was very liked at Hull House. It is impossible, however, to say who Keyser's close friends were. An interesting aspect of Keyser's life—unlike that of either Addams or Starr—was that she kept in close contact with her biological family, who lived in the Hull House neighborhood.

The religious differences between these three women are especially pronounced and merit further discussion. Addams had her own personal religious views and belonged to an evangelical Congregational church, yet she kept this information private. Publicly, she spoke on the commonalities shared between people regardless of their specific religious beliefs. She upheld an overriding spiritual emphasis on mystery and affirmed life, which she thought was basic to all people. In contrast, Starr found herself drawn to the spirituality of the Roman Catholic Church. The profundity of the Mass became central to her. Like many mystics before her, she experienced in the sacrament the great drama of life and death, hope and love. Her spirituality and spiritual leanings, however, were innately tied to creations of art and actions of political and social reform. The disciplines of confession and prayer were balanced in her life by an active involvement in art and politics.

As young women, Starr and Addams both found evangelical Christianity lacking because of its emphasis on personal salvation and creedal formulas. Both eventually joined Christian denominations because it offered community, not answers. As mature women, their dissatisfaction with traditional Protestant Christianity emerged in extremely different fashions. Addams veered away from intellectual conceptualizations of religious certainties; Starr grew to appreciate the history, ritual, and ultimate connectedness that such practices provided. Both Addams and Starr emphasized mystery, yet Starr found spiritual mystery best enacted in the sacraments and Addams found it best reflected in the experiences of life itself. Both women encountered difficulty in justifying their religious perspectives along with their activity and concern about the realities of social life. They were not "other-worldly," and they were not passive and patient in their attempts to change the world. Addams came to emphasize the spiritual elements of the Christian religion— some might argue she did so to the point of deChristianizing it (hence, the designation of Addams as a "secular saint")—and Starr did her best to claim from within the Christian religion a transforming spiritual path—some might argue she did so to the point of being too devoted.

The secular designation of Addams' religious perspective is a claim she would have rejected. In a 1911 article, Addams critiqued the church for appearing to be "totally unrelated to the world," and for not addressing problems such as industrialization, poverty, unemployment, agism, and lack of adequate health care. Addams wrote that when religious institutions fail to connect religious principles with real life experiences they fail to be a "living church." In interpreting the history of the Christian Church, Addams argued:

> Again and again during its history the church has been obliged to leave the temples and the schools in order to cast in its lot with the poor, and to minister without ceremony or ritual, directly to the needs of the sinner and the outcast.

She called for a "new religious expression" which would take into account scientific and humanitarian knowledge and still assert spiritual realities. "Is it not the office of religion to lift a man from personal pity into a sense of the universal compassion, from petty wrath to comprehension." She continued, "After all the business of religion is not only to comfort and conserve, but to prophecy and to fortify men for coming social changes." Addams sought cooperation between social reformers and church leaders. She praised the work done by the social arm of the newly formed Federal Council of Churches, the formation of sociology departments within theological seminaries, and the social welfare work undertaken by the Y.M.C.A. and other local church committees. She predicted that if such associations—based on mutual respect and willingness to learn from one another—would continue and expand, "we shall find ourselves united in a new religious fellowship and living in the sense of a religious revival."[92]

The religious views and spiritual emphases of Addams and Starr may be placed within the parameters of the social gospel movement. The social gospel and the social settlement movements were similar in their desire to bring Christianity back to a more grounded existence. There were differences between the two movements, however. The social gospel was male-dominated and emphasized theological proclamation; its key leaders were either clergymen or male academics. The social settlement movement was female-dominated and emphasized praxis and community; its key leaders were women who could not be official leaders within either institutional churches or educational institutions. While some social gospel leaders, such as Graham Tayler, were involved in the social settlement movement, women such as Addams and Starr were never defined as within the social gospel movment. This is not due to the incompatability between their work and beliefs but, rather, due to their gender.

By the second decade of the twentieth century, when Addams and Starr were in their fifties, the fundamentalist-modernist split within Christianity became pronounced, and the religious and spiritual insights of both Addams and Starr became unacceptable to either camp. Starr and Addams were neither modernists nor fundamentalists. They emphasized a spiritual and intellectual Christianity, a Christianity related to the world in practical ways yet, ultimately, a path of mystery. While little information exists on Keyser's religious views, she provides a more typical picture of a late-nineteenth-century woman's experience than either Starr or Addams. Keyser seems to have been a content and active member of the Ewing Street Congregational Church. She attended worship services, as did her family of origin, and did not seem to question the doctrines she heard. She seemed quite satisfied with her religious life. At her funeral service, the pastor of her congregation spoke of her life in ways typical of nineteenth-century feminine spirituality, that is, he remembered her for her goodness and her self-sacrifice. The struggles encountered by Starr, and perhaps the compromises made by Addams, are not apparent in the short religious life of Keyser.

Jane Addams, Ellen Gates Starr, and Mary Keyser were the first constellation of the Hull House galaxy. While Hull House grew in the scope of its work, in some ways these three women provided the range of the galaxy.

5

Constellation Two
—Shooting Stars

Alice Hamilton (above)
Julia Lathrop (top right)
Florence Kelley (bottom right)

After Addams, Starr, and Keyser moved into Hull House, their work was quickly supplemented by the presence of other talented women. While some of these women became residents, others supported and enlarged the work of Hull House while living in their own private homes. Still, residency was central to the operation of a social settlement house and Hull House, in part, became famous because it attracted such a core of competent and dedicated workers.

By 1894, fifteen people lived in Hull House, including two men whose rooms were in a house across the street.[1] *Hull-House Maps and Papers* records twenty residents as of January 1, 1895 (refer to Appendix). Approval of potential residents rested with those who already lived there. One of the purposes of the residents' meetings was to review the candidacy of other people who also desired to be residents. Such "initiates," as they were called, participated in the life and work of Hull House for six weeks, then came up for review.[2]

Initiates were not automatically approved. For example, a special residents' meeting was called on May 25, 1896, by Ellen Gates Starr to approve the residency of Mrs. Josefa Humpal Zeman. Zeman had already been a resident of Hull House, but had left to do other things.[3] Jane Addams then apparently invited her back. While some of the residents, including Florence Kelley, thought she would come back if encouraged, other residents (unnamed in the minutes) "felt that Mrs. Zeman would not be a desirable resident—and that her best sphere was in the Bohemian neighborhood." The motion to approve her second residency lost and she was not invited to resume residency.

Residency at Hull House was carefully monitored to include only those people believed to exhibit the proper qualities of service, commitment, and tolerance. In this sense, it was a tightly knit community upholding particular ideological and behavioral values. Although homogeneity was not explicitly sought in regard to age, class, and race, the necessity of sharing daily life resulted in efforts to regulate the overriding ideology of potential members and to ensure that the spheres of their intended work were compatible with the goals of Hull House. The commitment exhibited by residents grew with the length and degree of their association with the activities of the house and their interpersonal relations.[4]

Like other social settlements of its day, Hull House attracted a large number of college-educated women. Work and life in a settlement house provided an attractive vocational option for them, and had an indirect gatekeeping function. The community that developed at Hull House, therefore, had a club-like quality. Rebecca L. Sherrick argued that Hull House was more of a sorority than a home, and that it centered on Addams, who "assumed a comfortable role at the center of a group of women who held her views and followed her lead." Sherrick's analysis, however, did not take into account the powerful presence of Ellen Gates Starr at Hull House, nor, of other women who did not automatically bow to Addams' wishes. It does not explain, for example, why Addams' desire for Zeman to be admitted into residency was rejected by the residents of Hull House. While Addams was indeed the center and leader of Hull House, she did not override other residents' opinions, but fostered the expression and implementation of them.[5] Addams herself wrote that Hull House was held together by the "companionship of mutual interests." Hull House worked as a community because the particular interests of individuals were supported within a general structure that allowed for variety yet provided a prevailing social and spiritual vision.

However the community of Hull House is defined, it holds an especially important place in the development of independent living space for women in the late nineteenth century. It was not a commune. Women (and men) came and went as desired, married, and engaged in events outside of the house. It also was not a dormitory. Private living space was provided. The women who lived in Hull House proper had separate rooms, modestly furnished with usually a bed, bureau, desk, two chairs, bookcase, and pictures. Addams' room was more luxurious than the other women's rooms. She also had a sofa, two rocking chairs, and an expensive oil painting.[6] Addams had a habit of rearranging her room when she was depressed or disturbed. Louise deKoven Bowen wrote that residents of Hull House used to observe, "Miss Addams is low in her mind today. She is re-hanging all the pictures and changing everything."[7]

Due to the limited size of the main house, some residents lived in Hull House apartments which were built to accommodate the growing residential population. Apartments were occupied by both single women and married couples.

The Jane Club, established in 1891, was an apartment building solely for single, working women. Its import was in providing independent living space to women, many of whom moved to Chicago for employment. Article Two of its constitution stated its purpose:

> The object of the Jane Club shall be to secure and pro- mote the mutual comfort and improvement of its mem- bers, and, to this end, to provide and maintain a house or houses in the city of Chicago, at which its members may lodge and board; such house or houses to be man- aged on the co-operative plan, all resident members sharing the expenses, losses, and benefits, equally.[8]

During an era when women, particularly single women, did not live outside the bounds of biological families, Hull House was an acceptable and affordable place for them to live and from which to work. Dolores Hayden, a feminist historian of architecture, emphasized the role Hull House played in expand- ing independent living options for women and how this basic possibility enhanced the opportunity for them to pursue career vocations:

> Many of the professionals at Hull-House were single women, pioneers in their fields, who chose university training for a career at a time when this choice often implied a rejection of marriage and family. Dozens of such single-minded career women, like Addams herself, found that domestic life in a settlement solved the lo- gistic problems of spinsterhood, by providing a respect- able, adult home life, autonomous yet collective. It was more independent than living with relatives and more congenial than living alone.[9]

Perhaps related to Addams' and Starr's joining particular

churches for a sense of community, living at Hull House provided women with a daily sense of community—of sharing ideological and spiritual visions (if not religious doctrine), work, and
casual social interaction. In the growing residential life of Hull
House, Addams wrote, "[A]ll higher aims live only by communion and fellowship, [and] are cultivated most easily in the fostering soil of a community life."[10]

The common dining room and the opening of the Hull
House coffee house in July 1893 added to the community aspects of Hull House life. Indeed, Starr hardly ever cooked in
her own apartment, except for breakfast and serving tea to
guests. She had "[l]unch in the Coffee Shop and dinner in the
dining room." At dinner, she and Addams would sit at either
end of a long table, fulfilling their roles as Hull House founders
and hosts.[11]

The concept of residency was crucial to the operation of
Hull House. In this chapter, the lives, works, and beliefs of three
of the most prominent Hull House residents—Julia Lathrop,
Florence Kelley, and Alice Hamilton—are discussed. These
women came to Hull House at different points in their lives.
Although varied in their interests, skills, and personalities, they
became lifelong friends and colleagues. Other women lived at
the house longer and were likewise competent and capable, but
Lathrop, Kelley, and Hamilton became the most distinguished
former Hull House residents—they became the "shooting stars"
of the Hull House constellation.[12] Their reform vocations were
formed through their years at Hull House and the space and
energy it provided. When they left the house, they extended
their public service in larger societal arenas. While they might
be remembered today for their post-Hull House years, it is unlikely these achievements would have occurred without their
Hull House experience and formation.

Julia Lathrop

Julia Lathrop shared the most characteristics with Addams and
Starr of all the Hull House women, yet she developed her own
particular skills and vocational niche. Like them, she was an
Illinoisan. Born in Rockford in 1858, she was roughly two years

older than either Addams or Starr. She also attended Rockford Female Seminary in 1876-1877, one year prior to the arrival of Addams and Starr. She then transferred to Vassar College, where she received her degree in 1880.

Lathrop's father, William, had settled in Rockford in 1851 after emigrating from New York state. William Lathrop was a lawyer who became a leading Republican politician. He first served in the state legislature and then, in 1876, was elected to Congress. He was an abolitionist and supporter of political rights for women. Her mother, Adeline Potter Lathrop, was a member of the first graduating class of Rockford Seminary and came from a strong Congregational background. She was active in the Second Congregational Church of Rockford, an avid reader, and, like her husband, a determined suffragist and convicted abolitionist. They had met in Rockford and were married in 1857, only after William Lathrop had saved his first ten thousand dollars.[13]

Julia Lathrop was the eldest of five children, and spent much of her maturing years looking after her younger siblings. Later in life, she was criticized by opponents who desired to denigrate her child welfare policies. They sarcastically asked Lathrop how many children she had raised. Lathrop replied, "With a little help from my father and mother I have raised four."[14]

Lathrop's parents, though in agreement on many political matters, differed on the subject of religion. Her mother tended toward pietistic expression of faith. Her father leaned toward non-expression, or cultural expression of religion. Despite the fact that his sister, Martha, lived with the family while attending Rockford Seminary and after graduating became a missionary in India, William Lathrop did not uphold evangelical convictions. He even defended Abraham Lincoln from the "heckling" of Methodist preacher Peter Cartwright, during Lincoln's congressional campaign. At the same time, however, he supported the religious views of his wife, attended church as paterfamilias, and sent his children to Sunday School.[15] The Lathrop children, much to their mother's disappointment, never "became church members at the age considered proper for such a step."[16]

After graduating from Vassar College, Lathrop returned to Rockford and spent the next ten years working as her father's secretary and law assistant. She also worked for two other law practices, in which she bought stock and from which she made some additional money. Lathrop may not have experienced the internal struggles, which many white privileged women did in the late nineteenth century, of determining purpose or activity during her years after graduation. Jane Addams wrote, "There is no record of [Lathrop's] inner readjustments during the eighties, those first years after college so difficult for many gifted young people."[17] James Weber Linn, however, stated that Lathrop shared with other women of like characteristics the limitations of late-nineteenth-century gender constraints: "[Lathrop] found herself at thirty educated, cultivated, trained, and without the opportunity of responsibility."[18] Vocational discernment for nineteenth-century women was difficult given the lack of choices available to them.

Lathrop had no desire to teach, the most available option for a young, white, female college graduate of her day. Instead, she utilized her family connections, read law while working for her father, and did some administrative work at Rockford Seminary. She remained close to her family of origin and, apparently, did not find the "family claim" as overwhelming as Addams.

In the winter of 1888 and 1889, Addams and Starr returned to Rockford Seminary to promote their idea of a social settlement house. Lathrop and her father heard their pitch for support. Addams later reflected on that first meeting: "Mr. Lathrop although very friendly was not convinced of the usefulness of our plan but he assured us of his good will and made no objection when Julia decided to go to Hull-House." Lathrop, however, must have been impressed with the speeches of Addams and Starr and the encouragement she received from them to join their enterprise. In 1890, she decided to leave Rockford and her family for Chicago and Hull House. It is not entirely clear what motivated Lathrop to make this major move. Addams suggested that the Haymarket Riot of 1886 served as a catalyst in enlarging Lathrop's social concern, as it had for many middle- and upper-middle-class European Americans. No doubt part of Lathrop's societal leaning also grew from the inherited political and social concerns of her family.[19] Although Lathrop was not the first resident to join Starr and Addams in Chicago's nineteenth ward, she became an early and important resident.[20]

Shortly after Lathrop's arrival, she formed and led the Plato Club, which was one of the most popular programs at Hull House. A Sunday afternoon neighborhood discussion group composed mostly of older men, it debated philosophical and religious matters. Philosopher and educator John Dewey attended the group at Lathrop's invitation and sometimes gave lectures on topics such as social psychology. Lathrop did not always agree with Dewey even though he was "often outspoken when his opinions differed from those of Miss Lathrop."[21] Lathrop had no problem explaining and defending the merits of her own viewpoints in a predominantly male group, even when they differed with the opinions of someone as prominent as Dewey. From her earliest years at Hull House, Lathrop exhibited a gentle but firm sense of confidence in her own thoughts and actions.

Lathrop's interests moved very quickly from the theoretical to the practical. She began to investigate relief applicants in the Hull House neighborhood. She was the inspiration behind the publication of *Hull-House Maps and Papers,* in which she wrote a chapter on the charities of Cook County.[22] In 1893, she became the first Hull House resident to receive a state position after Governor John P. Altgeld appointed her to the Illinois Board of Charities. In this capacity she visited county "farms" and "almshouses." She advocated not only safer facilities, but also separate facilities for delinquent children, the mentally ill, the elderly, and the physically sick.[23]

In 1901, Lathrop resigned from her position as a member on the Illinois board. In her resignation letter submitted to Governor Richard Yates, she stated her opposition to partisan politics in the work of state charity and pleaded for "skilled and disinterested attention" to be directed toward reforming charitable institutions:

> I feel . . . that my continued presence on this Board will appear at least to indicate a complacency toward methods whose evil I have seen too long, and which I have tried earnestly, but of course vainly, to overcome.[24]

In 1905, Governor Charles Deneen reappointed her to the Board of Charities. She served until 1909, when the board was reorganized on nonpartisan principles.[25]

In the early years of Hull House, Lathrop and Addams were involved in the life and happenings of the neighborhood. Both she and Addams often found themselves doing things for which neither of them were trained. For example, one day they rushed to the aid of a neighborhood woman giving birth to an "illegitimate" child. After the birth Addams said to Lathrop, "This doing things that we don't know how to do is going too far. Why did we let ourselves be rushed into midwifery?" Lathrop replied:

> If we have to begin to hew down to the line of our ignorance, for goodness' sake don't let us begin at the humanitarian end. To refuse to respond to a poor girl in the throes of childbirth would be a disgrace to us forevermore. If Hull-House does not have its root in human kindness, it is no good at all.[26]

Lathrop's work was rooted in human kindness, whether she visited state penal facilities or aided in childbirth. Much of her compassion was directed toward children and immigrant families. She was instrumental in founding with Lucy L. Flower the first juvenile court in the United States. The court building was located across the street from Hull House, making it possible for court personnel to lunch at the settlement's coffee shop. Addams wrote that over lunch many unofficial discussions took place regarding both the theory and practice of the court system.[27] Lathrop also was a founder and trustee of the Illinois Immigrants' Protective League and active in the Chicago Woman's Club. Later in life, she and Addams both became members of the National Board of the League of Women Voters.

Lathrop was a kind and compassionate presence with Hull House. Unlike other residents, she made herself available to the many callers and visitors Hull House received. While the residents of Hull House very quickly established a system whereby certain individuals would be responsible to field such visitors (the residents referred to this responsibility as "toting"), Lathrop often let herself be drawn into conversations with them. Addams said that Lathrop took the time and energy to listen to Hull House visitors. Other residents observed her behavior and generally believed that Lathrop was wasting her time and energy with such interactions. In regard to one conversation Lathrop had with a distressed visitor, a resident said that it was a "great waste for as valuable a person as Julia Lathrop to spend so much time with such an obvious fool." But another resident said the "whole point of the conversation" was missed, since Lathrop was able to comfort the visitor in a way she probably had not been comforted since childhood.

Lathrop was very capable in her social reform work, yet she also was very pastoral and brought a humane presence to Hull House. She mentored younger residents, took time to be with them and listen to their concerns. She was especially appreciated for such gestures of simple kindness and openness. More so than all the early Hull House residents, Lathrop was known for her capacity for friendship, a quick wit, and an unfailing sense of humor. A Hull House supporter once donated a parrot to the kindergarten. The man who donated it was "extolling its virtues" to Lathrop, and said that it did not know any swear words. Lathrop replied, "That lack in his education will soon be rectified in our nursery." A young male resident at Hull House once said about Lathrop: "Miss Lathrop is so phenomenally quick in the uptake and on the return that she must think of a lot of awful mean things to say, but she never once says one."[28]

When Lathrop was away from Hull House, on trips throughout Illinois for charity meetings or the visiting of state facilities, her return was greatly anticipated by house personnel: "Julia Lathrop is coming! Julia Lathrop will be here for dinner!" residents said to each other.[29] Like other residents, Lathrop determined her own schedule and contributed to the overall work of the house. For years, she went to bed in the early evening, waking in the later evening to read and write while most of the other residents were asleep.

It is unlikely that Lathrop ever joined a Protestant congregation or was active in one. In fact, Addams recorded that Lathrop's aunt (who had been a missionary in India) was very disappointed that Lathrop failed to "openly profess adherence to a set creed." When her aunt visited Hull House, however, she was moved by the "good works" she observed. Lathrop said to Addams one night,

> The dear angel [her aunt] is so pleased by this sign of grace that she has momentarily forgotten her own doctrine of "by faith alone." I quite dread the moment when she shall remember it, for all her innocent pleasure may then vanish.[30]

Lathrop's own personal spirituality was rooted in "good works," actions of human kindness, and an overriding respect for the differing opinions of people. Although she held convictions, especially regarding the care of society's most neglected people, she was known for her restraint from pushing her opinions on others. James Weber Linn wrote that Lathrop's humor, ability to keep her temper, and overall patience with change served her well while working with people of vastly different opinions. In part, her philosophy was "[w]ait and see; but meanwhile, whatsoever your hand found to do, do it with your might. Cry if you must; laugh when you could; work and wait."[31]

In 1912, after more than twenty years at Hull House, Lathrop was appointed chief of the Federal Children's Bureau, a position Florence Kelley helped her to secure. She moved to Washington, D.C., and intensified her work on such issues as infant mortality, nutrition, juvenile delinquency, and child labor laws.[32] Hull House friends often stayed at her apartment when they were in the city for meetings or conferences, and Lathrop continued to visit them when she came through Chicago. Ten years later, she resigned and retired to live with her sister in Rockford, Illinois.

Lathrop's life slowed down with her official retirement, yet she remained active in select reform movements. She maintained close ties with Hull House women, especially Addams, Kelley, and Hamilton. She became the president of the Illinois League of Woman Voters and, at the time of her death in 1932, was in the midst of a personal campaign against capital punishment. The social issues addressed by Lathrop varied through the decades but always related to advocating tangible changes to benefit those with the least power in society, namely, women, children, prisoners, and the ill.

Upon her death, *The New York Herald Tribune* reviewed Lathrop's fifty years in public service and applauded her pioneer efforts in public welfare reform. It noted that she worked with a "spiritual zeal that never flagged."[33] The spiritual zeal uplifted in her obituary, however, was based not on evangelical Protestantism or strict Christian doctrine, but on an all-embracing appreciation of life and the needs of the most needy within society. Throughout her active life, Lathrop held central ideals regarding the betterment of humanity—ideals based on individual respect and friendship, as well as the humanizing of social systems. Like other progressives and social gospelers, she believed that societal conditions could be improved to more fully reflect the best of human nature. In the midst of a busy life, she retained close familial relations and reached out in kindness to people with whom she came in contact. Although a social scientist, she brought a "calm efficiency and a warm heart into cold-blooded 'scientific' charities."[34] Lathrop's vocation integrated both the action of doing and the aspect of being; what she did and who she was were balanced in how she lived in response to the needs of her time. Her life's purpose and motivation were based on a spiritual vision of human connectedness present in the simplest of human interactions and enhanced by social structures that would advance the well-being of all.

Florence Kelley

One of Julia Lathrop's best friends at Hull House was Florence Kelley. Kelley came to the house "[o]n a snowy morning between Christmas 1891 and New Year's 1892," while Lathrop was in Rockford visiting her family.[35] Kelley brought her three children, products of a marriage between her and a medical doctor, Lazare Wischnewetzky. Her life experiences were broader than most of the house's other women. She had lived abroad, been married, and was more politicized than any of the others. Addams wrote that Kelley "galvanized us all into more intelligent interest in the industrial conditions all around us."[36] Whereas

Lathrop was a pastoral presence in Hull House, Kelley was a galvanizer, and incited Hull House residents and associates into greater political understandings and actions.

During 1892, Kelley lived in a room at Hull House by herself. For a period she also shared a room with Dr. Harriet Rice, a black physician who lived at Hull House for a number of years. Kelley initially boarded her children at the home of Henry Demarest Lloyd and Jessie Bross Lloyd. The Lloyds lived in Winnetka, a wealthy suburb of Chicago, and were very much part of the work of social reform. Their house, called the Wayside, was known for its hospitality, "[T]here was never a time when somebody who needed harboring was not a regular member of the family, and seldom a dinner when guests were not in the majority."[37] The personal relationship struck between Kelley and the Lloyds lasted until the latters' deaths, and provided the basis for their socio-political alliances. For example, on Henry Lloyd's recommendation, Kelley was appointed the Chief Factory Inspector of Illinois in 1893. In turn, Kelley enlarged Henry Lloyd's education in the area of urban poverty. Frances Perkins, a friend of Kelley's and social settlement worker, noted that Kelley's friendship with the Lloyds was "perhaps the most valuable and cherished association of her life."[38] In the spring of 1892, Kelley took a Hull House apartment and moved in with her children. Like many other working women, Kelley continuously struggled between the demands of her work and the desire to spend time with her children.[39]

Kelley's actual journey to Hull House during the winter of 1891 was difficult because of the conditions of late-nineteenth-century Chicago roads:

> The streets between car-track and curb were piled mountain-high with coal-black frozen snow. The streetcars, drawn by horses, were frequently blocked by a fallen horse harnessed to a heavily laden wagon. Whenever that happened, the long procession of vehicles stopped short until the horse was restored to its feet, or, as sometimes occurred, was shot and lifted to the top of the snow, there to remain until the next thaw facilitated its removal.[40]

Kelley's life journey to Hull House was also impeded and enriched by many obstacles and experiences. Born in 1859 to a well-to-do Philadelphia family, Kelley's early years were filled with sickness and death. As a child, she did not regularly attend school because of frail health and a major bout with scarlet fever. Much of her early education was gleaned from reading through her father's library, an activity she started at age ten and completed seven years later. As the second born of eight children, five of whom died in infancy or early childhood, Kelley had firsthand experience with the inadequacy of child health care. She reflected in her autobiography:

> After the death in 1859, of my elder sister Elizabeth, aged two years, entries in the family Bible followed with pitiful frequency. There were, all told, five in twelve years: Marian in 1863, aged eleven months; Josephine in 1865, aged seven months; Caroline in 1869, aged four months; and Anna in 1871, aged six years.[41]

The irony for Kelley was that these sibling deaths occurred not on the frontier but "within four miles of Independence Hall." She wrote, "[t]hese tenderly cherished young lives were sacrificed, not to the will of God, as mothers were taught . . . [but] to the prevailing ignorance of the hygiene of infancy."[42]

Kelley's father, William, was initially trained as a jeweler, but became a lawyer and then a politician. He was elected to the House of Representatives in 1860 as a Republican, serving consecutively until his death in 1890. Like Lathrop's parents, he was a staunch abolitionist and supporter of women's suffrage. Kelley's mother, Caroline, was adopted by Isaac and Elizabeth Kay Pugh, after the early deaths of her parents. The Pughs were the grandparents Kelley so fondly remembered in her autobiography. While visiting them in their house in Germantown, Pennsylvania, Kelley first heard of the death of Abraham Lincoln.

The Pughs were Quakers. Isaac Pugh's sister, Sarah, was a well-known Quaker reformer and a good friend of Lucretia Mott. Kelley wrote that Sarah promoted the "antislavery movement, peace, woman suffrage, the single standard of morals for men and women, and free trade." As a child, Kelley was at first confused by her great-aunt's refusal to eat sugar and wear cotton clothing. In the tradition of John Woolman, Sarah Pugh told the young Kelley that "[c]otton was grown by slaves, and sugar also . . . so I decided many years ago never to use either, and to bring these facts to the attention of my friends." Ever precocious, Kelley asked her great-aunt whether she really thought slaves were freed by her refusal to use sugar or cotton. Aunt Sarah replied: "Dear child, I can never know that any slave was personally helped; but I had to live with my own conscience."[43] Whether or not this event actually took place the way Kelley remembered and recorded it, the idea of doing what one's conscience dictated, regardless of the end result, became the standard of Kelley's own life.

Kelley's ancestors came from a variety of religious traditions including Baptist, Presbyterian, and Episcopalian. Her father and mother were married in the First Unitarian Church of Philadelphia, where her father's funeral was later also conducted. The Quaker influence was most important to Kelley, perhaps because of its dual emphasis on mystical experience and social reform. She wrote that evangelical "conviction of sin" was not a value instilled by her family. While still a boy, her father protested against his sister's singing of "There is a Fountain filled with blood/Drawn from Immanuel's veins." He said, "I don't want to hear about blood."[44] As a Quaker, her mother not only supported abolition and women's suffrage, but temperance.

Nineteenth-century Quakers, though radical in many areas of society, were influenced by the dominant culture, especially in their anti-Catholic views. Kelley's mother was of this opinion. Kelley's son Nicholas remembered the election of Governor John Altgeld, a Catholic, and his grandmother's response to it:

> My mother's mother was of Quaker descent and of that school that would speak of such a subject as liquor or of members of the Catholic faith only in a whisper. When one of her old friends from Philadelphia asked her how her daughter could accept appointment from Governor Altgeld, she replied that she could not understand it, as she herself would no more utter his name than she would that of the devil.[45]

Unlike her mother, there is no indication whatsoever that Kelley had any dilemma regarding Altgeld's Catholicism; he was a man she greatly admired for his political and social vision. She supported him as he did her. She especially appreciated that he did not attempt to curtail her freedom of speech.

Most historians have interpreted Kelley's presence at Hull House as its major secularizing influence. Allen F. Davis wrote that Kelley "laughed at the 'Reading Parties' and hooted at the evening prayer sessions," and that she—more than anyone else—transformed Addams from a "philanthropist into [a] reformer."[46] It is true that Kelley had little patience for mere talk or pietistic platitudes. She had little use for institutionalized religion or for most preachers, because she experienced Christianity and its ordained clergy to be passive in the face of great injustices. She did not find within evangelical or orthodox Christianity an emphasis on the necessity for social reform, because it was too focused on individual sin and salvation. For these reasons, she directed Hull House's agenda toward what she believed to be practical political and social concerns. Kelley was not officially involved in any religious organization during her Hull House years. She joined the Society of Friends only in 1927, three decades after she left the house. It is likely, however, she always thought of herself as a Quaker, even when her immense energy and activities were funneled toward measurable reform and continuous advocacy for women and children. Historian Amanda Porterfield argued that Kelley's lifelong commitment to social justice issues was directly reliant on her Quaker heritage, and that "[t]hroughout her life Kelley assumed herself to be a Christian."[47] In public discourse, Kelley used highly moral—though not necessarily Christian—language to communicate her political, economic, and social goals. In this sense, she was similar to other nineteenth-century reformers who grounded their actual reform efforts in a Christian moral vision of how society ought to be.

At the age of seventeen, Kelley entered Cornell University. She wrote, "Entering college was for me an almost sacramental experience."[48] She thrived on the educational environment, the reading, the friends, the discussions. During her second year, she helped to found the social science club. Unfortunately, after spending Christmas holidays with her family in 1879, she returned to Cornell only to become very ill with a diphtheria infection. Due to inadequate care, she was not able to return to classes for three years. In March of 1882 she returned to Cornell, took her bachelor's examinations and submitted her thesis. Her thesis was on the connections between the law and the welfare of children, a project she researched at the Library of Congress while staying with her father in Washington, D.C., during recuperation from her illness. Cornell granted her the bachelor of arts degree that spring.

Kelley applied to the University of Pennsylvania to study law but was refused entrance due to her gender. She then decided to start an evening school for teenage girls in Philadelphia. While successful with the school, Kelley heard that the University of Zurich was admitting women students. She and her brother went to Switzerland and she enrolled at the university. Although she never received a degree from Zurich, she attended lectures, studied law, and was introduced to a variety of students. Most of the women students were Russian, and there was only one other U.S. woman there during her four-year stay.

Kelley wrote, "Coming to Zurich, the content of my mind was tinder awaiting a match."[49] She spoke in English, French, or German (never in Russian, which she says she was unsuccessful in learning). She attended socialist meetings. Describing the first socialist meeting she attended in Zurich, Kelley had a kind of conversion experience: "This might well have been a Quaker meeting. Here was the Golden Rule! Here was Grandaunt Sarah!"[50] While in Zurich, Kelley met a fellow socialist and medical student, Lazare Wischnewetzky, whom she married in 1884. They had their first son, Nicholas (nicknamed Ko), in 1885. After returning to the eastern United States in 1886, they had two other children, Margaret (born 1886), and John Bartram (born 1888).

On this phase of her life, Kelley wrote: "Having married a Russian physician, I returned to America in 1886 with him and my elder son, and the ensuing five years were devoted to domestic life." She did have two other children, but her description is not totally accurate. She worked on translating Friedrich

Engels' *The Condition of the Working Class in England in 1844* and Karl Marx's *Free Trade* speech into English, the first North American to do so. She also threw herself into the work of the Socialist Labor Party. But in 1887, she and her husband were expelled from the party because hard-liners did not trust their allegiance. While Kelley remained a lifelong socialist, she also remained very bitter toward U.S. socialists. Years later, when she was living at the Henry Street settlement in New York City, she and her friend Lillian Wald watched a Socialist march outside their window. Kelley said to Wald, "I belong there, but they put me out because I could speak English."[51] Her expulsion was more complicated than language; her forceful presence and leadership was threatening to the established Socialist Party of New York City.

Kelley hardly wrote of her marriage and its demise. Josephine Goldmark, her longtime friend and biographer, said that Kelley sought a divorce in the midst of her husband's inability to establish a medical practice and growing debt.[52] Historian Kathryn Kish Sklar wrote that in 1890 Kelley began to be physically abused by her husband, and a year later took her children and left him.[53] In part, Kelley came with her children to Illinois because the divorce laws were more lenient than in the eastern states. She also was familiar with the nascent social settlement movement through previous visits at the College Settlement in New York City. Kelley came to believe that the social settlement had good possibilities for her vocational interests. Without informing either Addams or Starr, she decided to move to Chicago and "look for work at Hull House." She soon divorced, assumed her given birth name, and adopted "Kelley" as the surname for her children.[54]

Kelley had great energy and drive in her adult years. Upon her arrival in Chicago she immediately opened an employment office in a corner of a Hull House building. She found much need for such a service in the neighborhood yet no adequate financial means to support it. She was hired in 1892 by the Illinois Bureau of Labor Statistics to look into the sweatshop system used by the garment industry. Her major concern was not the work done in poorly equipped factories, but the homework done by women and children. This investigation took her into the midst of the slums of Chicago, where children were taught to pull basting threads and sew buttons on garments as soon as they were able to sit in high chairs. Kelley found the use of such child labor to be abhorrent. She could not understand why other people accepted it as normal practice within industrialized society. She began to speak at working-class rallies and intensified her writing schedule, publishing in English (and German) journals and papers. A prophetic sense of right and wrong pervaded her words, whether spoken or written.

Kelley's investigative reports on the abusive labor practices she found within the Hull House neighborhood led her to further examine the employment of women and children. She and Mary Kenney, founder of the Jane Club at Hull House, guided commission members through their neighborhood to uncover the underground sweatshop systems. Kelley was appalled when one member of the commission refused to enter any sweatshop because he feared he would catch an infection and pass it on to his children.[55] Such selfishness had no place within Kelley's sense of social duty. She was a tireless advocate for children and women. Her unyielding dedication resulted in the passage of the 1893 Factory Act by the Illinois legislature, which limited work hours for women, prohibited child labor, and set standards and procedures for the inspection of tenement sweatshops.[56]

Due to Kelley's growing reputation and Henry Lloyd's recommendation, Governor John Altgeld selected her as the Chief Factory Inspector for the state. She hired a support staff of twelve people, including Mary Kenney and Alzina Stevens, another Hull House resident. Altgeld received complaints that he appointed a woman to such a top-level position, but he defended Kelley and said she was the "best qualified in the country for the job." In this position, Kelley emphasized the elimination of child labor (and connected it to the need for compulsory education for children), the improvement of conditions in work places, and the enforcement of the eight-hour work day for women.[57] As a way to ensure that her reforms would be taken to court and legally enforced, she enrolled as a law student at Northwestern University. Granted credit for her reading of law with her father and her studies at Zurich, she attended night classes for one year and was shortly admitted to the Illinois bar.

When Altgeld lost his reelection bid in 1897, Kelley lost her political appointment. For the next two years, she continued her work in informal ways by writing and speaking on labor and socialism while holding an evening job at the John Crerar Library to financially support herself and her family. She was worried about finding a suitable permanent job. In May 1899, she finally accepted an offer to become Head of the National Consumers' League, an advocacy organization based in New York City. Kelley moved with her children to the Henry Street Settlement, where she lived for the next twenty-seven years.

With her departure, Hull House lost one of its most vocal and energetic residents. The relationship between Kelley and Lathrop was especially missed. Being very different in temperament and method, Lathrop and Kelley provided sparks to the Hull House community. James Weber Linn wrote of the differences between these two strong and capable women:

Mrs. Kelley was a fighter; Miss Lathrop was a diplomat. Both were brilliant, imaginative, humorous, and troubled by injustice; both had great powers of persistence in daily routine; both had studied law, and been admitted to the bar. But Miss Lathrop had endless patience; Mrs. Kelley a kind of fiercely joyous impatience. Miss Lathrop glowed with determination, Mrs. Kelley burnt with eagerness. Miss Lathrop could bide her time, Mrs. Kelley must ón [sic]. The logical disciplined minds of both were accompanied by gentleness in Miss Lathrop, and high-spiritedness in Mrs. Kelley. Even their wit was different, one flashed, the other scorched. When both were at Hull House together, arguing some problem of correcting a social injustice, and disagreeing as they often did on the best method of procedure, it is doubtful if any better talk was to be heard anywhere.[58]

Alice Hamilton wrote about the relationship shared between Kelley and Lathrop: "[They were] great friends but very different. Florence was a 'rough-and-tumble fighter for the good life for others.' Julia was quiet—she never lost her head nor her temper." Hamilton added that both affected Jane Addams in different ways as well: "Florence often inspired Addams to get out into the workable world and fight some social wrong. Julia gave her companionship."[59] Indeed, Kelley was one of the few residents who actually teased Jane Addams, especially about her growing reputation as "Saint Jane." Kelley once said to Addams, "Do you know what I would do . . . if that woman calls you a saint again? I'd show her my teeth, and if that didn't convince her, I would bite her."[60] Kelley had a great deal of respect for Addams and once remarked that she was the cult figure that tied the Hull House crew together. Kelley was called the "most salient, salty character" of the galaxy of Hull House women. She was impatient and hot-tempered. She lacked tolerance. Immune to trivialities, she dressed very plainly and always wore black clothes, a symbol of her Quaker heritage.[61]

When Kelley left Hull House to become Secretary of the Consumers' League, she was on her way to becoming one of the most influential social reformers in the history of the United States. She intensified her writing, travelling, and lecturing schedule. Not fussy about where she spoke, Kelley was a popular speaker on women's college campuses and at women's clubs, but she also spoke in Protestant congregations and Jewish synagogues, and at ethical and missionary societies. Frances Perkins stated that Kelley did not care whether her audiences were large because educating one person was significant enough to her. Kelley travelled cheaply, and stayed in low-budget hotels or with local households. As spokeswoman for the Consumers' League, she pushed consumers to utilize their buying power by forcing manufacturers to uphold humane standards of employment. She was not known for her administrative skills, but she was a persuasive orator and leader. Much like Ellen Gates Starr, people either liked or disliked her, were drawn to her or found her abrasive. She was far from being the kind, meek, and gentle stereotype of Victorian womanhood. Some people were even afraid of her temper.[62] But more people were inspired by her convictions: "Everyone was brave from the moment she came into the room," was Newton Baker's reflection on powerful presence wielded by Kelley in her work for social reform.[63]

Kelley's connections were immense, as was her involvement in political and social organizations. She was crucial in advocating the formation of the Federal Children's Bureau and the subsequent appointment of her friend, Julia Lathrop, to head it up. She, along with Jane Addams, was involved in the initial organization of the National Association for the Advancement of Colored People, as well as the Woman's International League for Peace and Freedom. Kelley—like other women of her generation—opposed the Equal Rights Amendment because she feared it would destroy the protective gains she had worked so hard to get for women.

Activity dominated Kelley's life, yet she maintained close contact with her friends and colleagues from her Hull House years. While she sustained an intense professional schedule until 1930, as she got older she realized a need to get away from her work for some periods of time. She felt this especially after the death of her daughter, Margaret, who died in 1905 of a heart attack just as she started her studies at Smith College. Immediately after Margaret's death, Kelley threw herself more intensively into her work, until she finally collapsed of exhaustion. Two years later, in 1907, she bought property in Maine. Buying property went against her principles as a socialist, and her friends had great fun reminding her of the inconsistency between her political ideology and her capitalistic purchase of private property; Kelley ignored their ribbings. For at least six weeks each summer she relaxed in Maine, away from the hustle and bustle of her normal life. Josephine Goldmark wrote that Kelley needed this time for quiet and solitude, for sailing and blueberry picking:

> Thus that cold Maine Coast, alternately fog-drenched or sun-baked, blown upon by all the winds of heaven, gave to [Kelley's] stormy spirit that sense of identification with the cosmic forces which is religion to many natures. Each year the 6 weeks in Maine fortified Florence Kelley for her strenuous winter program. . . . [She would return to New York, saying] "I am back at work with my battery recharged."[64]

This was Kelley's first private, personal home—she had lived in social settlements for most of her adult life—and she enjoyed

decorating and furnishing it. The house itself was rather eccen-
tric, perhaps reflective of Kelley's own personality and values.
Frances Perkins observed that Kelley haphazardly added rooms
on to the house during the years, so that eventually "[o]ne had
to go out of doors and around the house in order to go upstairs
to bed."[65] But this was where Kelley was most comfortable in her
later years. It was in Maine that she formally joined the Society
of Friends. True to her initiating spirit, she even started a Quaker
meeting in her house.[66] She died in 1932 after being diagnosed
with a terminal illness, and was buried near her Maine home.

Felix Frankfurter, a Supreme Court justice and friend of the
Hull House women, wrote that Kelley had "probably the largest
single share in shaping the social history of the United States
during the first thirty years of this [the twentieth] century."[67]
She certainly had much influence in raising the consciousness
of people regarding the injustices of uncontrolled economic
growth. She was especially successful in developing political
strategies and legal legislation to protect the welfare of women,
children, and working men. She was a remarkable woman, energetic, stubborn, and unforgiving of opposition, disregardful
of her personal appearance, yet remembered for her wonderful
flute-like voice. Her association with Hull House and its key
residents added depth to their collective experience, widened
their world view, and prodded them into broader actions. She
was much more of a free spirit than most of the other Hull
House women, with the exception of Starr, who exhibited a
similar driving passion for social justice. Starr's passion, however, was blatantly rooted within the Christian religion whereas
Kelley's passion drew upon a spiritual moral vision which had
no room for quietism and no patience with mere religious talk.
The time Kelley spent at Hull House, and the skills and the
friendships she honed while there, greatly impacted her later
reform activities. Through Hull House, Kelley's ward of reform
widened to include the whole United States.

Alice Hamilton

During the fall of 1897, Alice Hamilton arrived in Chicago to
move into Hull House and begin her first professional job as

professor of pathology at the Woman's Medical School of North-western University. On her first evening at Hull House, Hamilton ate dinner with Jane Addams, Julia Lathrop, Florence Kelley, and former Governor John Altgeld. It was a startling dinner for Hamilton, who had been raised in a politically conservative and privileged environment. Although she was excited to be at Hull House, she initially was intimidated by many of the residents, visitors, and the environment in general. She was unsure about her own unique contribution to settlement life and felt insecure when she compared herself to the other women. She tired from the multitudinous duties and expectations of the house.

Of all the Hull House residents, Hamilton found Kelley especially intimidating. She quickly grew "tremendously fond" of her, however:

> Mrs. Kelley was one of the most vivid personalities I have ever met. She used to make me think of two verses in the Old Testament: the one in Job about the war horse who scents the battle from afar and says among the trumpet, "Ha,Ha"; and the one where the Psalmist says, "The zeal of thine house hath eaten me up." It was impossible for the most sluggish to be with her and not catch fire. A little group of us residents used to wait for her return from the Crerar Library, where she was in charge evenings, and bribe her with hot chocolate to talk with us. We had to be careful; foolish questions, half-baked opinions, sentimental attitudes, met with no mercy at her hands.[68]

Hamilton immediately appreciated Lathrop—who was to become a lifelong friend—and soon accompanied her on some visits to asylums. Hamilton learned from Lathrop the importance of tact, and found her to be the "most companionable person, with a sense of the absurd and a way of telling absurd stories." Lathrop's "Mark Twain-like twists into high philosophy or sudden nonsense at the close" was very different from Kelley's quick and "sweeping logic."[69]

Ten years their junior, Hamilton observed in Lathrop and

Kelley different styles of reform. She learned from both of them, but particularly appreciated Lathrop:

> Julia Lathrop did not see herself as the center of what she was doing; she really was not thinking at all of her relation to it. Florence Kelley was more stimulating; Julia Lathrop never roused one to a fighting pitch, but then fighting was not her method. (Neither was it mine. I have always hated conflict . . . this led me to cowardice . . . never with [Lathrop].) [Lathrop] taught me . . . that harmony and peaceful relations with one's adversary were not in themselves of value, only if they went with a steady pushing of what one was trying to achieve.[70]

James Weber Linn remembered that Hamilton seemed to have come to Hull House just before Kelley moved to New York City, and that, in some ways, Hamilton took Kelley's place, not that the two women were anything alike. Linn wrote:

> Mrs. Kelley was a propagandist, Alice Hamilton a scientist; the one relied for reform on action, the other on investigation. Yet when the one went and the other came, the social life of Hull House lost little of its old color or fun.[71]

During the short time period Kelley and Hamilton overlapped at Hull House, Hamilton struck up a special relationship with Kelley's son, Nicholas, who was called Ko. Ko, then a young teenager, and Hamilton (along with several other residents) went bicycling together—a great fad of the late nineteenth century—and enjoyed one anothers' company. Hamilton found it hard to say goodbye to Ko when he went to join his mother in New York City.[72]

Like Kelley and Lathrop, Hamilton did not stay at Hull House for all her working years. But more than twenty years at the house greatly shaped her interests and influenced the direction of her long and creative life. She came to Hull House as a twenty-nine-year-old, well-educated but with little practical experience, well-intentioned but with no idea how to imple-

ment her dreams. She left the house at age fifty-one, a highly
reputed reformer and scientist on her way to becoming the first
woman professor hired by Harvard Medical School.

Hamilton was born in 1869 in New York City. Her mother,
Gertrude Pond Hamilton, had gone there to visit her own
mother and to have her second child. But Hamilton stated in
her autobiography that she really belonged to Indiana, which
was where her parents lived and she was raised.[73] She was one
of four sisters born within six years of each other—a brother
was born when Alice was seventeen years old. The Hamiltons
were a closeknit family. Her father, Montgomery, was a graduate
of Princeton and an avid reader. He operated a wholesale grocery store in Fort Wayne, where his family had settled as immigrants from Northern Ireland. Hamilton remembered her
mother as less intellectual than her father but "more original
and independent in her approach to life." Hamilton had a very
close relationship with her mother, and viewed her as an "extraordinary woman for her day and generation." In part, Hamilton thought her mother's independence came from the fact
that she spent much of her childhood in Germany and France,
and thereby was "free from the Victorian prudery which was
considered essential to a lady."[74]

The Hamilton sisters—Edith, Margaret, Norah, and Alice—
received their primary education at home because their mother
objected to the long hours of public education and their father
did not like the curriculum of public schools.[75] They received
a solid education and studied many subjects, including Greek,
Latin, history, literature, and religion. Hamilton wrote of the
religious education they received, an education that covered
orthodox theology and heresies:

> The religion we were taught was sober, not colored with
> the fervent evangelism which was so prevalent in those
> days. My father . . . had a passion for theology. There
> was a time I knew more about Arianism, Socinianism,
> Gnosticism, and the other heresies than I knew about
> the history of my own country. He insisted that my sister
> Edith and I learn the Westminster Catechism, and many
> a struggle we had over the heathenish production. It

was a struggle to memorize the words—we never both-
ered with the meaning. My mother, Episcopalian as she
was, sometimes protested against giving such strong
meat to babes, but apparently one can shovel very tough
particles into a child's mind without causing indigestion.
. . . Luckily for Margaret and Norah, my father was tired
of the Catechism when they came along, and they es-
caped it.[76]

In addition to memorizing the Westminster Catechism for
her father, Alice and her sisters learned the Psalms, the Sermon
on the Mount, and the first chapter of the Gospel of John.
Hamilton later wrote that they knew the Bible better than they
knew any other book.

The Hamilton family attended the First Presbyterian
Church in Fort Wayne and, on special occasions such as Christmas, went to the German Lutheran Church, which was the congregation of their maids and hired men. When Hamilton was
ten years old, the family bought property on Mackinac Island
in northern Michigan where they spent summers. There they
attended the Episcopal Church, where they were "steeped in
the collects and the Litany and the *Te Deum*." Hamilton said,
"We learned to love the service better than we had ever loved
the Presbyterian."[77]

Reflecting on the kind of religion taught to her and her
siblings, Hamilton connected her nascent investigatory skills to
her early explorations in the field of religion:

Religion, as it was taught to us, had little authoritarian-
ism; certainly credulousness was not encouraged. The
first piece of "research" I ever undertook was when I was
about twelve years old. My father set me the task of
finding proof of the doctrine of the Trinity in the Bible.
His own belief was that this doctrine was a later addition
to the Gospels, and he had no hesitation in setting me
on an inquiry which might bring me to the same conviction.

Hamilton said, however, that while academic engagement in the

Biblical text was expected and encouraged, the centrality of the Bible for ethics was fully accepted:

> We never questioned the rightfulness of truth-telling, honorable dealing, unselfishness, self-control. . . . Actions were right or they were wrong, and when they were wrong we knew that the eyes of the Lord are in every place beholding the evil and the good.[78]

After receiving their primary education at home, the Hamilton sisters were all sent to Farmington, Connecticut, to attend Miss Porter's School, a finishing school for elite young women. Alice Hamilton attended in the years 1886 to 1888. She enjoyed the school even though she found "some of the teaching we received was the world's worst."[79]

After Miss Porter's School, Hamilton decided she needed to train for a job that would provide a living wage; the family's resources were limited after 1885 because her father's business failed. She had a strong desire to do something with her life and to achieve a sense of independence. Her older sister, Edith, decided to go into teaching, and became the famed classicist. Her sister, Norah, was a talented artist even though she struggled with mental illness for much of her life. Alice chose medicine, not because she was "scientifically-minded," but because as a doctor she "could go anywhere . . . to far-off lands or to city slums—and be quite sure that I could be of use anywhere."[80]

Hamilton did not have the necessary educational credentials to immediately enroll in medical school, so she first studied physics and chemistry under the tutorage of a high school teacher. She then entered a "third-rate medical school" in Fort Wayne for one year to study anatomy. Having in this manner convinced her family, especially her father, of the seriousness of her vocational goals, she enrolled at the Medical School of the University of Michigan in Ann Arbor and graduated with a Doctor of Medicine in 1893.

Hamilton found little resistance to women students at Ann Arbor, since the University of Michigan had admitted women students for twenty years. She greatly enjoyed her studies. She especially appreciated the fact that living in Ann Arbor provided

her with her "first taste of emancipation," with no one concerned about her comings and goings or her whereabouts.[81]
While a medical student, Hamilton decided not to go into private medical practice but to specialize in bacteriology and pathology.

Upon graduation, she realized there was a severe shortage
of intern options for women doctors of medicine. She found
two hospitals willing to accept her. From 1893 to 1894, she in-
terned at the Northwestern Hospital for Women and Children
in Minneapolis and at the New England Hospital for Women
and Children in Boston. Boston first introduced Hamilton to
"life in a big city." While in Boston, she met a Russian intern,
Rachelle Slobodinskay, who later married Victor Yarros; both
became lifelong friends of Hamilton and long-time residents at
Hull House.[82]

Following her intern positions, Hamilton and her sister,
Edith, went to study at the University of Leipzig for a year. Hamilton did not like Germany. She found the sexism of German
men worse than what she had encountered in the United States.
She also found the antisemitism repugnant, the militarism
alarming, and the disregard for religion among most Germans
repulsive.[83] In addition, she did not learn anything new in her
studies. They returned to the United States in the fall of 1896.
Edith accepted a headmistress position at the Byrn Mawr School
in Baltimore, and Alice did additional postgraduate work at
Johns Hopkins Medical School. In 1897, Alice received her first
job offer, which was to teach pathology at Northwestern University's Woman's Medical School: "I accepted it with thankfulness, not only because it meant employment in my own field,
but because it was in Chicago. At last I could realize the dream
I had had for years, of going to live at Hull-House."[84]

Hamilton and her sisters had never "heard much about social
reform in . . . [their] sheltered youth." But her cousin, Agnes,
had stumbled across Richard Ely's books and was excited about
Christian socialism, the social gospel, and the settlement movement he described. In 1895, before leaving for Germany, Alice,
her sister, Norah, and their cousin, Agnes, heard Jane Addams
speak at the Methodist Church in Fort Wayne. "I only know that
it was then that Agnes and I definitely chose settlement life."[85]

Getting accepted into Hull House, however, was a hurdle for Hamilton. The house was at the height of its popularity and many applicants desired admittance. Upon getting the job offer from the Woman's Medical School, Hamilton met with Addams to talk about the possibility of living at Hull House. Addams informed her that no rooms would be available for that fall. During this interview, Hamilton also met Florence Kelley for the first time, that "vivid, colorful, rather frightening personality whom [she] later came to adore." Hamilton then visited the Chicago Commons, where she received even less encouragement. Hamilton wrote that the Taylors were not at home when she arrived and that the resident to whom she spoke told her she would be of little use to the settlement if the only time she could devote would be her evenings.

In a letter to her cousin, Agnes, Hamilton wrote, "I had to give up all idea of going to Hull House or Chicago Commons and I am dreadfully disappointed." Hamilton's initial rejection made her "feel so small." She was also intimidated by the surroundings of Hull House and the Commons, finding them to be "tremendously cultured," and the people all seemed to be "specialists." Hamilton wrote, "I know I never would be accepted by them." Her greater fear, however, was to be initially accepted and then voted out after the probational period.[86]

Despite the setback, Hamilton was determined to combine settlement life with her medical career. She believed "professional work, teaching and pathology, and carrying on research, would never satisfy [her]." She felt she "must make for [her]self a life full of human interest."[87]

Unknown to Hamilton, between her initial meeting with Addams and her coming to Chicago in the fall of 1897, Kelley talked to Addams about accepting Hamilton as a Hull House resident. Kelley told Hamilton in October 1897 that she hoped Hamilton liked Hull House because she was "partly responsible" for her being there, since she "urged Miss Addams very strongly" to accept her. When Hamilton asked her why she did this, Kelley responded that she had met Hamilton's cousins while in Fort Wayne, and that she "knew if [Hamilton was] anything like them, we had better have you in Hull House." This conversation further intimidated Hamilton. She wrote to her Fort Wayne cousin, "I am not at all like you. . . . I don't even know whether I believe in not 'buying sweaters' clothes."[88]

Not knowing about Kelley's recommendation of her to Addams, Hamilton was surprised to receive a letter from Addams during the summer of 1897 while she was at Mackinac Island. Addams invited Hamilton to live at Hull House because a room had become available. In jubilation, Hamilton immediately accepted the offer.

During her first few years at the house, Hamilton taught during the days and helped with assorted duties during the evenings. She toted visitors around, led classes, and established a well-baby clinic. "My part in [Hull House] was humble enough," Hamilton said of her early years there. But the work took its toll. She wrote:

> About January [1899] I began to get very tired and I think my work at the school would have been just about all I could manage, but you know how it is refusing to do things at Hull House. You simply cannot. And so my work at school was done lifelessly and my work at the House, with weariness and irritation, and along with it all I had a bitter feeling inside that my own work was going to the winds, that I never could be a scientist. . . . You see how it was, can't you? how I was trying to do three things at once and failing in all of them.[89]

On the insistence of her friend, Rachelle Yarros, Hamilton finally took a couple days off to rest. She considered leaving Hull House so she could better pursue her scientific career. While thinking about making that change, Hamilton said that Addams was "genuinely distressed at the thought of my going away." Addams told her she could stay at Hull House and "do nothing at all, that she was sure it would be better for me in a place where I was happy and had people I liked around me than in a lonely boarding-house." Hamilton decided to remain at Hull House, yet lamented: "If only I were strong! But I am not. I tire so easily and then I cannot sleep and my work goes to pieces and then I think I shall have to give up everything."[90]

While Hamilton found her first few years at Hull House

physically exhausting, she also learned much. She began to be politicized. She learned about the "inequalities in our democratic country." She became suspicious and fearful of the police, and felt hostile toward mainstream newspaper reporters.[91] These realities were new to Hamilton given her upper-middle-class upbringing, as new as it was to associate with people whom she was raised to believe were radicals and revolutionaries. It is no wonder Hamilton felt tired and overwhelmed; she not only was working long hours but she was undergoing a radical reorientation regarding political and societal realities. In later years, Hamilton joined the picket lines in labor disputes. Unlike Starr, however, Hamilton usually picketed in the mornings. She did not necessarily want to avoid arrest, but she wanted to avoid being dragged by the police.[92]

In 1902, the Woman's Medical School was closed. Hamilton found a new position as a bacteriologist at the Memorial Institute for Infectious Diseases. There she began to investigate the typhoid epidemic in the nineteenth ward, and also worked to eliminate the cocaine industry, a problem which came to the attention of Hull House residents. While she did important work during these years, it was not until 1908 that she read a book that shaped her vocational direction. The book was *The Dangerous Trades* [1902], by Sir Thomas Oliver. Through this book, Hamilton learned of the field of industrial diseases. This nascent field intrigued Hamilton and became her area of specialization. Upon the recommendation of Charles R. Henderson of the University of Chicago, Hamilton received appointment to the Illinois Commission on Occupational Diseases. The state appointment enabled her to develop her knowledge of industrial hazards by engaging in field research. In 1910, she supervised the investigation into the "poisonous trades" and focused on lead poisoning. Through on-site inspections and interviews with workers, Hamilton exposed the inadequate safety conditions of early-twentieth-century factories. Hamilton had at last found a way to utilize her scientific skills in making the world a better place. She had become a scientific reformer.

In 1919, Hamilton received an invitation from the Medical School of Harvard University to become the Assistant Professor of Industrial Medicine. After much negotiation, Hamilton accepted the offer on the basis that she teach half the year so she could have the opportunity to do research and visit Hull House the remainder of the year. As the first woman professor at Harvard, she was never fully accepted by the administration or her faculty colleagues. She was prohibited from participating in graduation ceremonies because "under no circumstances may a woman sit on the platform." She was not allowed to use the Harvard Club, which was male only, and was told she could never claim her quota of football tickets. Hamilton was not disturbed by the discrimination she received at Harvard, but was rather amused by it. Her friends, however, were angered. Hamilton did not push for her legitimate rights at Harvard because it was something that did not bother her. Despite Harvard's attempts to limit Hamilton's presence on campus, she received much publicity for being its first woman professor. When newspapers made much of her appointment, Hamilton replied: "Yes, I am the first woman on the Harvard faculty. I'm not the first woman who should have been appointed."[93]

During her Harvard years, Hamilton bought a home in Hadlyme, Connecticut. She rested there during the summers, was visited by family members and the women of Hull House, including Jane Addams and Mary Rozet Smith. With her sister, Margaret, she lived there permanently after her retirement from Harvard in 1935. Hamilton long outlived the first generation of Hull House women; she did not die until she was one hundred and one years old. She remained active well into her eighties, first acting as a consultant to the Department of Labor and then becoming president of the National Consumers' League. In 1949, she revised her 1934 textbook, *Industrial Toxicology*. Like Kelley in her initial opposition to the Equal Rights Amendment, Hamilton came to support it in the 1950s. She also came to support the official recognition of the People's Republic of China, as well as to denounce McCarthyism and the U.S. military involvement in Vietnam.[94] As Hamilton aged, she grew in self-confidence and became more forthright in stating her political and social opinions. As a result of her apparent increasing radicalism, Hamilton was accused of being a communist, and was placed under surveillance by the Federal Bureau of Investigation in the 1950s.[95] In the 1960s—as a woman in her nineties—Hamilton had no patience with what she viewed as that decade's emerging conservatism, which advocated the return to private charity, uncontrolled capitalism, and persecution of labor unions. "I think that those who hold such views must have been young during our great depression," Hamilton wrote. "I was in my sixties and saw it from the world of the working class."[96] Her ability to see the world from the perspective of the least power- ful—and her sense of solidarity with those struggling within the dominant economic and social order—was directly tied to her learnings at Hull House.

In later life, Hamilton expressed less certainty about her religious views, although she increasingly used examples from the Bible in her correspondence. Madeline Grant suggested that Hamilton and Addams never asked each other what they believed or what they thought of immortality:

> To both, religion was a growing, ever-changing, deeply personal process. Each had that peace of mind to live with the eternal uncertainty of life hereafter. All the mys- teries of life—kindness, beauty, spiritual truth—were not increased by defining them, but by believing them, liv- ing them. What the Greek laborer had said about Jane Addams could equally well have been said of Alice: "Her no just one religion, her all religions."[97]

In 1959, more than twenty-five years after Addams' death, Hamilton wrote, "Somehow, I do not know how or when, I lost my belief in individual immortality." She continued, "I don't mean I disbelieve it, I simply do not know. When death comes, I shall know." She then quoted Paul's words, "Now we see through a glass darkly, but then face to face. Now we know in part but then shall we know even as we are known." Finally, she concluded, "My whole relation to God and to Christ has become cloudy, and I think will be till I die and then really know."[98] Perhaps her lack of certitude regarding orthodox Christian teachings was related to the years she spent employing scientific methodology. She was not willing to outrightly reject something that did not have sufficient proof, but neither was she willing to wholeheartedly accept something solely on the basis of faith.

And she saw no reason to say she believed in something when she knew that, in her heart, she did not know. This inability to full-heartedly believe has usually been defined within a secularization model of North American religious history. It is more appropriately understood as a striving to claim the core spiritual dimensions of Christianity without succumbing to doctrinal rigidity, which limits one's perceptions and dictates one's analysis of what is known and unknown.

Hamilton outlived all her early Hull House friends, as well as her sisters. She disliked the loneliness of this aspect of aging. She eventually lost her hearing, and though she grieved this loss, she believed that with time she would adjust. She also grieved when the Hull House complex was sold to the city in 1963 to be bulldozed as part of the site for the new University of Illinois at Chicago campus; with this change, a significant part of her personal history was destroyed. She hoped she would die quickly, and did not want to linger in illness. Unfortunately, she was bedridden for the final four years of her life, and finally died of a stroke in 1970. In her century of life, Hamilton saw great changes in U.S. public and social policy. Some of these changes directly resulted from her efforts as scientific reformer and teacher. Hamilton, like Lathrop and Kelley, sought an active life of meaning and responsibility; she ultimately desired to contribute in transforming the United States into a more humane, compassionate, and just society.

Discussion

Julia Lathrop, Florence Kelley, and Alice Hamilton are examples of women who received their initial vocational experiences at Hull House but went on to become involved in larger spheres of society. They were tremendously skilled and respected in their areas of expertise and made a great impact in their society. They were truly reformers.

Women have played a substantial role within reform movements in North America.[99] From the efforts of women in the abolition movement to their efforts in promoting moral reforms such as temperance and the elimination of prostitution, women have labored long and hard to implement changes within the social structures of their time. Their motivations generally included both an ideal that the world was improvable and a belief that they individually could make a difference through leading lives of active service. Individual service included convincing other people—women and men—of the righteousness of their positions and seeking support in the struggle to improve the conditions of the less fortunate. While the "cult of true womanhood" attempted to severely limit women's involvements to immediate concerns of home and family, and women's spirituality was deemed properly pietistic rather than political, women used the common ideology to extend their concerns into larger spheres of social and political life.[100]

Many women experienced difficulty discerning and living their vocations. They wanted to live what they called "useful" lives, but their options were limited. In a century when most women married, it was a rebellious act in and of itself to not marry—or in the case of Kelley, to divorce and not remarry. If a woman did not marry and was not independently wealthy, her vocational crisis intensified as cultural norms still dictated primary obligation to her biological family.[101]

The Christian religion as institutionalized within nineteenth-century North America contributed to the vocational conflict women experienced by giving them a mixed message. On the one hand, Christian literature and preaching advocated the obedience and submissiveness of Christian women, and upheld their life purpose as mothers and helpmates to men. On the other hand, Christian practice baptized male and female "into the freedom of Christ," and Christian doctrine stated that all people were created in God's image. The one clear message women in the nineteenth century received, however, was that Christians were to love their neighbor. The conflict within themselves—and often with dominant society—arose in identifying one's neighbors and the boundaries of their neighborhood.

Few women in the nineteenth century directly addressed the gender contradictions within Christianity or the patriarchal assumptions and teachings espoused in its name. Yet some, like Elizabeth Cady Stanton, were keenly aware of it.[102] Many women, especially married women, lived within the tension of institutionalized Christianity. They did not experience it as too overwhelming, found ways to work within its boundaries, were simply not aware of other possibilities, or believed that their secondary roles were in fact, by nature, God-intended. The reform vocations of such women were usually exerted through church-connected organizations: local ladies' aids, women's clubs, missionary societies, deaconess orders.[103]

Women active in the social settlement movement, unlike their more religious sisters, labored outside the structural boundaries of institutionalized Christianity. This does not mean, however, that they did not understand their work and lives as vocation. Lathrop, Kelley, and Hamilton show unrelenting vocational drives. As advocates for those most abused and forgotten by the wealthy and powerful in society—the incarcerated, the working poor, the neglected and wayward children—these women used their voices, skills, and lives to fulfill vocations typically considered secular. Kelley talked about her vocational direction as a relatively young woman, when, in the 1880s, she said:

> The question that forces itself upon us, and imperatively demands an immediate answer, is this: in the great strife of classes, in the life-and-death struggle that is rending society to its very foundations, *where do I belong?* [*italics added*][104]

Kelley continued, "Shall I cast my lot with the oppressors. . . ? Shall I spend my life in applying palliatives. . . ? Shall I fritter away the days of my youth investigating the deservingness of this or that applicant for relief. . . ?" She concluded with an insight into her holy vocation: "Shall I not rather make common cause with these my brothers and my sisters to make an end of such a system?"

Vocation is not limited to activity or placement within institutionalized Christianity. Given the prohibition of the formal leadership of women in nineteenth-century church structures, it is especially crucial that vocation be defined in a broad rather than narrow way. The word vocation comes a Latin word meaning summons or call, and is tied to another Latin word meaning voice. Lathrop, Kelley, and Hamilton all lived as though they had been summoned or called to a purpose greater than themselves, and they found and used their voices in extending this purpose. In other words, Lathrop, Kelley, and Hamilton are not simply examples of emerging career or occupational options for white, middle-class women. Nor is it accurate to say that reform itself became their religion.[105] While they needed to financially support themselves, they engaged in reform work for the betterment of others. They had a vision of how the world could be, and understood their lives as contributing to a new way of shared life. This vision came from their understandings of the true purpose of Christianity.

The vocational directions for these three women developed over time, with experience, and with mutual support. Unlike some of their more overtly religious sisters, they neither had startling moments of illumination which clarified the direction of their life work nor did they passively await their vocational callings. They were more like pilgrims than mystics, and their vocational callings were formed by searching and activity.[106] Kelley came to Hull House with a clear vocational direction, but no idea of how she was to implement it. Lathrop and Hamilton came with vague vocational notions. All three left the house as mature reformers. The community of Hull House shaped the vocational directions of its residents because it allowed for diversity under a uniting spiritual vision of social and political involvement. As a community of reform, it shaped the vocations of many individuals by summoning a vision of how the world ought to be, by calling individuals to utilize their lives in implementing the vision, and by giving women, especially, the experience of knowing and using their voices.

One must ask, however, about the religious or spiritual underpinnings of their reform works. Both Lathrop and Hamilton were raised in evangelical Protestant environments, yet they did not, and perhaps could not, retain the religion of their youth. As their world views enlarged, their religious evangelical roots became too constraining to explain the mysteries of life. Rather than engaging in theological aerobics, both came to emphasize the social ethics or "works" of their evangelical rearing: love, service, care, friendship. Kelley, who was raised in a quasi-Quaker environment, seemed in her early years to operate with no theological or spiritual agenda—socialism and labor were her focus. Yet in her later official alliance with the Society of Friends, Kelley placed emphasis on spiritual experience yoked with principles of social justice.

Though all three women were strong individuals, their personal vocations were tied to their relationships of friendship and mutual support. All became friends for life despite the fact that they were very different in personality and leadership style. Late night debates over steaming cups of hot chocolate were a highlight of informal social interaction at Hull House when the three of them lived there. After moving apart, they continued to visit one another, stayed in each others' homes while on business trips, and vacationed together when time allowed. Lathrop, perhaps more than either Kelley or Hamilton, was also intentional about mentoring younger residents and helped them claim their own unique selves and vocations. Kelley, as the only mother among them, raised her children not in a middle-class environment dictated by values of isolated and insulated nuclear households, but utilized the support of friends who provided care and guidance for her growing children. Their vocations, as vocations must, combined all segments of their lived lives.

It is a sad commentary on the lack of societal memory that none of these women are widely known today. Their contributions as reformers are significant in and of themselves, and show great accomplishment. Perhaps they are not remembered because they were ambitious and successful. In her discussion on women's lives as presented through biography and autobiography, Carolyn G. Heilbrun suggested that when the vocational realities of women's lives are either ignored or classified as exceptional, they are not able to function as models for next generations.[107] If the lives of Lathrop, Kelley, and Hamilton were viewed as normal in their strivings for purpose and accomplishment, they would have a power not presently granted them. These three women offer models for how women and men can discover and utilize their own vocational lives. As the "shooting stars" of Hull House, they formed a unique vocational constellation. They burned brightly as they left the galaxy of Hull House to become part of larger institutions and movements.

6

Constellation Three
—Wealthy Stars

Helen Culver (above)

Louise deKoven Bowen (top right)

Mary Rozet Smith (bottom right)

JANE ADDAMS AND ELLEN GATES STARR did not set out to found an institution. They believed their work would be impeded through institutionalization, a commonly held view in the settlement movement. Institutionalization would slow down the response capabilities of residents and inhibit recognition of the particularities of differing situations. It would force residents to rely on procedural guidelines and policies rather than personal insight based on observation and experience. Anti-institutionalism reflected values of the nineteenth-century Romanticist Movement and indicated an emerging emphasis on pragmatism. Ironically, the very success of Hull House led to its institutionalization.

Institutionalization became official in 1895 when, after the incorporation of the Hull House Association in 1894, a Board of Trustees was appointed to oversee the operation. The Hull House Association Charter, the policy statement of the institution, described what the settlement had successfully been doing during its five-year history: "To provide a center for the higher civic and social life; to institute and maintain educational and philanthropic enterprises, and to investigate and improve the conditions in the industrial districts of Chicago."[1]

The first Hull House Board of Trustees was composed of Mary Wilmarth (Vice-President), Allen Pond (Secretary), William Colvin (Auditor), Helen Culver, Edward Butler, and Mary Rozet Smith. Jane Addams was named President, a position she retained until her death. The trustees were valuable because of their social connections in the city of Chicago and because of their financial donations. In 1895, for example, William Colvin gave $500 to Hull House and Louise DeKoven Bowen gave $750. In 1896, Mary Rozet Smith gave $1,000 and Mary Wilmarth $200.[2]

The trustees did not mirror the constituency of Hull House, but came from and tapped into the privileged leadership of Chicago. With the exception of Addams herself, none of the first board of trustees lived at Hull House or were from the nineteenth ward. The trustees usually ratified the desires of Addams, and cancelled meetings if she was absent. The creation of the board of trustees showed the need for Hull House to have an official standing and connection with the Chicago elite in order to function on an institutional level. Although the trust-

ees were intensely interested in the work of the house and contributed not only money but also time, their ultimate importance was their identity as wealthy Chicago elite and as
well-connected individuals. Neighborhood people were not represented on the board, reflective of the major class divisions
within the late-nineteenth century. Even though Hull House
existed to bridge class divisions, it reinforced them by excluding
neighborhood people from its highest governing board.

This is not to say that the board members were not capable,
fascinating, and dedicated individuals. Mary Jane Hawes Wilmarth was one prominent trustee who rose to civic leadership
through the woman's club movement. Born in 1837 in New
England, she came to Chicago as a young women and married
Henry Wilmarth, who died in 1885.[3] Wilmarth desired to live
at Hull House as a resident when it opened in 1889, but her
family thought such an arrangement would be inappropriate
for a woman of her standing. Wilmarth instead kept an apartment in the Congress Hotel (built where the Wilmarth's home
once stood and on property she still owned), and served as a
Hull House trustee until her resignation in 1908.[4] Later in life,
Wilmarth divided her time between Chicago and a second
home in Lake Geneva, Wisconsin. A generation older than the
typical settlement worker, she supported the work of the house
for thirty-years and died in 1919.

Wilmarth was especially close to Ellen Gates Starr and maintained an affectionate relationship with her. In correspondence,
Wilmarth often punned Starr's name, addressing letters to "My
dear Ellen, my Star." After Starr visited Wilmarth in 1913, and
after years of Wilmarth's financially supporting Starr, Wilmarth
wrote Starr a letter which concluded, "I love to love you." These
words expressed the maternal affection Wilmarth felt toward
Starr. Indeed, while Wilmarth supported Hull House and
thought highly of Jane Addams, her special connection always
remained with Starr.[5]

Helen Culver and Mary Rozet Smith were also original female trustees. They became important to Hull House for different reasons. Culver was a wealthy businesswomen who quite
skeptically rented part of one of her properties to Addams and
Starr in 1889. Only gradually did she become a staunch sup-

porter and participant in the work of Hull House. Smith, who wandered into the house during its first year of operation, became a steady presence and wealthy supporter of Hull House. More importantly, she became the intimate friend and companion of Jane Addams.

The original male trustees—William H. Colvin, Allen Pond, and Edward Butler—represented the male philanthropist portion of Chicago society. Colvin was a prominent Chicago businessman and served as director of the World's Fair of 1893. He was concerned especially about the working class of Chicago, supported university extension courses at Hull House, and financed the settlement's coffee house and billiard room. After his death in 1896, he was replaced by John Dewey.[6] Dewey served as a trustee for one seven-year term. Allen Pond, along with Irving K. Pond, was one of the architects of the Hull House complex first utilized to build the Butler Art Gallery in 1891. Edward Butler provided the money for the Art Gallery and, like Colvin, was a wealthy Chicago businessman. At his resignation in 1912, Julius Rosenwald, another wealthy Chicago man, took his place.

Louise deKoven Bowen was not an original trustee, but became one in 1903 when she filled the position vacated by John Dewey. By that time, she was already active in the settlement, especially in her capacity as president of the Hull House Woman's Club. Bowen, with her strong personality, money, and willingness to work long hours, was influential in the Hull House circle in the 1890s. She was more politically conservative than Addams, Starr, Kelley, or Lathrop, but always supported their work and was a key interpreter of Hull House to the larger city.

Given the composition of the first board of trustees, it is difficult to accept what Addams herself said regarding them:

> There were women of sentiment, afraid they were going to be sentimental and so tending to be hard-boiled; and there were hard-headed business men, afraid they were going to be hard-boiled, and so tending to be sentimental.[7]

Addams appears to have been engaging in Victorian gender stereotyping. Her comments do not reflect what is known about

Culver and her financial and personal astuteness. Neither she nor Bowen after her could be labelled as sentimental. Addams' comments, however, may adequately describe Wilmarth and Smith, who in some ways more adequately reflected Victorian conceptions of womanhood.

Addams also said that the presence of John Dewey as a trustee was especially appreciated for he acted as a "lubricant" between sentiment and practicality. Dewey himself provided insight into the workings of the trustees and said the responsibilities of the board were to rubber-stamp Addams' suggestions. Dewey said the board would simply "say to Miss Addams, what her friends have always said, 'You are all right; go ahead.'" Dewey argued that while Hull House became an institution, it did so "without becoming institutionalized."

The institution certainly revolved around the person and leadership of Addams. The trustees were friends and colleagues of Addams, and they trusted her to know what was best. Addams' world view was first enlarged by neighbors and then radicalized by residents such as Florence Kelley and Alzina Stevens. She, in turn, influenced the trustees so they could better support social and political changes at the turn of the century.

To become an institution without becoming institutionalized is a rare if not impossible occurrence. Yet Dewey's point is substantiated by Alzina Stevens, an important Hull House resident and labor organizer from the mid-1890s to her death in 1900. Stevens wrote that many people criticized Hull House because they perceived its work to be inconsistent. Stevens cited the fact that Hull House supported nursery facilities for working mothers, yet it also advocated societal changes which would render working mothers unnecessary for family survival. It did not support relief or charity as essentially helpful to the poor, yet it found itself distributing relief during times of economic strife.[8] Inconsistency is contradictory to the movement toward institutionalization, a point to which Dewey was perhaps alluding. The policy set forth in the settlement's charter was not meant to curtail actions or to make them consistent, but to encompass the many activities deemed necessary in a complex society.

While the board of trustees did not determine the exact actions of Hull House residents and their programs, it did in-

Constellation Three — Wealthy Stars   151

stitutionalize the settlement by legitimizing its presence within an extremely class-conscious culture. It was perhaps even necessary to the survival of Hull House that prominent and wealthy Chicagoans were utilized as trustees. These people (or "friends" as they were sometimes called) provided legitimization, and in turn, were transformed. Being a trustee was an education that changed the social and political ideals of many elite Chicagoans, even if it did not convince them to give away their wealth and privilege or to become socialists and radical reformers.

In this chapter, biographical sketches are provided for three Hull House Trustees: Helen Culver, Mary Rozet Smith, and Louise deKoven Bowen. These women were similar in their standing as significant trustees of Hull House and in their wealth, but dissimilar in their life situations. They provide examples not only of nineteenth-century elite female philanthropy, but also insight into women's attempts to be active contributors—monetarily, socially, and personally—to the betterment of their society. Though not residents of the settlement, they were crucial supporters and friends of the Hull House residents. In fact, nonresidency proved to be an asset. The personal homes of Smith and Bowen provided places for special meetings and fancy dinner parties, as well as retreat space for residents in need of respite. The topic of friendship is especially significant in this chapter. The presence of these women and their relationships with Hull House women points to the importance of friendship as a powerful component in individual and social transformation, and as a grounding for vocational and spiritual identities. As reiterated by North American feminists in the 1970s, the personal is political.

Helen Culver

Herma Clark wrote of the uproar caused in February 1889, when Charles J. Hull, a wealthy and widowed Chicago real estate tycoon, died while on a business trip. In his last will and testament, he left his entire estate to his "spinster" cousin and coworker, Helen Culver:

> There has been great interest in Chicago concerning the will of Charles J. Hull recently probated, by which

Miss Helen Culver, a cousin of Mr. Hull, is declared sole heir and executor. The estate is said to be worth more than a million dollars. The dead man, a childless widower, had only nephews and nieces to inherit his great fortune.[9]

By the time of Hull's death, Culver had been his business manager for more than twenty years and was known for her financial expertise. Yet the idea of a woman controlling such a large estate shocked the sensibilities of many late-nineteenth-century people. Known as the first businesswoman of Chicago, and probably the first woman notary public of the State of Illinois, Culver was remarkable for her day.[10] She became a great Chicago benefactor. She especially supported Hull House and the University of Chicago. Her rise to financial independence and wealth while in her fifties reflects the sometimes surprising and diverse vocational journeys of nineteenth-century women.

Culver was originally from Little Valley, in Cattaraugus County, New York, an area that was still frontier in the early nineteenth century. The Erie Canal, completed in 1825, had barely opened up the area when she was born in 1832. Culver's ancestors had come to New England in 1635 with John Winthrop, Jr. Her grandfather, Noah Culver, moved to Little Valley, New York, from Vermont. In 1825, Culver's father, Lyman, married Emeliza Hull, the oldest sister of Charles Hull. Culver was their fourth child. Charles Hull, twelve years Helen's senior, was visiting his sister's family on the day of Helen's birth.[11]

Culver's mother died when Helen was five years old. Her father subsequently remarried and had a second family before his death in 1851. Culver received her primary education from a local school, enjoyed reading, and especially studied a textbook on rhetoric. She loved being outdoors and developed a special love for nature. At the age of fourteen she took up teaching, while also pursuing a higher grade education at the newly opened Chamberlain Institute. With her father's death, Culver and her older siblings gave up their inheritance claim to their father's second family. Consequently, Culver had to find independent financial means to subsist. She migrated westward with an older brother in 1853, moving to Sycamore, Illinois, to join their grandfather, who had earlier begun homesteading in this frontier area some sixty miles northwest of Chicago. She started teaching day and evening classes in an abandoned schoolhouse. In 1854, she went to Chicago to look for a less demanding teaching job. When she arrived in Chicago, she found only six public schools and secured a position in School Number Six. Shortly after, she was promoted to Assistant Principal in Grammar School Number Three, where she remained for a few years before being promoted to a high school position.

Part of Culver's reasoning for moving to Chicago was that her cousin, Charles Hull, and his family, were living there. In 1856, the Hull family built a house on the outskirts of town, a two-story buick building surrounded by grass and trees. They lived in this house for more than ten years. The house, which was originally built in the spacious suburbs, was quickly engulfed by the expanding city. It became surrounded by wooden buildings, tenements, factories, a saloon, and a mortician's shop. After the Hull family moved out of the house, it was leased to the Little Sisters of the Poor, a Catholic convent. It was eventually subdivided to contain a cabinet shop and various apartments.

Mrs. Hull died in 1860. Before her death, she asked Culver to quit teaching and look after Charles and his two children. Culver submitted to the "family claim" and quit her teaching job. She assumed her new role as the Culver housekeeper and caretaker. Her biographer, Thomas Goodspeed, wrote that Culver was as successful in these duties as she was in teaching. During her domestic years, however, Culver continued her studies and read profusely.[12] She would not let household duties keep her from learning and thinking.

The outbreak of the Civil War in 1861 greatly affected Culver, who, in 1863, volunteered for the United States Sanitary Commission. Along with two other Chicago women, she went to Murfreesboro, Tennessee, where she oversaw a nursing hospital. Herma Clark recreated the scene of Culver at the railroad station on her way to Tennessee and described Culver's "gentle and dignified bearing, and her air of complete self-command."[13] Serving in the Civil War introduced Culver to the "horrors of war," something she remembered throughout her years.[14]

Upon returning to Chicago, Culver once again assumed family duties. Hull's son, Charles Morley, died during the cholera epidemic of 1866. Culver went to Oberlin College in Ohio to tell his sister, Fredrika, of his death. While there, she met Martha Ellen French, a friend and classmate of Fredrika's. French would become Culver's close friend for fifty years.

Culver and Hull soon gave up maintaining their household at the Hull mansion on Halsted Street, and Culver began to help Hull with his business. With this change in duties, Goodspeed said that Culver "awoke to the discovery that she possessed business gifts hitherto unsuspected." One might say she discovered her vocational niche. Culver took charge of Hull's Chicago office, an especially important job since Hull spent increasingly more time travelling, buying and developing property throughout the United States. Culver left Chicago in the winter of 1871 and 1872 and temporarily moved to Savannah, Georgia, were she helped Hull develop property for the newly emancipated African-American population. True to her teaching spirit, she worked during the day in the development office and at night founded and operated a school for more than 300 black men, women, and children. After returning to Chicago, she resumed full responsibility for Hull's local operations. Known by her work associates as a seemingly tireless worker, she spent most of her waking hours in the office; in the evenings, she taught in the office school she kept.[15]

In 1874, tragedy again struck the Hull family with the death of Hull's daughter, Fredrika. Once again, like her mother before her, Fredrika made Culver promise to stay with her father. Due to his travelling schedule, Hull decided to live in a hotel while in Chicago. He and Culver only reestablished a home together in 1884 when his health gave out, at which point Martha French came to live with them. French and Culver lived together for thirty years. French, also a teacher by training, was Culver's "companion and assistant, particularly in her philanthropic work."[16] Hull died in 1889, after being sick for a number of years. Goodspeed explained why Hull left his full estate to Culver, "[Hull] felt that [Culver] had so much to do with accumulating his fortune that it belonged to her as much as to himself."[17]

Culver became a wealthy businesswoman through inheritance. She managed properties in Chicago, as well as in Baltimore, Savannah, Houston, Jacksonville, and Lincoln, Neb. It was to Culver, then, that Addams and Starr went in 1889 when they found a building in Chicago's nineteenth ward that they thought would be perfect for what they called their "scheme." Upon learning that the property was the original home of the recently deceased Charles Hull and had just become the property of Helen Culver, Addams approached Culver to see if they could rent part of it. Culver was initially skeptical about the venture of Addams and Starr, but agreed to rent three rooms of the house to them. "The conviction of [Hull House's] usefulness grew on Miss Culver." She eventually not only donated the house to the settlement, but the entire block. She not only became a member of the first board of trustees, she also gave $50,000 for the boys' building and made monthly contributions to the work of the house.[18]

Addams and Starr did not name their social settlement "Hull" House at its inception. Rather, they referred to it as a Toynbee Experiment or a Chicago Toynbee Hall. But Hull's name stuck to the old mansion, which was a landmark on the near west side of Chicago. The house retained its popular name, reflective of its first owner and Culver's donation of it to the settlement venture.

Thomas Goodspeed suggested that Culver saw in Hull House the "opportunity of true philanthropy." This may be true, but it is possible to interpret Culver's growing support of Hull House as her recognition that it institutionalized many of her lifelong vocational interests related to education and helping the less fortunate. She became a personal friend of Addams and supported her through the years. Even though she did not always agree with Addams, Addams said that she always accorded her "freedom and generous support."[19]

W. W. Grinstead, who was Culver's lawyer and business associate from 1891 to 1904, recognized her strong administrative abilities. He found that she had a "fair, even temperament [and a] wonderful memory." She was a "leader rather than a driver, courteous, [and] easy to approach."[20] She may have been sentimental, as Addams suggested in her reflection on the first board of trustees. Culver was concerned about helping the less fortunate, but she also was practical about how that could be accomplished. After all, she was a successful businesswoman. In the mid-1890s, when Culver was in her sixties, she began to train Charles Hull Ewing, Hull's nephew, to be her business associate. Ewing eventually took over her business. (He also replaced Culver as Hull House trustee when she resigned in 1920.)

In the late 1890s, Culver bought a piece of property, a "neglected farm" in Lake Forest, just north of Chicago, where she could once again enjoy the outdoors. She and French set up their own home. Later, she also bought a home in Sarasota, Florida, where she and French spent their winters. Culver gradually lost her sight, but before that happened, she memorized her favorite poems. Her friends and companions continued to read to her until her death.

Culver's adult religious affiliation was Unitarian, though many in her family of origin were Quaker. Her cousin and benefactor, Charles Hull, was active in the Unitarian Church and an admirer of the Reverend David Swing. Hull had little respect for orthodox theology and evangelical views. He called the doctrine of substitution a "fable," believing that "grace and growth are elements of the soul, and never can be eternal." He believed that individuals were to exemplify the spirit of Jesus; this was the core of his faith and led him to support abolition, prohibition, and women's suffrage.[21] His unorthodox religious and radical political views probably contributed to his willingness to leave his estate in the hands of his female cousin, also an unorthodox practice in the nineteenth century.

Culver embodied similar social and political views as Hull. She displayed the late-nineteenth-century philanthropic view of service and usefulness to the world reflective of a Quaker spirituality and background. Her service in teaching night classes and during the Civil War reflected her ideals of contributing to the larger society. As a member of the Church of the Unity, pastored by Dr. Robert Collyer until he became pastor of Theodore Parker's congregation in Boston, she formally aligned herself with a liberal Christian theology. She exemplified the progressive, practical, and positive belief that society would improve through increased knowledge and education. At the 1897 dedication of the Hull Biological Laboratory at the University of Chicago, for which she donated one million dollars worth of property as well as additional gifts of money, Culver said:

> I have believed that I should not do better than to choose as [Hull's] heirs and representatives those lovers of the light, who, in all generations and from all ranks, give their lives to the search for truth, especially those forms of inquiry which explore the Creator's will as expressed in the laws of life and the means of making lives more sound and wholesome.[22]

Like many other progressives, Culver equated the increase of science with the ability to learn the truth and then uphold it. Truth, to her, was the core of all religious endeavors, and was an expression of spirituality in and of itself: "Moral evils grow less as knowledge of their relation to physical life prevails—and that science, which is knowing—knowing the truth—is a foundation of pure religion."[23]

Culver was similar to many nineteenth-century women in her acceptance of responsibilities to care for family members and maintain households. This was a duty expected not only of married women and mothers, but also of single women. In fact, family duty expanded for single women as their services were called upon by extended family relations. The fact that Culver resigned her teaching position to care for her cousin and his family showed that even she, an apparently independent and self-sufficient woman, was not immune to the family claim or the family culture of her era.

Unlike many nineteenth century women, however, family devotion did not engulf her world. Culver, through luck, hard work, and ability, became a respected and successful businesswoman. Her vocation was not just her business, however, as she believed that with wealth came responsibility. With Martha French, her companion in living, Culver engaged in philanthropic endeavors involving both time and money. Through her participation as a trustee and her huge financial donations to Hull House, as well as to the University of Chicago, she helped reform her environment on the progressive ideal of education as a tool toward social improvement and perfection.[24] Her commitment to Hull House, and her connections with its leaders, was a tangible expression of her personal, social, and spiritual ideals.

Mary Rozet Smith

Alice Hamilton said of Mary Rozet Smith that she was a "supremely lovely figure," and Jane Addams' closest friend, who "left no mark on history but . . . left a deep mark on all who knew her." Hamilton continued,

> [S]he had a genius for personal relations. I suppose that means quick insight, warmth, and a "heart at leisure from itself." She was one of those persons whose biographies are never written but had a deep abiding influence on their time. Her large, gracious home on Walton Place was a refuge for Miss Addams—who could hardly have carried on had she not been able to slip away from the West Side to it now and then—and a place of refreshment for many of the rest of us. And to Hull House her coming was not only a joy but a sustaining help in time of trouble and perplexity for all the years up to her death in 1934.[25]

Mary Rozet Smith was from a prominent Chicago family. Her father, Charles Mather Smith, was a successful manufacturer, and her mother, Sarah, was a philanthropist in her own right, having come from a wealthy Philadelphia family. Smith was born in 1868 and educated at the private and prestigious Kirkland School. She spent most of her teenage years travelling abroad in Europe with her father and mother. A friend of Jennie Dow, Hull House's first kindergarten teacher, Smith drifted into Hull House in 1890, as James Weber Linn described it, to "see whether there was anything she could do there. She was barely twenty; tall, shy, fair, and eager."[26]

Smith quickly became active in Hull House activities, taking special interest in children and leading clubs such as the Dramatic Association. Unlike blazing reformers such as Starr and

Kelley, and more like Keyser, Smith was never involved in social or scientific investigation or in overt political reform work. She never picketed in labor disputes and was never arrested by the police. She preferred to remain behind the scenes of action, in the background of the other Hull House women, especially Addams.[27]

Despite Smith's quiet, low-key demeanor, she was a noticeable presence at Hull House. She brought a respectable and Victorian, ladylike bearing to the house, whether she was working with children or talking with visitors. She was gracious and hospitable to all people, neighbors and visitors alike. Louise deKoven Bowen, however, believed Smith participated in one negative aspect of the house, that of tobacco smoking. Bowen described the moment of Smith's first cigarette, an event that might be interpreted as Smith not wanting to offend a distinguished Hull House guest:

> One evening at Hull-House, I think we made a step downward. Mrs. Emily Pankhurst, the most prominent English Suffragist, was visiting there. We had just finished dinner when she asked Miss Addams if she might smoke. Now, we had never had any smoking at Hull-House. I don't think its walls had ever been polluted by a cigarette or cigar. . . . [Mary Rozet Smith had a cigarette with Pankhurst and] she always smoked from then on.[28]

Mary Smith not only provided Hull House with an additional helping hand. As an original trustee, she was crucial in enlisting monetary gifts for the work of the settlement. She had connections to Chicago society and money through her family and friends. For example, Eleanor Smith, who launched the very successful Music School of Hull House, originally came to it in 1892 because she was a friend of Mary Rozet Smith. Not surprisingly, Mary Rozet Smith provided the money to start the school.[29]

Smith recruited her immediate family to the work of Hull House. Before the death of her father, who went blind in his last years, she convinced him to donate large sums of money for building projects. She got her mother, Sarah, an invalid for many years, interested in supporting the children of the Hull House neighborhood. After the death of Sarah Smith, the Smith family donated a pipe organ in her memory. At the dedication service of the organ, Jane Addams posthumously thanked Sarah Smith for her devotion to Hull House. Addams expressed thankfulness not only for the time and interest Sarah gave to Hull House, but that she allowed Mary to become involved. Reflective of the pervasive family claim upon single women, Addams said that Sarah willingly shared the "time and services of her daughter, when she would gladly have claimed this companionship for herself." Addams stated that even before Mary Rozet Smith inherited the family home on Walton Street, Sarah had opened its doors for Hull House residents to come and relax. Indeed, the Smith residence was known as a place of retreat, a "kind of annex to Hull-House."[30]

Mary Rozet Smith's greatest contributions to Hull House were not her Chicago connections or money, but her unwavering support of Jane Addams. James Weber Linn wrote that "the friendship of Mary Smith soon became and always remained the highest and clearest note in the music of Jane Addams's personal life."[31] Historian Robyn Muncy identified Smith as the "great woman behind a great woman."[32] Smith and Addams were each other's primary relationship. They shared mutual friends and their friends treated them like a married couple. Louise deKoven Bowen, for example, described the relationship between the two women as a kind of marriage relationship. She related how Smith habitually followed Addams around with a "shawl, pocket handkerchiefs, crackers if she thought Miss Addams might be hungry, or anything else she might want, and was always ready to supply Miss Addams' needs, whatever they were."[33] Correspondence to Addams was often directed through Smith. Smith did much of the social networking of their relationship and maintained communication with friends and associates throughout the United States. While this division of duties may have happened because Addams was busy doing more "public" events, it is more accurate to suggest that Smith had a greater capacity for maintaining friendships than did Addams. She was a friendlier, more amiable person than Addams.

If compared to a traditional heterosexual marriage, it is possible to identify Smith as fulfilling the role of supportive wife and Addams that of a famous husband in need of care and special attention. Yet this comparison does not quite hold. During the early years of their relationship—times of dire financial situations for the newly formed Hull House—Smith provided impromptu financial support to keep it going. Minutes from the residents' meeting in January 1895 indicate the financial challenges of Hull House during its early years: "The glory of the new year has brought no insignificant shadow of gloom upon us as we find the murky fingers of debt holding us with tenacious grasp."[34] Smith may have been the loving, "behind-the-scenes" spouse, but she was the one with the money in the bank and a relatively open purse when it came to supporting the needs of Addams and the house. Addams, though aware of the potential problems of mingling financial matters with personal friendship, could not help but grow to love Smith.

In his biography on Jane Addams, historian Allen Davis addressed the relationship between her and Smith. He said that while Addams' close relationship with Ellen Gates Starr was important in the years prior to Hull House, it was more of an intellectual relationship than one based on friendship. With Smith, Addams became emotionally attached. Part of the emotional connection was due to Smith's unconditional acceptance of Addams, a quality not shown by Starr.[35]

The relationship between Smith and Addams was central to their lives. They spent as much time together at Hull House as possible. Addams often stayed at Smith's Walton Street home when she needed to get away from her duties and the public spotlight of Hull House. They communicated regularly through letter writing when apart, related news about activities and people, and, in some letters, expressed their longing for each other. They travelled together when circumstances allowed. Historian Blanche Wiesen Cook claimed that Addams wired hotels ahead of their arrival to request a "large double bed for their hotel room."[36] In 1904, Addams and Smith bought a home and property together near Bar Harbor, Maine, just a quarter of a mile from the summer mansion of their friend, Louise Bowen. Bowen took charge of the house for them, and saw that it was initially furnished and thoroughly cleaned each spring.[37] The summer house was a special place for Smith and Addams, and they spent part of every summer there while their health lasted. In this shared home, they received many visitors and relaxed with other Hull House women who were also in the area, including Bowen, Kelley, and Hamilton.

Given the life history of Addams' ill health and the fact that Smith was nearly ten years Addams' junior, everyone expected Addams to die before Smith. This did not happen. Alice Hamilton rushed to the bedside of Smith (as she also attended to Addams in times of sickness) just before Smith's death in 1934 at the age of sixty-five: "When I came out here I told Mary that she must get well, that she could live on without J.A. but J.A. could not live without her." Smith died the next day.

Hamilton was especially concerned for Addams' future, not only because of the emotional attachment between her and Smith, but because of practical implications. Hamilton wrote that with Smith's death, Addams no longer had a patron: "What are we to do? Here is J.A. ordered to bed for four more weeks at the least—and we are in a house that is not Mary's, it is her heirs'—the servants, the heat, the food—it is no longer Mary who gives them to us." Hamilton herself was shaken over Smith's death, and wrote, "I can't look at my grief over Mary because I should lose my grip."[38] Addams spent the summer of 1934 at Hamilton's home in Connecticut, and lived the remaining year of her life with Bowen in her Chicago house.[39]

Upon Smith's death, every letter that Addams had ever sent to her was discovered in Smith's desk drawers, revealing a forty-year relationship of devotion and trust. Addams, as all her friend's feared, was greatly affected by Smith's death. James Weber Linn said that with Smith's death, Addams' "spirit dimmed," and though she "walked as steadily as ever," she walked as if in the "twilight."[40]

The life and work of Smith provides a striking contrast with some of the more prominent women of Hull House such as Kelley and Hamilton, who became famous through their amazing accomplishments and reform vocations. While Smith participated on numerous civic boards and organizations and was involved in racial justice issues, she preferred to work behind the scenes. She was not college educated like many of the other

Hull House women, and "people interested her more than causes or schemes, and children perhaps more than any other sort of people." Smith was perhaps more tolerant of people than even Addams, Linn observed, but always "remained shy at heart." Linn suggested that if Smith had anything that might be classified as a career, it was her "decision to be primarily concerned in making life easier for Jane Addams."[41] Like many women, Smith's vocation was innately tied to her personal relational commitments. What makes Smith's relational vocation different from other late-nineteenth- and early-twentieth-century women was that her primary commitment did not fall within the boundaries defined by biological family or male association. Smith was committed to the social settlement ideal, but her base committment was to the person of Jane Addams. It is no wonder that Addams' life without Smith proved heartbreaking and she lived only one year longer than her best friend and companion.

Most twentieth-century historians have not known how to interpret the relationship between Smith and Addams. Allen Davis wrote that such close female relationships have to be understood in relation to nineteenth-century "separate spheres" ideology. At the same time, he claimed the question as to whether or not women such as Addams and Smith were lesbian was "essentially irrelevant." Given our post-Freudian twentieth-century society, Davis said:

> The romantic words, the love letters, the terms of endearment can be easily misinterpreted, but it is important that many unmarried women drew warmth and strength from their supportive relationships with other women.[42]

In a footnote attached to the above-quoted sentence, Davis related a discussion he had with Alice Hamilton—when she was in her nineties—about the possibility of lesbian relationships at Hull House. In his words, she "denied that there was any open lesbian activity. . . but agreed that the close relationship of the women involved an unconscious sexuality." Davis went on to say that since Hamilton believed such relationships were unconscious, she deemed them unimportant; she said his very asking her about the subject showed the "separation between [his] generation and hers." Hamilton's comments are not surprising. Her letters simply assume the presence of significant and close female relationships while they provide some record of the heterosexual dating practices within Hull House, and uplift numerous marriages that occurred from within the community.[43]

One possible interpretion of the relationships shared by women such as Smith and Addams (and Culver and French) is to understand them within nineteenth-century ideals regarding romantic relationships or homoerotic friendships between women.[44] Such relationships, however, occurred not only between single women (as Davis limits their occurrence), but between women regardless of their marital standing. Affectionate relationships occurred between mothers and daughters, teachers and students, cousins and school friends. Virtually any kind of special relationship between women became suspect in the early decades of the twentieth century. The rise of the male-dominated medical profession, the emerging insistence on romantic and companionate heterosexual marriages, and a backlash against feminism in the 1920s, led all women into the closet, so to speak, afraid to show love and affection to other women for fear that they would be labeled lesbian, butch or dyke, or "manly women."

What, then, are we to make of the relationship between Smith and Addams? Can it simply be upheld as a friendship, in the same way that Addams and Kelley, Lathrop and Hamilton, Starr and Wilmarth, were friends? To do this does not grant their relationship enough significance given what is known regarding their shared lives. On the one hand, Davis's argument is true. Labelling the sexuality of Hull House women as being homosexual or heterosexual, lesbian or straight, is a reflection of our late-twentieth-century psycho-social-sexual culture. Perhaps it is enough, then, to clearly indicate the intimate and long, loving, and supportive partnerships shared between women such as Smith and Addams, Culver and French. Additionally, it is an exercise in historical futility to attempt to establish the sexual activities of such women or classify their sexual

behaviors given the lack of concrete data existent on such private encounters. In this sense, then, Davis is correct. Smith and
Addams lived in a different world than today. Their "Boston
marriage," as such long-term companionate relationships between women were often called in the nineteenth century, may
or may not have been explicitly sexual.[45]

On the other hand, as Blanche Wiesen Cook pointed out,
"[i]f we lived in a society where individual choice and the diversity of our human rhythms were honored, the actuality of lesbianism would in fact be irrelevant."[46] Cook argued that labelling
such possible relations irrelevant serves to uphold dominant
heterosexism. Given the Victorian sexual mores in which Smith
and Addams lived, it is also much more acceptable to think of
them as asexual rather than sexual, or, in other words, to believe
they were properly celibate rather than pervertedly lesbian.

The question of what makes a relationship between two
women lesbian is a contemporary debate: Is it based on sexual
contact? And if so, how is sexual contact defined? Is it based on
emotional interdependence? shared finances or household? Is
it a political stance against patriarchy? Can a woman be both a
"woman identified woman" and be sexually involved with men?
The contemporary questions go on and on. Most current literature defines lesbianism as broader than a woman's sexual activity. Lillian Faderman, in her historical analysis of romantic
relationships between women from the Renaissance to the present, defines a lesbian relationship as a "relationship in which
two women's strongest emotions and affections are directed toward each other. Sexual contact may be part of the relationship
to a greater or lesser degree, or it may be entirely absent."[47]

Some recent publications uplift individuals such as Smith
and Addams as lesbian, and are important contributions in providing role models for contemporary lesbians and gays. These
works, though sometimes propagandist in style, attempt to crack
dominant, heterosexual society by arguing for the lesbian or
gay identity of famous historical figures. As a result of such
reinterpretations, the homophobia of our current North American society may perhaps be lessened, so that a fuller range of
love relationships shared between women may be accepted and
appreciated.[48]

Given what is known about the relationship between Smith and Addams, it was not "essentially irrelevant" as Davis concluded. Their relationship helped them form the meaning of their lives and became central to their vocations at Hull House. Because they lived in a pre-Freudian era, they did not have to hide the centrality of their partnership from peers or co-workers. Women like Hamilton and Bowen, and men like James Weber Linn, were not suspicious of their relationship, and did not think it abnormal. Rather, all who knew Addams and Smith acknowledged their relationship and rejoiced that they had one another in their lives.

If Smith and Addams were alive today and shared a relationship similar to that which they shared one hundred years ago, they would be understood as lesbian. Furthermore, they would probably have to identify themselves as such to the larger society and would encounter discrimination because of their mutual love and shared life. Indeed, the Hull House settlement—as primarily women's space—would likely receive more criticism and denunciation from the religiously conservative and politically right than it did a century ago. Smith and Addams, and all their Hull House women friends, could still claim an innate feminine character which legitimized their concerns and activities. Though their presence threatened the status quo—as has the presence of all women who have worked and lived together striving for social change—nineteenth-century understandings of womanhood protected them against the most harsh condemnations. While dominant Christianity as a religious system curtailed their leadership, the spirituality of Christianity enabled them to live without having to defend or explain their female associations.

Louise deKoven Bowen

Louise deKoven Bowen is probably the best example of an elite woman getting involved in philanthropy and social reform in the late nineteenth and early twentieth centuries. She and Smith shared a number of similarities including wealth, familial Chicago connections, and lack of a college education. Unlike Smith, Bowen did not prefer the shadows but sought the spotlight. Her work at Hull House and related activities in social and political work were very public. Indeed, Bowen was often in the society pages of the Chicago papers and she appeared to thrive on such publicity. Although on the politically conservative end of the spectrum when compared with most of the other Hull House women, involvement in Hull House enlightened Bowen to the need for political and social changes. She was always supportive of Hull House and came to be very supportive of Jane Addams. A privileged white woman, Bowen was changed by her friendship with Addams and the more radical residents of the house.

Bowen was born in 1859 and was the only child of John and Helen (Hadduck). She inherited wealth from both parents. Her father was a successful banker, and her mother was the grand-daughter of an early Chicago land investor who owned much of the property that was to become the area of Chicago's downtown Loop.[49] Her grandfather, Edward H. Hadduck, came to Chicago in 1835. Bowen wrote that when her grandfather arrived in Chicago, he saw so many "possibilities for a young man" that he went back to Ohio to marry, and returned immediately to make his fortune. Her grandparents initially lived in Fort Dearborn. Bowen wrote that her grandmother often talked of these early years:

> I have often heard my grandmother tell of the trials of living in the same room with fifty other people, and how difficult it was to get water and how she had to sneak out of the Fort down to the river, to avoid the Indians of whom she was very much afraid.[50]

Bowen attended Dearborn Seminary from ages five to sixteen. After finishing her formal schooling, she spent two years reading the "cyclopedia" as a way to increase her knowledge. Like other women of her class, she also took lessons in music and art. Still, Bowen found that her formal education was inadequate: "By the time I made my entry into society I was ignorant in everything and accomplished in nothing."[51]

Bowen was raised going to church every Sunday and was a lifelong member of the St. James Episcopal Church.[52] As a child, she was "passionately devoted" to her Sunday School teacher and, when she became old enough, volunteered to become a teacher herself. The only class offered to her was the fourteen- to sixteen-year-old "bad boys" class. Their former teacher had quit because they were too rowdy for her. Although Bowen was only sixteen years old, she handled the class with an air of authority and some physical prowess unacceptable today:

> When I sat down I said I had never had a class before and knew nothing of the rules of the school, but that I intended to be obeyed and that I would not tolerate rough-housing. . . . One big boy immediately kicked the boy next to him. I told him to be quiet, but as he kicked again I thought it was time for action, and seizing the big boy by the collar I pulled him off the bench and out into the aisle, down toward the door, which, when I opened and cast him out. The whole affair was so unexpected—that is, being seized by a girl and dragged down the aisle before the whole school—that the boy did nothing but kick. . . . When I returned to the class everyone was quiet as a mouse. I began the lesson, and from that time on I never had one bit of trouble with the boys.[53]

Bowen taught the class, which called itself "The Soldiers of Christ," for eleven years. It grew to one hundred students. In addition to teaching these boys she invited them over to her family's mansion three times a week to play billiards, visited them at their homes, and helped them to find jobs. The first boy's club in Chicago, which was formed on Huron Street, was an outgrowth of her Soldiers of Christ class.[54]

Bowen, reflecting on her early life experiences, wrote that in her youth the church was the "only outlet for social work." As an adult, she began to feel guilty that she was not participating in church work. She found out, however, that the church would not utilize her skills:

> Later in life, when I had had a good deal of experience in social work, I had a pang of conscience that I was

doing no church work. I went to my rector and asked for something to do. After thinking the matter over he offered me the chairmanship of the Chancel Committee, the same work I had done when I was an inexperienced girl. This work I declined on the ground that my experience should have fitted me for something more responsible.[55]

Like all women in nineteenth-century mainstream Christian churches, Bowen was not allowed to function in anything more than a secondary position. She found in settlement work the opportunity to engage in service which she did not find within the church. Bowen, in writing of her involvement in Hull House, said:

I often felt at this Hull-House club [the Woman's Club] that not even in church did I ever get the inspiration or the desire for service, so much as when I was presiding at the meeting of the club and sat on the platform and looked down on the faces of 800 or 900 women gathered together, all intensely in earnest and all most anxious perhaps to put over some project in which they were interested. The club also proved to be a liberal education for me.[56]

Historian Rima Lunin Schultz argued that Bowen was influenced not only by a general Christian attitude of social service, but by a particular sense of social stewardship.[57] Describing her family socialization, Bowen wrote:

I had been brought up with the idea that some day I would inherit a fortune, and I was always taught that the responsibility of money was great, and that God would hold me accountable for the manner in which I used my talents.[58]

Bowen inherited money from her family of origin as well as from her wealthy husband, Joseph Bowen, whom she married in 1886. They had four children, born between the years

1887 and 1893. While she had heard of Jane Addams and Ellen Gates Starr prior to 1893, it was only after the birth of her last child that Bowen visited Hull House and met Jane Addams. Addams, recognizing an opportunity to enlist the support of a wealthy and skillful Chicagoan, immediately asked Bowen to join the Hull House Woman's Club, to lend it her leadership, and teach the women parliamentary procedure. Before Bowen could teach the other women parliamentary procedure she first had to learn it herself. She soon became president and remained with the club for seventeen years. When Bowen assumed leadership of the woman's club in 1893, it was a fledgling group that had existed only two years. Under Bowen's leadership, it grew into one the strongest Hull House clubs. When she resigned in 1910, it was to become president of the Chicago Woman's Club. Bowen recognized that the skills she learned through her work at Hull House were crucial in her later civic work:

> My first speeches were made at Hull-House. I had never spoken before and felt very nervous when I got on my feet; I found it difficult to collect my thought. It was, however, good practice to do admidst [sic] so much confusion; frequently when I was speaking, the door of the room would be thrown open and some of the residents (who were doing what they called "toting"—that is, showing people around Hull-House) would say, "This is the Hull-House Woman's Club, that is Mrs. Bowen, the president, on the platform," and it was very difficult not to listen to the comments of the visitors, as I was trying to put my own thoughts in order.[59]

Bowen developed a special relationship with Jane Addams, and she and Mary Rozet Smith often travelled to meetings together. Addams helped Bowen write her first speech, and taught her other, less concrete things. For example, Bowen related one incident in which she helped a woman who never expressed her gratitude. Bowen shared her displeasure with Addams, who asked: "Is that the reason you helped her, because you wanted gratitude?"[60] Bowen believed Addams had a real skill in helping people develop their gifts:

> Miss Addams had a rare way of putting people in a position of responsibility and then letting them work out their own plans; she always commended them for what they had done although, in a very wise way she managed to let them see the imperfections of their plan and how much it might be bettered another time. She had a marvelous influence over the people who went to Hull-House, she could almost always make anyone get up and speak.[61]

Bowen expanded her areas of interest beyond the woman's club. She became involved with Julia Lathrop on the Juvenile Protection Association committee, succeeded Lathrop as president, and was a mainstay of the organization for thirty five years. James Weber Linn wrote that it was Bowen, not Lathrop, who made the early juvenile court system work. Bowen raised money for salaries and for constructing the court building and detention home. She also established standards for employees.[62] After the death of her husband in 1911, Bowen conducted studies on delinquency and the growing problem of race relations between African Americans and European Americans in Chicago.[63]

Bowen became skillful in using her class privilege. She "squeezed money out of the rich, and bullied decent laws out of the politicians." When the "ultra-exclusive" Fortnightly Club withdrew its invitation for Jane Addams to speak due to her perceived radicalness, Bowen used her position as a member to call a special meeting. As a privilege of membership, she brought along Addams to speak. Bowen claimed she did not particularly like chairing meetings and hosting dinners, yet she often did so as a way to solicit support from the Chicago elite: "You could lead the conversation around to some project you were particularly interested in, and then, a few days later, send a letter asking for a contribution and be pretty likely to get it."[64]

Bowen's wealth and position in the society pages of Chicago newspapers was perceived both positively and negatively by her

contemporaries. Bowen related an incident regarding the Hull
House Woman's Club:

> For many years I went to these club meetings, driving
> in a buggy and wearing my most simple clothes, but
> afterwards I found this was a mistake, the women
> wanted good clothes, they liked to see me dressed
> smartly, they liked to have me drive up in a motor and
> see it standing in front of the club house on Polk Street.
> I always told my friends that I had to keep up a number
> of social activities in order to get my name in the papers
> to please the Hull-House Woman's Club. Many a time
> they would say, "We saw your name in the paper as being
> at the opera." "We were glad to know our club president
> was at a ball." "It is a pleasure to know we have for
> president a lady who goes so much into society."[65]

Yet other people expressed abhorrence at Bowen's wealth and
extravagance. Bowen related an incident in which she and Addams were chairing a "High Cost of Living" meeting for the
Woman's Fair Price Commission of the state of Illinois. She
wrote that a man in the audience asked "how much [she] had
paid for the fur coat [she] was wearing." Before she could reply,
he also asked if she "had brought [her] grocery bill with [her]."
She refused to answer such personal questions, but later in the
meeting, she and Addams had to quickly vacate the stage after
it was rushed by the questioning man and his friends.[66]
    The wealth of Bowen was tremendous. The house she and
her husband built at 1430 Astor Street in Chicago had forty
rooms that were "tastefully decorated." Bowen put in an elevator
in the 1930s to accommodate Addams, who was becoming more
ill. Bowen's summer house in Bar Harbor, Maine, was no little
cottage either, but contained a dining room that would seat
forty to fifty people, six bedrooms on the second floor and five
on the third floor. Eight maids' rooms were also on the second
floor. It had ten baths, two porches, a swimming pool, gardens,
tennis court, and tea house.[67] It is not surprising that at least
some working people interpreted Bowen as insincere.
    Bowen came to understand Addams as "a middle person

between wealthy and working classes." A remarkable strength about Addams' leadership was her ability to cross class boundaries—something other white, privileged people either could not do or did not want to do—as her regular commutes from the homes of Bowen and Smith to the nineteenth ward symbolized. Bowen never fully became such a middle person, although her life was tremendously broadened through her Hull House involvement:

> My whole acquaintance with Hull-House opened for me a new door into life. I met many prominent people there, because anyone who came to Chicago always wanted to visit the House. I have dined there with many celebrities, and always found it most interesting, and on the other hand I have made many good friends among working people and have come in contact with problems and situations about which I would have otherwise known nothing.[68]

Bowen's friendship with Jane Addams enlarged her world view even though she never completely agreed with Addams. Alice Hamilton, for example, wrote that Louise deKoven Bowen was "always a prop and a stay to Miss Addams, even when, as in 1917, she did not agree with Jane Addams' anti-war stand, for her generosity . . . [was] one of the spirit as well as of the purse."[69] While Bowen always maintained, to her death in 1953, the caste of wealth and social elitism, she had begun to understand social and economic injustice:

> [I]t was most interesting to realize that although the people I met at Hull-House lived a life far removed from the kind I led, yet, after all we are all cast in the same mold, all with the same emotions, the same feelings, the same sense of right and wrong, but, alas, not with the same opportunities.[70]

One of the working-class people who influenced Bowen was Alzina Stevens.[71] Stevens, a resident of Hull House, was a particularly powerful labor organizer and became the first state probation officer in 1899. Born into a poor family in 1849, Stevens went to work at the age of thirteen in a textile factory, where she witnessed a co-worker fall to death in an elevator shaft and where she herself lost a finger due to an injury that became infected. Stevens came to Hull House, was hired by Kelley as one of her factory inspectors, and became involved in advocating the 1897 Illinois labor law. Stevens was not afraid of disrupting the wealthy or the influential. As a factory inspector, she had a major conflict with Marshall Field, the magnate store owner:

> [Stevens] discovered bales of cheap women's coats and jackets in a smallpox-infected tenement house and, before burning them, removed the Marshall Field label. Armed with her evidence, [she] confronted the merchant. Field offered no excuse. He arraigned Mrs. Stevens as a "termagant," "no lady," and "unsexed woman," and advised her to go home.[72]

Stevens did not go home and did not let the wrath of wealthy capitalists like Marshall Field distract her from her work. Due in large part to her own life experiences, Stevens was successful in introducing wealthy trustees such as Bowen to the needs of the working classes. She also educated other privileged residents like Alice Hamilton. Stevens, for example, took Hamilton to speeches given by such radicals as William Dudley Haywood and Emma Goldman, and introduced Hamilton to Eugene Debs.[73] Although Stevens unexpectedly died in 1900, she made a tremendous impact on the likes of Bowen and Hamilton. Through her and other women and men, they began to know of the struggles of working people.

Bowen had the opportunity to use her wealth and power in ways that would help working people. As a stockholder in numerous large companies, Hull House residents pressured Bowen to use her position to exert change. For example, when Alice Hamilton informed her about the "prevalence of lead-poisoning and tuberculosis among the workers" of Pullman Company, Bowen forced the company to at least open a hospital for its workers. Likewise, when Bowen learned that the International Harvester Company was employing women on its night shift, she lobbied Cyrus H. McCormick to stop women's work at night and to introduce a minimum weekly wage for women. It was not unusual for Bowen to receive anonymous letters that threatened her life or those of her children as she pushed for various reforms.[74]

Bowen also began to understand the oppression of racism. While the African-American population was minimal in Chicago until the 1920s, and the Hull House neighborhood never contained a high black population, the house sponsored meetings for black women, supported the Black Clubwoman's movement, and backed W.E.B. DuBois. Hull House had one black resident in the 1890s, Dr. Harriet Rice, who was in charge of the dispensary. For reasons yet undetermined, Dr. Rice's residency at Hull House was not pleasant or long.[75] Jane Addams and Ida B. Wells discussed lynching in the late 1890s; they agreed on the inappropriateness of its violence but disagreed on its causes. By the second decade of the twentieth century, however, Bowen—like other white women—began to show more awareness of racism. She wrote in 1913, "The life of the colored boy and girl is so circumscribed on every hand by race limitations that they can be helped only as the entire colored population in Chicago is understood and fairly treated."[76] While she advocated segregation of African Americans and European Americans, her work with Hull House and the juvenile court system gave her an understanding of race issues uncommon to most white people of her class.[77]

Other people recognized Bowen's ability to often stand alone from other members of elite Chicago society. In 1922, Bowen was asked to run as the Republican candidate for mayor of Chicago. Three reasons were given to support her possible candidacy: (1) she had no interest in or use for the Ku Klux Klan, (2) she had no interest in or use for the Chicago political machine, and (3) her name would "make nice society items for the [news]papers."[78] Needless to say, Bowen declined the pressure exerted on her to run for political office. She was satisfied with the informal influence she exerted through Hull House, the Chicago Woman's Club, and the Juvenile Protective Association.

Bowen's involvement in Hull House was substantial. Like Florence Kelley, she had a forceful personality and did not mince words, personal opinions, or actions. James Weber Linn remarked that Bowen's personality "pervaded" Hull House, and the only person who ever equalled Bowen in directness was Kelley.[79] At the celebration of her eightieth birthday, Bowen remarked in her speech:

> Some of my friends have insinuated that at times I have stepped where angels feared to tread, and I can only say that, under the circumstances, as I look over this room I marvel that I have so many friends left.[80]

Bowen's strong personality, wealth, and desire to be a central figure in Hull House's administration "sometimes caused consternation" among other Hull House participants. Yet after Addams' death, Bowen became president of the Hull House Association. Her strong leadership ensured that it would continue to function even after the death of its unifying and charismatic leader.

With the exception of Alice Hamilton, Bowen outlived the other Hull House women of the the 1890s. Her health remained remarkably good and she remained active until her mid-eighties. Her final years were spent mostly doting on family members and writing two autobiographical accounts. *Baymeath*, a family memoir was privately published in 1945. This work was written in letter form to a grandson who was serving "somewhere in Burma" during the Second World War; she wrote it for the express purpose of letting her descendants know how "their great-grandparents lived, thought and acted."[81] Her more general autobiography, *Open Windows: Stories of People and Places*, was published in 1946. This work reviewed her life and activities, and included many stories about her relationship with Jane Addams. In 1953, Bowen died of a stroke in her Chicago mansion.

Discussion

The presence of Culver, Smith, and Bowen was crucial to the operation of Hull House in its first decade and into the twentieth century. They formed a unique constellation among the Hull House galaxy because they operated as nonresidents, wealthy supporters of the enterprise, and interpreters of the work of the house to the broader community. Though not necessarily reformers in a strict definition of the word, they were capable and personally committed to making an impact on their social and political environment. Even though Culver, Smith, and Bowen shared the characteristics of wealth, class, and race, they made different contributions to the house.

Culver was older than the other Hull House women, and unlike Smith and Bowen, came from a poor farming background. She earned the money she inherited, unlike Smith and Bowen, who were born into wealth. Smith was the youngest woman of the group and the least desirous of public recognition. She preferred to remain in the background, and her vocation centered on personal interactions with the Hull House neighbors and residents. Her primary place came to be seen as the personal support and special friend of Jane Addams. Bowen, a skilled organizer with a powerful personality, was a wife and the mother of four children. Like the residents of the house, she too maintained an intense schedule of meetings and activities. She was a planner and a doer. She loved being in the society columns of the Chicago papers and used her position as an elite Chicagoan to advocate basic changes to benefit the less fortunate of the city.

All three women deviate from nineteenth-century Victorian stereotypes of true womanhood. They were skillful at managing and raising money, and did not draw their authority from or base their involvement in the larger society from the private realm of their home. They were active in their society. With the encouragement of Addams and other Hull House women, and through personal encounters with the women, men, and children of the nineteenth ward, they became convinced of the social settlement ideals and used their money to maintain and extend the work of the house. They were not just monetary philanthropists, however. They became advocates for a better social and civic life, for increased educational programs, and for fairer work conditions in an industrial era. Nor were they simply patrons who solely delighted in associating with some of the more radical fringe in their society or rubbing elbows with the poor. They spent many waking hours at Hull House and throughout the city, laboring in various ways for the institution. Their leadership skills, and their sense of personal power, developed through their association with Hull House. Bowen especially found opportunities in public speaking and organizing that she found in no other nineteenth-century organization in the city. None of these wealthy women always understood the implications their involvements, yet they showed a willingness and an openness to be changed by their interactions—to learn more about their world.

These women experienced Hull House as a place—a new kind of space—where personal and spiritual transformation occurred. They found it a place where they could be of service to their society from their particular locations within that society. Hull House, unlike Christian churches of their day, directed their energies, helped identify and use their gifts. Bowen, a worshipping Episcopalian, expressed dissatifaction with her church because it would not—or could not—utilize the skills she had to offer. She found her greatest spiritual experiences in the work she did at and through Hull House. By the end of her life she came to understand her work at Hull House and on various civic committees as preceding the emerging profession of social work. She spoke of her work in secular rather than sacred terms, and very much perceived it as due to public and civic duty rather than Christian piety. Still, she appreciated Addams not only as an amazingly capable and facilitating leader, but also as a "deeply religious person."[82] Perhaps if the Christian religious traditions of her day, including the male-dominated social gospel movement, had allowed women such as Bowen greater responsibilities, she would have understood her work and concerns as spiritually grounded. She might have realized that her vocation of public service was based on Christian ideals. Not content to fulfill what she considered trivial church duties, Bowen attended worship but found her spiritual outlet through a social settlement rather than through her Christian congregation.

The importance of women's friendship as a transforming agent becomes clear when these three women are placed within the Hull House galaxy. The dynamism of Hull House related to the encompassing social and spiritual vision it provided, but just as importantly, it was tied to the basic relations of friendship it fostered. Through Hull House, wealthy women such as Culver, Smith, and Bowen met and sometimes became friends with radicals, immigrants, and laborers. Through Hull House, women such as Starr and Lathrop found and became mentors. Many of the women of Hull House, such as Hamilton and Kelley, became friends for life, and some, like Smith and Addams, found their life/love companions. Friendships with men such as John Dewey and Henry Lloyd were important, too, to name only a few of the male friends of Hull House. The variety of friendships shared between the Hull House women was broad. While a basic sense of equality was present in their relations, their friendships were not identical in form or degree. To point out the significance of friendship relations among the Hull House women does not make them all the same or indicate that everyone involved in Hull House became friends or even talked about personal matters in the house dining room. The common thread to the friendships formed, however, was that they served to enlarge, not diminish, each woman's world.

In her book *A Passion for Friends*, Janice G. Raymond argued that one of the most important aspects of women's friendship is that it "gives women a point of cystallization for living in the world."[83] This sense of worldliness that friendship offers women—or involvement in actual, physical aspects of human life including what has typically been called the public realm—counteracted late-nineteenth-century patriarchal ideology, which attempted to limit women's interactions and activities. Raymond continued by saying that friendship gives women a location from which to act, and in so doing, "provides women with a common world that becomes a reference point for location in a larger world." In this sense, a "sharing of personal life is at the same time a grounding for social and political existence."

The friendships made and nurtured at Hull House enlarged the personal worlds of each woman. They helped each woman identify her unique vocation, and served as a basis for her social and political involvements. Despite differences in personality and leadership styles, and despite interpersonal conflicts, friendships emerged because people gathered together on shared tasks under a common vision. That many of these women worked, thought, strategized, and travelled together was significant. That many of them lived in the same house and ate in the same dining room was also significant, because such practical arrangements reinforced the commonality of their ties. That many of them were single or divorced women and did not have children, allowed them to share work-related tasks as well as relaxing times. The women of Hull House did not become friends for pragmatic purposes only, and they had other significant friends connected to but outside the Hull House community. But these particular women came to care deeply for one another and desired the best for one another even as they worked to improve their world. Despite busy and hectic schedules, they organized their lives so that they would have time—at least in the summers—to simply be together, enjoy one another's company, and renew their spirits for the work they felt called to do. They were often present with one another in times of illness and approaching death. When death occurred and grief followed, they provided mutual comfort and practical support.

Aristotle suggested that a friend was simply "another self" (even though he did not believe women had the capacity for friendship).[84] This may be true for the women of Hull House. The friendships shared by these women, however, enlarged their identities because they were not etheral or self-absorbed. Their friendships stimilated them to seek greater knowledge and activity in the world. Their personal connections energized them into new ideas and broader stances. Their friendships formed their vocations, grounded their spirituality, and integrated the whole of their lives.

This discussion on Culver, Smith, and Bowen, completes the three constellations of the galaxy of Hull House women. While not reformers in the strict sense of the word, as were Lathrop, Kelley, and Hamilton, and while not the initial settlers of Hull House, as were Addams, Starr, and Keyser, they were significant in the work and support they offered the house. When these nine women are interpreted as a galaxy of stars, it is clear that their interactions were intertwined in complex ways.

Both attracting and repelling forces are needed to hold the

stars of the universe in place, and so it was with the women of Hull House. They encompassed a vast array of personal experiences and embodied a spectrum of political methods, skills, religious doctrines, and spiritual motivations. Desirous of lives that would make a difference in the face of the overwhelming social milieu of the late nineteenth and early twentieth centuries, they decided that activity in the world was better than non-activity, and that learning was better than merely accepting the dominant status quo. Their association with Hull House placed them in the same galaxy. Despite differences, they held to a shared vocational outlook: that their lives could make a difference, and that they could offer something to make the society in which they lived more just. Their spirituality was based on cherishing life and recognizing its ultimate sense of mystery; it was a spirituality based on their interpretation of Christianity, and it was both profoundly individual and social.

Conclusion

THE HULL HOUSE GALAXY HAD a broad and glorious range: from the pivotal persona of Jane Addams to the unrelenting activism of Florence Kelley and the philanthropic leadership of Louise deKoven Bowen; from the radical political, artistic, and religious stances of Ellen Gates Starr to the gentle, witty, and determined actions of Julia Lathrop and the quiet, supportive presence of Mary Rozet Smith; from the kindheartedness and home-centeredness of Mary Keyser to the scientific, medical expertise of Alice Hamilton and the astute business capacities of Helen Culver. The Hull House galaxy was a powerful presence in late-nineteenth-century society.

The women of Hull House in the 1890s made history. They did not merely fulfill traditional female roles but sought lives of meaning and activity. Passivity was not an option chosen by them in light of the pressing problems and multifold changes within their society. Rather, they pushed at the boundaries allotted to them by the religious, social, and political institutions of their day. As predominantly white women of privilege, they utilized their social locations, educational opportunities, and monetary resources to participate in extraordinary actions of change. None of them began life filled with confidence or grandiose ideas about themselves or the changes they would make. None of them had women role models on whom they could model their lives. Rather, each woman struggled to find her own voice and power, and to develop confidence and skills. Shaped by a Christian idealism of service, they had an intense desire to be useful. With time, practice, and mutual support, they made their voices heard and their actions count. They built political and social networks that facilitated reforms to especially benefit women and children. Despite vast differences in personality and a spectrum of individual interests, they joined together in a common effort to make their society more neighborly.

Under the gathering leadership of Jane Addams, Hull House became an extraordinary space for personal exploration and joint ventures. It was a home and yet it was a work place; it was located within a specific neighborhood, yet the boundaries of that neighborhood stretched across the United States. Some of the women who came to Hull House knew what they wanted to do with their lives; most did not. At Hull House they found more than enough activity to keep them occupied (sometimes too much activity to maintain their health). They also developed relationships of support and challenge. At Hull House they had opportunities to acquire broader understandings and philosophies of life. They learned from the experiences of other people—from the poor and disenfranchised to the newly arrived immigrants and the incarcerated. They became involved with those who were hurting and those who were abused and those who were the discardable humans in their society. Their concerns ultimately encompassed improving the whole world. They came to embrace basic standards for all humanity—the opportunity of all people to live without want of food, decent housing, and health care, the chance for all people to learn to read and write and be partakers as well as creators of works of art and philosophy, and most importantly, the ability of all people to have lives of meaning and love. The shared vision of the women of Hull House was extraordinary in its optimism and scope.

The women of Hull House were part of a movement that was initially Christian. By the time of their deaths, the Christian base was all but gone. Christianity, as they experienced it, did not provide satisfactory answers to basic questions and strivings: What is it to be Christian? And how are Christians to live in the world? A transcendent, creedal religion was not enough for the women of Hull House. A secondary role within Christianity did not satisfy them either. Religious devotion and confessional statements for most of them, therefore, with the exception of Ellen Gates Starr, lessened in importance as their service to humanity increased. The divisiveness within Christianity and its inability to fully address pressing social problems contributed to a growing perception regarding the irrelevancy of the church to "modern" society. Claiming the remnants of a feminine spirituality, the women of Hull House desired Christianity to motivate people into kindness and provide personal meaning within a world community. Institutional Christianity seemed unable to do that.

What became important to the women of Hull House was a spirituality based on the loving of God through the loving of one's neighbor. Julia Lathrop exemplified this quality in her emphasis on "good works" over confession of faith. Jane Addams upheld the sacredness of life and spiritual mystery; she sought social justice and supported diversity even though she was a member of an evangelical Protestant congregation. Ellen Gates Starr, with her spiritual journey taking her eventually into the Roman Catholic fold, also focused on mystery and the need of theology to address practical social issues. Starr, unlike the other women of the house, found sacramental liturgy a means to uphold both God's immanence and transcendence. Florence Kelley, though not officially a Quaker until late in life, found sacramental qualities in the work of social justice, in the redeeming of the world through political and social actions.

The religious qualities of the women of Hull House, if acknowledged, have usually been compared to those of the philosophers John Dewey and William James. Many of the women of Hull House could similarly—and more successfully—be compared to the emerging liberal tradition within North American Protestantism. The Reverend David Swing and Professor Shailer

Mathews, two prominent Chicago religious leaders and contemporaries of the Hull House galaxy, deemphasized creeds and desired to make Christianity applicable to their society.[1] By continuing to compare these women, especially Addams, to so-called secular philosophers rather than to religious leaders, the incorrect opinion that they acted with no theological underpinnings and desired to rid themselves and society of religion is reinforced. Such was not the case. The women of Hull House in the 1890s desired to implement the religious teachings of their day, but found they needed to reimagine the tradition and focus on spiritual rather than doctrinal aspects. Yet even liberal Christianity as it developed would not have satisfied most of the Hull House women. They sought a Christianity that was both spiritual and intellectual, personal and social, prayerful and political. In other words, they wanted a Christianity that would pull together the facets of their own lives.

Hull House itself became a quasi-spiritual community, and Addams a reluctant seer. Addams' vision was that of a truly democratic society where differences would remain but cooperation would be the functioning criteria for human interactions. Addams' vision could not have been communicated without the presence of other women who helped one another direct their energies and idealism into vocational callings. New fields of service were forged by these women which took them beyond the boundaries of church and patriarchal familial structures. Hull House uplifted and supported individuality even as joint actions of societal betterment were undertaken. The women brought unique personalities, skills, and talents, and their individuality was not lost but encouraged. Yet it was as connected human beings that they got their strength and endurance. Crucial to their developing vocations and spiritualities were the friendships formed. These relationships were based not only on loving, supporting, and critiquing one another, but on making the world more just and loving. Their friendships varied in degree and intensity, and changed over the years, but accounted for much of their power. The women of Hull House substantiate Mary Hunt's insight, that "it is hard to find an example of a woman who made social change apart from a group of friends."[2]

In the end, however, why study the women of Hull House? The obvious answer to this question is that they played a significant role within the historical time period of the late-nineteenth and early-twentieth centuries. The fact that even their names have been largely forgotten within shared historical memory, makes discussion on their lives more pertinent. The less obvious answer is that through studying them we learn not only of past events but of present time. As we approach the end of the second millennium, debate continues regarding the practical implications of Christianity as a religious system and what it is to be Christian in a pluralistic and needful world. Individuals struggle to discern the meaning of their lives and how to be active in perpetuating goodness and justice from their particular contexts. In the midst of a densely populated world, the search continues for authentic relationships and communities that broaden rather than narrow one's world. The women of Hull House show the complexities related to activity in the world. Their lives indicate that the triad of spirituality, vocation, and friendship are interrelated.

On the first night that Addams, Starr, and Keyser slept at Hull House, they inadvertently left the back door not only unlocked but wide open. The door to Hull House remains open for further study and exploration.

Notes

Introduction

1. Robert N. Bellah *et al.*, *Habits of the Heart* (Berkeley: University of California Press, 1985); *The Good Society* (New York: Alfred A. Knopf, 1991).

2. Refer to Amanda Porterfield, *Feminine Spirituality in America: From Sarah Edwards to Martha Graham* (Philadelphia: Temple University Press, 1980), 155f; Denise Lardner Carmody and John Tully Carmody, *The Republic of Many Mansions: Foundations of American Religious Thought* (New York: Paragon House, 1990), 153f.

3. Carol Ochs, *Women and Spirituality* (Totowa, N.J.: Rowman and Allanheld, 1983), 8f.

4. Refer to Rosemary Skinner Keller, ed., *Spirituality and Social Responsibility: Vocational Vision of Women in The United Methodist Tradition* (Nashville: Abingdon Press, 1993) for essays on the connections between vocation and social responsibility.

5. Mary E. Hunt, *Fierce Tenderness: A Feminist Theology of Friendship* (New York: Crossroad, 1991), 29.

6. For a concise overview of the Beguines, refer to Fiona Bowie, ed. and introduction, *Beguine Spirituality: Mystical Writings of Mechthild*

of Magdeburg, Beatrice of Nazareth, and Hadewijch of Brabant (New York: Crossroad, 1990), 3–45. Refer also to Janice G. Raymond, *A Passion for Friends: Toward a Philosophy of Female Affection* (Boston: Beacon Press, 1986), Chapter Two for an excellent discussion on the Beguines within the history of the Christian Church.

7. Refer to Cynthia Grant Tucker, *Prophetic Sisterhood: Liberal Women Ministers of the Frontier, 1880–1930* (Boston: Beacon Press, 1990).

Chapter 1

1. Daniel Levine, *Jane Addams and The Liberal Tradition* (Madison: State Historical Society of Wisconsin, 1971), 57. By 1906, Hull House was the second-largest institution in Chicago (measured by programs and buildings), exceeded only by the University of Chicago.

2. Guy Szuberla, "Three Chicago Settlements: Their Architectural Form and Social Meaning," *Journal of the Illinois State Historical Society* Vol. LXX, No. 2 (May 1977): 114–129, argued that its very design communicated middle-class values of democracy and order in a fluctuating, often chaotic, urban environment.

3. On the activities or "objective value" of Hull House refer to these works by Jane Addams: "The Objective Value of a Social Settlement," in *Philanthropy and Social Progress*, ed. Henry C. Adams (New York: Thomas Y. Crowell and Company, 1893), 27–56; "Hull-House, 1889–1909" (Chicago: Privately printed, 1909?); *Twenty Years at Hull-House* (New York: Phillips Publishing Company, 1910). By Jane Addams and Ellen Gates Starr, refer to "Hull-House: A Social Settlement" (printed in pamphlet form on February 1, 1894, revised January 1, 1895). Refer also to Allen F. Davis and Mary Lynn McCree, eds., *Eighty Years at Hull-House* (Chicago: Quadrangle Books, 1969); and Mary Ann Johnson, ed., *The Many Faces of Hull-House: The Photographs of Wallace Kirkland* (Urbana: University of Illinois Press, 1989). The Hull House Scrapbooks, containing much information about the activities of Hull House, are at the Special Collections Library, University of Illinois-Chicago.

4. For example, refer to Hilda Satt Polacheck, *I Came A Stranger: The Story of a Hull-House Girl* (Urbana: University of Chicago Press, 1989).

5. Jill Conway, "Jane Addams: An American Heroine", *Daedalus* Vol. 93, Pt. 1 (Spring): 766.

6. *If Christ Came to Chicago: A Plea for the Union of All Who Love in the Service of All Who Suffer* (Chicago: Chicago Historical Bookworks, 1978 [1894]), 407–429. It ought not be surprising that Stead ranks

Hull House very highly in his evaluation of the life and times of late-nineteenth-century Chicago.

7. The *Hull-House Bulletin* was published from 1896 to 1906. It was replaced with the more formal *Hull-House Yearbook*.

8. "Mrs. Joseph T. Bowen, Hull House, 1939–1940", Scrapbook, UIC-Special Collections.

9. "Hull-House: The Realization of an Idea, 1889–1945", nd (1945?), Board of Trustees Papers, UIC-Special Collections.

10. Robert A. Woods and Albert J. Kennedy, eds., *Handbook of Settlements* (New York: The Russell Sage Foundation, 1911), xiv.

11. James Weber Linn, *Jane Addams: A Biography* (New York: D. Appleton-Century Company, Inc., 1935); Margaret Tims, *Jane Addams of Hull-House: 1860–1935* (London: George Allen and Unwin Ltd, 1961); Conway, "Jane Addams: An American Heroine"; Christopher Lasch, editor, *The Social Thought of Jane Addams* (Indianapolis: Bobbs-Merrill Company, Inc, 1965); John C. Farrell, *Beloved Lady: A History of Jane Addams' Ideas on Reform and Peace* (Baltimore: Johns Hopkins Press, 1967); Cornelia Meigs, *Jane Addams: Pioneer for Social Justice* (Boston: Little, Brown and Company, 1970); Levine, *Jane Addams and The Liberal Tradition*; Allen F. Davis, *American Heroine: The Life and Legend of Jane Addams* (New York: Oxford University Press, 1973); Anne Firor Scott, "Jane Addams," in *Making The Invisible Woman Visible* (Urbana: University of Illinois Press, 1984): 107–141. Martin Marty, *Modern American Religion: The Irony of It All, 1893–1919* (Chicago: University of Chicago Press, 1986), 82, says that Addams took on an image of "secular sainthood." Jean Bethke Elstain is currently writing a new biography on Addams.

12. Jill Conway, "Women Reformers and American Culture, 1870–1930," *Journal of Social History* Vol. 5, No. 2 (Winter 1971–1972): 166–177.

13. Gerda Lerner, "Placing Women in History: Definitions and Challenges," *Feminist Studies* Vol. 3, No. 1/2 (Fall 1975): 5f. A reprint is also found in Gerda Lerner, *The Majority Finds Its Past: Placing Women in History* (New York: Oxford University Press, 1979).

14. Linn, *Jane Addams*, 130.

15. Addams, *My Friend, Julia Lathrop* (New York: Macmillan, 1935).

16. Grant, *Alice Hamilton: Pioneer Doctor in Industrial Medicine* (New York: Abelard-Schuman, 1967).

17. Sicherman, *Alice Hamilton: A Life in Letters* (Cambridge: Harvard University Press, 1984).

18. Edward T. James, ed., 3 vols. (Cambridge: The Belknap Press of Harvard University Press, 1971). Many of the Hull House women

have entries in the forthcoming, *Historical Encyclopedia of Chicago Women*, eds. Adele Hast and Rima Lunin Schutz.

19. Goldmark, *Impatient Crusader: Florence Kelley's Life Story* (Urbana: University of Illinois Press, 1953); Blumberg, *Florence Kelley: The Making of a Social Pioneer* (New York: Augustus M. Kelley, 1966).

20. *The Autobiography of Florence Kelley: Notes of Sixty Years* (Chicago: Charles H. Kerr Publishing Company, 1986); "Coming to Terms with Florence Kelley: The Tale of a Reluctant Biographer," in *The Challenge of Feminist Biography: Writing the Lives of Modern American Women*, ed. Sara Alpern *et al.* (Urbana: University of Illinois Press, 1992), 17-33; *Florence Kelley and the Nation's Work: The Rise of Women's Political Culture, 1830-1900* (New Haven: Yale University Press, 1995).

21. Sherrick, "Private Visions, Public Lives: The Hull-House Women in the Progressive Era" (Ph.D. diss., Northwestern University, 1980).

22. Sklar, "Hull House in the 1890s: A Community of Women Reformers," in *Signs: Journal of Women in Culture and Society* Vol. 10, No. 4 (Summer 1985): 658-677.

23. Robyn Muncy, *A Female Dominion in American Reform, 1890-1935* (New York: Oxford University Press, 1991).

24. Fish, "The Hull House Circle: Women's Friendships and Achievements," in *Gender, Ideology, and Action*, ed. Janet Sharistanian (New York: Greenwood Press, 1986), 185-227.

25. Fish, "Hull House Circle," 189.

26. Fish, "Hull House Circle," 202.

27. John P. Rousmaniere, "Cultural Hybrid in the Slums: The College Woman and the Settlement House, 1889-1914," *American Quarterly* Vol. 22 (1970): 46.

28. The emerging availability of higher education for women had a tremendous impact on the lives of middle- and upper-middle-class women in the last years of the nineteenth century. Refer to Helen Lefkowitz Horowitz, *Alma Mater: Design and Experience in the Women's Colleges From Their Nineteenth-Century Beginnings to the 1930s* (New York: Alfred A. Knopf, 1984); and Barbara Miller Soloman, *In The Company of Educated Women: A History of Women and Higher Education in America* (New Haven: Yale University Press, 1985).

29. Davis, *Spearhead for Reform: The Social Settlements and the Progressive Movement, 1890-1914* (New York: Oxford University Press, 1967), 38.

30. Levine, *Jane Addams and The Liberal Tradition*, 31.

31. *The New Radicalism in America, 1889-1963* (New York: Alfred A. Knopf, 1965).

32. Refer to Addams, "Filial Relations," in *Democracy and Social Ethics* (Cambridge: Belknap Press of Harvard University, 1964), 71–101; and Joyce Antler, "'After College, What?': New Graduates and The Family Claim," *American Quarterly* Vol. 32: 409–434, who addressed Addams' distinction of family versus social claim. Antler argued that the family claim on educated, middle-class women—as shown by their close relations with their mothers—had a positive effect on women, as well as a negative effect; the family claim provided emotional support for the new roles they were attempting to assume within society. In other words, the family claim was not entirely negative, but was sometimes positive in supporting the social claim.

33. Rousmanier, "Cultural Hybrid"; Estelle Freedman, "Separatism as Strategy: Female Institution Building and American Feminism, 1870–1930," in *Feminist Studies* Vol. 5, No. 3 (Fall 1979): 512–529.

34. Trolander, *Professionalism and Social Change: From the Settlement House Movement to Neighborhood Centers, 1886 to Present* (New York: Columbia University Press, 1987), 12f.

35. Degler, *At Odds: Women and The Family in America From the Revolution to the Present* (New York: Oxford University Press, 1980), 320f.

36. T.V. Smith and Leonard D. White, *Chicago: An Experiment in Social Science Research* (Chicago: University of Chicago Press, 1929); Mary Jo Deegan, *Jane Addams and The Men of the Chicago School, 1892–1918* (New Brunswick, N.J.: Transaction, Inc., 1988).

37. Deegan, *Jane Addams and the Men*, 66f.

38. Chambers, *Seedtime of Reform: American Social Service and Social Action, 1918–1933* (Minneapolis: University of Minnesota Press, 1963).

39. For an example, refer to Vivia H. Divers, *The 'Black Hole' or The Missionary Experience of a Girl in the Slums of Chicago, 1891–1892* (Chicago: Privately published, 1893). This is not to suggest that evangelical Christianity was not also interested in the well-being of humanity. Refer to Timothy L. Smith, *Revivalism and Social Reform in Mid-Nineteenth-Century America* (New York: Abingdon Press, 1957); Norris Magnuson, *Salvation in the Slums: Evangelical Social Work, 1865–1920* (Metuchen N.J.: Scarecrow Press and The American Theological Library Association, 1977).

40. Carson, *Settlement Folk: Social Thought and the American Settlement Movement, 1885–1930* (Chicago: University of Chicago Press, 1990), 198.

41. Refer to Marlene Stein Wortman, "Domesticating the Nineteenth-Century American City," *PROSPECTS: An Annual of American Cultural Studies*, ed. Jack Salzman, Vol. 13: 531–572 (New York: Burt

Franklin and Company Inc.); Muncy, *Creating a Female Dominion*, 30; and Josephine Donovan, *Feminist Theory: The Intellectual Traditions of American Feminism* (New York: Continuum Publishing Company, 1985), 54f. For more general works on separate spheres ideology, refer to Barbara Welter, "The Cult of True Womanhood, 1820-1860," *American Quarterly* Vol. 18 (Summer 1966): 151-174; Nancy Cott, *The Bonds of Womanhood: "Women's Sphere" in New England, 1780-1835* (New Haven: Yale University Press, 1977); Joan B. Landes, "Women and The Public Sphere: A Modern Perspective," *Social Analysis* No. 15 (August 1984): 20-31; Linda K. Kerber, "Separate Spheres, Female Worlds, Woman's Place: The Rhetoric of Women's History," *Journal of American History* Vol. 75, No. 1 (June 1988): 9-39.

42. Addams, "Subjective Necessity," 18f.

43. Addams, "Subjective Necessity," 20.

44. Elshtain,"A Return to Hull House: Reflections on Jane Addams," *Cross Currents* Vol. XXXVIII, No. 3 (Fall 1988): 260.

45. Elshtain, "A Return to Hull House," 264, 267.

46. Kalberg, "The Commitment to Career Reform: The Settlement Movement Leaders," *Social Service Review* Vol. 49, No. 4 (December 1975): 614.

47. Muncy, *Creating a Female Dominion*, 30.

48. Trolander, *Professionalism and Social Change*, 49f.

49. Amos Griswold Warner *et al.*, *American Charities and Social Work*, 4th ed. (New York: Thomas Y. Crowell Company, 1930); Lionel Charles Lane, *Jane Addams as Social Worker, The Early Years at Hull House* (D.S.W. diss., University of Pennsylvania, 1963); Chambers, *Seedtime of Reform*; Kathleen Woodroofe, *From Charity to Social Work: In England and the United States* (London: Routledge and Kegan Paul, 1968).

50. Chambers, *Seedtime of Reform*, 148.

51. Philpott, *The Slum and The Ghetto: Immigrants, Blacks, and Reformers in Chicago, 1880-1930* (Belmont Cal.: Wadsworth Publishing Company, 1991), 79f.

52. Philpott, *The Slum and The Ghetto*, 92f.

53. Lissak, *Pluralism and Progressives: Hull House and the New Immigrants, 1890-1919* (Chicago: University of Chicago Press, 1989).

54. For example, refer to Richard N. Juliani, "The Settlement House and the Italian Family," in *Italian Immigrant Women of North America*, eds. Betty Boyd Caroli, Robert F. Harvey, and Lydio F. Tomasi (Ontario: Multicultural Historical Society of Ontario, 1978), 103-123.

55. Mink, "The Lady and the Tramp: Gender, Race, and the Origins of the American Welfare State," *Women, The State, and Welfare*, ed. Linda Gordon (Madison: University of Wisconsin Press, 1990),

92-122. Refer also to Bettina Aptheker, *Woman's Legacy: Essays on Race, Sex and Class in American History* (Amherst: University of Massachusetts Press, 1982).

56. Philpott, *The Slum and The Ghetto*, xvii.

Chapter 2

1. Marty, *Modern American Religion: The Irony of It All, 1893-1919* (Chicago: University of Chicago Press, 1986), 76.

2. For a more detailed discussion on the origins of the social settlement movement refer to Allen F. Davis, *Spearheads for Reform: The Social Settlements and the Progressive Movement, 1890-1914* (New York: Oxford University Press, 1967), 3f.; Robert A. Woods and Albert J. Kennedy, *The Settlement Horizon: A National Estimate* (New York: Russell Sage Foundation, 1922), 1-72; and C. R. Henderson, *Social Settlements*, Part One (New York: Lentilhon and Company, 1899). For specific sources on Toynbee Hall refer to Werner Picht, *Toynbee Hall and the English Settlements* (London: G. Bell and Sons Ltd., 1914); J. A. R. Pimlott, *Toynbee Hall: Fifty Years of Social Progress, 1884-1934* (London: J.M. Dent, 1935); Asa Briggs and Anna McCartney, *Toynbee Hall: The First Hundred Years* (London: Routledge, Chapman and Hall, 1984); Standish Meacham, *Toynbee Hall and Social Reform* (New Haven: Yale University Press, 1987). For the life of Samuel Barnett refer to Henrietta O. Barnett, *Canon Barnett: His Life, Work, and Friends*, 2 vols. (Boston: Houghton Mifflin, 1919).

3. Jacobs, *Three Types of Practical Ethical Movements of the Past Half Century* (New York: MacMillan Company, 1922), 64.

4. Stated by Daniel Levine, *Jane Addams and The Liberal Tradition* (Madison: State Historical Society of Wisconsin, 1971), 38.

5. Davis, *Spearheads for Reform*, 3.

6. Jacobs, *Three Types of Practical Ethical Movements*, 54-105.

7. Jacobs, *Three Types of Practical Ethical Movements*, 60, 83.

8. Ronald C. White Jr. and C. Howard Hopkins, *The Social Gospel: Religion and Reform in Changing America* (Philadelphia: Temple University Press, 1976), 176.

9. In 1858, the United States had a total income of $16.6 billion. By 1900, its income was $126.7 billion. Refer to Michael W. Hughey, *Civil Religion and Moral Order: Theoretical and Historical Dimensions* (Westport: Greenwood Press, 1983), 101f., for a discussion on this era as a time of the "decline of the old middle classes." The population of the United States increased from 31,500,000 to more than 117,000,000 between 1860 and 1926. U.S. Census Reports.

10. Marty, *Modern American Religion*, 76.

11. Mark A. Noll, *A History of Christianity in the United States and Canada* (Grand Rapids: Wm. B. Eerdmans Publishing Co., 1992), 360f.

12. Refer to Robert T. Handy, *Undermined Establishment: Church-State Relations in America, 1880-1920* (Princeton: Princeton University Press, 1991), who argued that the Protestant religious and cultural hegemony lessened between 1880 and 1920.

13. Ely, *Social Aspects of Christianity and Other Essays*, New and enlarged edition (New York: Thomas Y. Crowell and Company, 1889). For recent analyses of the limitations of the social gospel movement refer to Ralph E. Luker, *The Social Gospel in Black and White: American Racial Reform, 1885-1912* (Chapel Hill: University of North Carolina Press, 1991); and Susan Curtis, *A Consuming Faith: The Social Gospel and Modern American Culture* (Baltimore: Johns Hopkins University Press, 1991).

14. Ely, quoted in *The New Encyclopedia of Social Reform*, ed. W. D. P. Bliss (New York: Funk & Wagnalls Company, 1908), s.v. "Church and Social Reform," by W. D. P. Bliss, 205-221.

15. Robert A. Woods and Albert J. Kennedy, eds., *Handbook of Settlements* (New York: Russell Sage Foundation, 1911).

16. For example, refer to S. Chalvet, *Social Settlements in France* (Paris: Centre D'Informations Documentaires, 1936).

17. Lathrop, *National Conference of Charities and Correction Proceedings*, 1896, 106-110. (Reprinted also in Lorene Pacey, *Readings in the Development of Settlement Work* [New York: Association Press, 1950], 41-45.)

18. Lathrop, "What the Settlement Work Stands For," 108.

19. Addams, "A Function of the Social Settlement" in *ANNALS of the American Academy of Political and Social Science* (AAPSS) Vol 13 (May 1899), 325.

20. Refer to Addams' essay, "The Subjective Necessity for Social Settlements," *Philanthropy and Social Progress: Seven Essays*, ed. Henry C. Adams (New York: Thomas Y. Crowell and Company, 1893), 1-26.

21. Cole, *Motives and Results of the Social Settlement Movement*. Publications of the Department of Social Ethics in Harvard University, No. 2 (Cambridge: Harvard University, 1908), 3.

22. Cole, *Motives and Results*, 4.

23. Ozora Stearns Davis, "Mansfield House University Settlement" in *Hartford Seminary Record* Vol. IV, No. 2 (Dec. 1893), 64f. Refer also to Charles Stelzle, *Christianity's Storm Centre: A Study of the Modern City* (New York: Fleming H. Revell Company, 1907), 140f., who

identified social settlements he considered to be aggressively evangelical in their work.

24. Addams, "Social Settlements in Illinois," *An Illinois Reader*, ed. Clyde C. Walton (DeKalb: Northern Illinois University Press, 1970), 323-335. (Originally published in *Transactions of the Illinois State Historical Society*, 1906, 162-171.)

25. Simkhovitch, "Settlements' Relation to Religion," *AAAPSS* Vol. XXX, No. 3 (Nov 1907), 490.

26. Addams, "The Social Situation: Religious Education and Contemporary Social Conditions," *Religious Education* Vol. VI (June 1911), 145-152.

27. Hodges, "Religion in the Settlement," *National Conference of Charities and Correction Proceedings* (1896), 151.

28. Letter from Richard Ely, June 3, 1895, in Hull House Scrapbook III—Clippings and Publications, 1895-1897, UIC-Special Collections.

29. Henderson, *Social Duties from the Christian Point of View* (Chicago: University of Chicago Press, 1909), 182f.

30. Henderson, *Social Duties*, 192f.

31. Henderson, *Social Duties*, 194.

32. "The Catholic Church in Chicago and Problems of an Urban Society: 1893-1915" (Ph.D. diss., University of Chicago, 1948), 36f.

33. Quoted in Walsh, "Catholic Church in Chicago," 37. The South End House in Boston encountered similar fears and suspicions from the Roman Catholic Church. Refer to Edward S. Shapiro, "Robert A. Woods and the Settlement House Impulse," *Social Service Review* Vol. 52, No. 2 (June 1978): 223.

34. Walsh, "Catholic Church in Chicago," 130f.

35. Hegner, "Scientific Value of the Social Settlements," *American Journal of Sociology* Vol. 111, No. 2 (Sept 1897): 181.

36. On Jewish women and social reform, refer to Linda Gordon Kuzmack, *Woman's Cause: The Jewish Woman's Movement in England and The United States, 1881-1933* (Columbus: Ohio State University Press, 1990). Chapter 4 (pp. 79-106) focuses on settlement reformers.

37. Addams, "The Social Situation," 146.

38. Addams, "The Reaction of Modern Life Upon Religious Education," *Religious Education* Vol. IV (April 1909): 25f.

39. Mathews, "The Significance of the Church to the Social Movement," *American Journal of Sociology* Vol. IV, No. 5 (March 1899): 603-620; and "The Christian Church and Social Unity," *American Journal of Sociology* Vol. V, No. 4 (Jan. 1900): 456-469.

40. Barnett, "The Ways of 'Settlements' and of 'Missions,'" *Nineteenth Century* 42 (Dec. 1897): 975.

41. Barnett, "Ways of 'Settlements' and of 'Missions'," 977f.

42. Addams, "Social Settlements in Illinois," 332.

43. Addams, "Social Settlements in Illinois," 332.

44. Addams, "Social Settlements in Illinois," 331.

45. Taylor, "The Social Settlement Religion and the Church," in *Christianity and Social Adventuring*, ed. Jerome Davis (New York: Century Co., 1927), 167. For a biography on Taylor, refer to Louise C. Wade, *Graham Taylor: Pioneer for Social Justice, 1851–1938* (Chicago: University of Chicago Press, 1964).

46. Taylor, "Social Settlement Religion and the Church," 167.

47. Taylor, "Social Settlement Religion and the Church," 174f.

48. Samuel Nicholas Reep, "The Organization of the Ecclesiastical Institutions of a Metropolitan Community" (Diss., Graduate Divinity School of the University of Chicago, 1910), 27f.

49. Henderson, *The Social Spirit in America* (Freeport, N.Y.: Books for Libraries Press, 1972 [1897]), 306f. The influence of the institutional church movement can still be seen when examining church structures—many churches added gymnasiums and stages to their building structures in the late nineteenth and early twentieth centuries as ways to offer more social activities for their membership.

50. Refer to Christine Wilson, *Thirty Neighborhood Houses: A Survey of Thirty Presbyterian Neighborhood Houses* (New York: Board of National Missions of the Presbyterians Church in the U.S.A., Department of City, Immigrant and Industrial Work, 1925).

51. Refer to Rev. George Whitefield Mead, *Modern Methods in Church Work; The Gospel Renaissance* (New York: Dodd, Mead and Company, 1897); and Edwin L. Earp, *Social Aspects of Religious Institutions* (New York: Eaton and Mains, 1908).

52. Huggins, *Protestants Against Poverty: Boston Charities, 1870–1900* (Westport: Greenwood Publishing Corporation, 1971), 44f.

53. Berreth, "Settlement Ideas for the Church," (B.Div. diss., Chicago Theological Seminary, 1945), iv.

54. "Social Settlements," *Chicago Times-Herald*, May 14, 1899. Hull House Association: Scrapbook Clippings, May 1899-Dec 1899, UIC-Special Collections.

55. Kinceloe, "City Missions, Institutional Churches and Neighborhood Houses," in *The Place of the Church in a Century of Progress, 1833–1933* (Chicago: Chicago Church Federation, nd [1933?], 23. Refer also to David John Hogan, *Class and Reform: School and Society in Chicago, 1880–1930* (Philadelphia: University of Pennsylvania Press, 1985).

56. Kinceloe, "City Missions, Institutional Churches", 23.

57. Refer to Louise C. Wade, "The Social Gospel Impulse and Chicago Settlement-House Founders," *Chicago Theological Seminary Register* Vol. LV, No. 8 (April 1965): 1-12, who examined the connectedness of the social gospel and social settlement movements.

58. Kinceloe, "City Missions, Institutional Churches," 23.

59. Rauschenbusch, "The Stake of the Church in the Social Movement," *American Journal of Sociology* Vol. III, No. 1 (July 1897): 26.

60. Henderson, *Social Settlements*, 83.

61. Starr, "Settlements and the Church's Duty," *The Church Social Union* [Boston: Office of the Secretary, The Diocesan House], No. 28 (Aug. 15, 1896): 4.

62. Starr, "Social Settlements and the Church's Duty," 11f.

63. Hodges, "Religion in the Settlements," 153.

64. Barry, "The Relationship of the Social Gospel to the 'settlement idea'" (B.Div. diss., Chicago Theological Seminary, 1941), 112.

Chapter 3

1. For an early history of Chicago, refer to Jacqueline Peterson, "The Founding Fathers: The Absorption of French-Indian Chicago, 1816-1837," in *Ethnic Chicago*, revised and expanded edition, ed. Melvin G. Holli and Peter d'A. Jones (Grand Rapids: William B. Eerdmans Publishing Company, 1984), 300-337.

2. Refer to William Cronon, *Nature's Metropolis: Chicago and the Great West* (New York: W. W. Norton and Company, 1991) for an analysis of the growing importance of Chicago in the developing of the west. For an overview of Chicago history, refer to Bessie Louise Pierce, *A History of Chicago*, 3 vols. (Chicago: University of Chicago Press, 1937-1959). For an excellent summary of Chicago at the turn of the nineteenth century, refer to Louise C. Wade, *Graham Taylor: Pioneer for Social Justice, 1851-1938* (Chicago: University of Chicago Press, 1964), Chapter 3, "The Challenge of Chicago," 51-82.

3. Appendix, "Foreign-born, White Foreign Stock, and Minority Population of the City of Chicago, 1890," in Holli and Jones, eds., *Ethnic Chicago*, 548f. The official population of Chicago was 503,185 in 1880, 1,099,850 in 1890.

4. Refer to James Gilbert, *Perfect Cities: Chicago's Utopias of 1893* (Chicago: University of Chicago Press, 1991), and Stanley Appelbaum, text, *Chicago World's Fair of 1893: A Photographic Record* (New York: Dover Publications, Inc., 1980).

5. Richard Hughes Seager, ed., *The Dawn of Religious Pluralism:*

Voices from the World's Parliament of Religions (LaSalle, Ill.: Open Court, 1993), and Jeanne Madeline Weimann, *The Fair Women: The Story of the Woman's Building, World's Columbian Exposition, Chicago 1893* (Chicago: Academy Press, 1981).

6. The term "white city" was used to describe the architecture of the 1893 fair. It came to symbolize not only the color of the buildings, but also the color of the participants in the fair and the attempt of dominant middle-class society to conceal the immense social problems and disparity between people in Chicago.

7. For the philanthropic views of such influential men of Chicago, as well as their biographical beginnings, refer to Kathleen D. McCarthy, *Noblesse Oblige: Charity and Cultural Philanthropy in Chicago, 1849-1929* (Chicago: University of Chicago, 1982).

8. Holli and Jones, eds., *Ethnic Chicago*, 548.

9. The African-American population in Chicago was minimal through the first decade of the twentieth century when blacks began to migrate to Chicago and were hired as strikebreakers. Migration increased prior to and during World War I, when many blacks from the southern states began to move to northern cities. Refer to James Grossman, *Land of Hope: Chicago, Black Southerners and the Great Migration* (Chicago: University of Chicago Press, 1989). Refer also to Allan H. Spear, *Black Chicago: The Making of a Negro Ghetto, 1890-1920* (Chicago: University of Chicago, 1969).

10. For an appraisal of the work of Hull House among the Greek community in Chicago, refer to Andrew T. Kopan, "Greek Survival in Chicago: The Role of Ethnic Education, 1890-1980," *Ethnic Chicago*, revised and expanded edition, eds. Melvin G. Holli and Peter d'A. Jones (Grand Rapids: William B. Eerdmans Publishing Company, 1984), 138-145.

11. Albert Halper, ed., *This is Chicago: An Anthology* (New York: Henry Holt and Company, 1952), viii.

12. Quoted in Helen Lefkowitz Horowitz, *Culture and the City: Cultural Philanthropy in Chicago from the 1880s to 1917* (Lexington: University Press of Kentucky, 1976), ix, n. 1.

13. Refer to George S. Phillips, *Chicago and Her Churches* (Chicago: E. B. Myers and Chandler, 1868), Chapter 1, "The Jesuit Missionaries," 9-28, and Chapter 4, "Early Religious History," 115-142.

14. Victor Edward Marriott, *The Chicago Primer: Church and City Approaching a New Era* (Chicago: Chicago Congregational Union, 1932), 11f.; Louise Christopher, "Henry Whitehead, Circuit Rider," *Chicago History* Vol. 5, No. 1 (Spring 1976): 2-11; Perry J. Stackhouse,

Chicago and The Baptists: A Century of Progress (Chicago: University of Chicago, 1933). Refer also to George A. Lane, *Chicago Churches and Synagogues: An Architectural Pilgrimage* (Chicago: Loyola University Press, 1981). The oldest church structure still standing in Chicago is St. Patrick's, built from 1852–1856.

15. Thomas James Riley, *The Higher Life of Chicago* (Chicago: University of Chicago Press, 1905), 115, Table of denominational strength in Chicago in 1902.

16. Kevin J. Christiano, *Religious Diversity and Social Change: American Cities, 1890–1906* (Cambridge: Cambridge University Press, 1987), 161, Appendix B. In 1890, church membership in Chicago was 388,145 out of a total population of 1,099,850; in 1906, church membership was 833,441 out of a total population of 2,049,185.

17. On anti-Roman Catholicism during the mid-part of the nineteenth century, refer to Richard Wilson Renner, "In a Perfect Ferment: Chicago, the Know-Nothings, and the Riot for Lager Beer," *Chicago History* Vol. 5, No. 3 (Fall 1976): 161–170. On the debate within the Roman Catholic community as to their participation in the World's Parliament of Religions, refer to James F. Cleary, "Catholic Participation in the World's Parliament of Religions, Chicago, 1893," *The Catholic Historical Review* Vol. 55, No. 4 (January 1970): 585–609.

18. Hannah G. Soloman, *Fabric of My Life* (New York: Bloch Publishing Company, 1946), 29f. Soloman's family was influential in starting Reformed Judaism in the city. As well, she and her sister, Henriette, were the first Jewish women asked to join the Chicago Woman's Club in 1877. She was also active in forming the Maxwell Street Settlement.

19. Soloman, *Fabric of My Life*, 262.

20. Darrel M. Robertson, *The Chicago Revival, 1876: Society and Revivalism in a Nineteenth-Century City*, Studies in Evangelicalism, No. 9 (Metuchen, N.J.: Scarecrow Press, Inc., 1989). Robertson argues that Moody's 1876 revival appealed very powerfully to middle-class, Anglo-American and Protestant values, and served to incite religious and social tensions in the city (156f.). Refer also to Rev. H. B. Hartzler, *Moody in Chicago or the World's Fair Gospel Campaign, Account of Six Months' Evangelical Work in the City of Chicago and Vicinity During the Time of the World's Columbian Exposition, Conducted by Dwight L. Moody and His Associates* (New York: Fleming H. Revell Company, 1894).

21. Riley, *Higher Life in Chicago*, 107.

22. Dolan, *The American Catholic Experience: A History from Colonial Times to the Present* (Notre Dame: University of Notre Dame Press, 1992), 326.

23. Riley, *Higher Life in Chicago*, 114.

24. Warren E. Thompson, *Building a Christian Chicago: A History of the Chicago Congregational Union, 1882-1932* (np., 1932), 2.

25. Sheldon, *In His Steps: "What would Jesus do?"* (Chicago: Advance Publishing Co., 1897).

26. Dolan, *American Catholic Experience*, 324.

27. Horowitz, *Culture and The City*, Appendix B, 235f.

28. McCarthy, *Noblesse Oblige*, 75f., n.1. Quote credited to Isaac N. Arnold addressing the Chicago Historical Society, 1877.

29. Muriel Beadle and the Centennial History Committee, *The Fortnightly of Chicago, The City and Its Women: 1873-1973* (Chicago: Henry Regnery Company, 1973); Henriette Greenbaum Frank and Amalie Hofer Jerome, compilers, *Annals of the Chicago Woman's Club for the First Forty Years of its Organization, 1876-1916* (Chicago: Chicago Woman's Club, 1916).

30. *Higher Life of Chicago*, 54f. and Appendix, Table I; Bessie Louise Pierce, compiler and ed., *As Others See Chicago: Impressions of Visitors, 1673-1933* (Chicago: University of Chicago Press, 1933), 313f. Refer also to Karen J. Blair, *Clubwoman as Feminist: True Womanhood Redefined, 1868-1914* (New York: Holmes and Meier, 1980).

31. McCarthy, *Noblesse Oblige*, 39f.

32. Rosemary Skinner Keller, "The Deaconess: 'New Woman' of Late Nineteenth Century Methodism," *Explor: A Journal of Theology* Vol. 5, No. 1 (Spring 1979): 33-41. Also refer to Edward T. James, ed., *Notable American Women, 1607-1950: A Biographical Dictionary* (Cambridge: Belknap Press of Harvard University Press, 1971), Vol. 2, s.v. "Meyer, Lucy Jane Rider," by Robert Moats Miller.

33. Quoted in McCarthy, *Noblesse Oblige*, 93f.

34. For a discussion of Jane Addams' involvement in Chicago public school reform, refer to Allen F. Davies, *American Heroine: The Life and Legend of Jane Addams* (New York: Oxford University Press, 1973), 130f.

35. Refer to David John Hogan, *Class and Reform: School and Society in Chicago, 1880-1930* (Philadelphia: University of Pennsylvania Press, 1985), 52f.

36. McCarthy, *Noblesse Oblige*, 103f.; Robertson, *Chicago Revival*.

37. *The Age of Reform* (New York: Alfred A. Knopf, 1955), 151f. When and why people begin to define as problems issues that previously had been acceptable, is a complex philosophical and sociological question beyond the scope of this project.

38. Refer to Louise deKoven Bowen, *The Woman's City Club of Chicago* (np., 1922), 9.

39. Letter, EGS to Mary [Blaisdell], February 23, 1889. Quoted by Mary Lynn McCree, "The First Year of Hull-House, 1889-1890, In Letters by Jane Addams and Ellen Gates Starr," *Chicago History* (Fall 1970): 104.

40. *Twenty Years at Hull-House* (New York: Signet Classic, 1981 [1910]), 75. The Rev. David Swing had been the pastor of the Fourth Presbyterian Church of Chicago before he was accused of heresy in 1874 by a professor at McCormick Seminary. Although Swing was acquitted of the charges, he resigned from Fourth Presbyterian, withdrew from the Presbytery and became pastor of the Central Church of Chicago, an independent congregation. Refer to *One Hundred Years: The Fourth Presbyterian Church of Chicago, Ill.* (n.d., n.p., 1971), 10. Refer also to David Swing, *Sermons* (Chicago: W. B. Keen, Cooke and Co., 1874).

41. The multifaced work of Hull House residents in the early years of the 1890s is best reflected in their book, *Hull-House Maps and Papers* (Boston: Thomas Y. Crowell and Co., 1895).

42. Harvey Warren Zorbaugh, in his classic work, *The Gold Coast and the Slum: A Sociological Study of Chicago's Near North Side* (Chicago: University of Chicago Press, 1929), criticized the Chicago social settlement movement, saying "[it] never has succeeded in restoring to the really disorganized areas of the city the neighborhood sentiment" (262f). Despite this criticism, Zorbaugh concluded, "the settlement has been the greatest single factor in interpreting the slum to the rest of the city" (263n).

43. For example, refer to "A Galaxy of Stars," Hull House Scrapbook, Vol. 3 (Clippings and Publications, 1895-1897), UIC.

44. *Communities of Resistance and Solidarity: A Feminist Theology of Liberation* (Maryknoll, N.Y.: Orbis Books, 1985), ix.

Chapter 4

1. Flora Kaplan, compiler, *Nobel Prize Winners: Charts, Indexes, Sketches* (1939), UIC-Special Collections; "America's Twelve Great Women Leaders During the Past Hundred Years, as Chosen by the Women of America," *The Ladies' Home Journal and The Christian Science Monitor* (Chicago: Associated Authors Service, 1933). Other women on the list included Susan B. Anthony, Mary Baker Eddy, Helen Keller, Frances E. Willard, and Mary E. Woolley.

2. Edward Wagenknecht, *Chicago* (Norman: University of Oklahoma Press, 1964), Chapter 5, 105-122.

3. *Modern American Religion: The Irony of It All, 1893-1919* (Chicago: University of Chicago Press, 1986), 82.

4. Christopher Lasch, ed., *The Social Thought of Jane Addams* (Indianapolis: Bobbs-Merrill Company, Inc., 1965); John C. Farrell, *Beloved Lady: A History of Jane Addams' Ideas on Reform and Peace* (Baltimore: John Hopkins Press, 1967).

5. Addams, *Twenty Years at Hull-House* (New York: Signet Classic, 1981 [1910]), 27. Rebecca L. Sherrick, in "Private Visions, Public Lives: The Hull-House Women in the Progressive Era" (Ph.D. diss., Northwestern University, 1980), 177 and 190, points out the Horatio Alger quality of Addams' autobiography. All autobiographical works need to be read with an awareness of the genre.

6. Hazel P. Cederborg, "Early History of Rockford College," (M.A. thesis, Wellesly College, 1926), 70 and 79. For a biographical sketch on Sill, refer to Edward T. James, ed., *Notable American Women* Vol. 3 (Cambridge: Belknap Press of Harvard University Press, 1971), s.v. "Sill, Anna Peck," by Jill Ker Conway.

7. *Twenty Years*, 50.

8. *Twenty Years*, 49.

9. *Twenty Years*, 51.

10. "Cassandra", *Rockford Seminary*, 30th Commencement (1881), 36-39. Rockford Seminary was accredited as a degree granting institution in 1882, so Addams received her degree one year after completing her course work.

11. Refer to Christopher Lasch, *The New Radicalism in America, 1889-1963* (New York: W. W. Norton and Company, 1965), 3-37, for an interpretation of Starr's and Addams' letters in the period between 1881 and 1889. Lasch argued that Addams came to reject an intellectual theology based on the rationalism of her day and, finally, could only accept experience over knowledge: "[Addams came to the conviction] that the only god she could worship was a god of love—a god, that is, of doing rather than of knowing" (29).

12. *Twenty Years*, 68.

13. *Twenty Years*, 68f.

14. *Twenty Years*, 61; James, ed., *Notable Women* Vol. 1, s.v. "Addams, Jane," by Anne Firor Scott. For an analysis of common maladies among middle- and upper-middle-class women in the nineteenth century, read Carroll Smith-Rosenberg, *Disorderly Conduct: Visions of Gender in Victorian America* (New York: Oxford University Press, 1985).

15. "Woman's Conscience and Social Amelioration," in *The Social Application of Religion*, ed. Charles Stelzle, The Merrick Lectures for 1907-1908 (Cincinnati: Jennings and Graham, 1908), 39-60.

16. Refer to *Democracy and Social Ethics* (Cambridge: Belknap Press of Harvard University, 1964 [1902]), Chapter 3, "Filial Rela-

tions," 71–101. Addams' health was never excellent. She suffered from bouts of depression, tiredness, kidney and bladder infections. She had a heart attack in 1931, and finally succumbed to cancer in 1935.

17. Conway, "Jane Addams: An American Heroine," *Daedalus* Vol. 93, No. 2 (Spring 1964): 773.

18. Refer to Lasch, *New Radicalism*, 3f., who argued that Addams' religion—and personality—as inherited from her father, was "almost stoic in its insistence on absolute self-dependence."

19. Scott, *Making the Invisible Woman Visible* (Urbana: University of Illinois Press, 1984), 113.

20. *Twenty Years*, 73.

21. *Making the Invisible Woman Visible*, 113.

22. *Twenty Years*, 73f.

23. Addams never denied the two-pronged purpose of social settlement work, as if fulfilling personal needs lessened more altruistic concerns. Refer to her essays, "The Subjective Necessity for Social Settlements," and "The Objective Value of a Social Settlement," in *Philanthropy and Social Progress*, Henry C. Adams, ed. and intro. (New York: Thomas Y. Crowell, 1893),1-26, 27-56. Neil Coughlan argued that Jane Addams borrowed almost verbatim from John Dewey for her "Subjective Necessity" speech; refer to *Young John Dewey* (Chicago: University of Chicago Press, 1975), 89. The fact is that Addams and Dewey were close friends and shared similar ideas.

24. Helen Campbell, "Jane Addams of Hull House, Chicago: Her Personality and Philosophy of Life," *The Congregationalist* (*Christian World*), May 4, 1901.

25. Kathleen D. McCarthy, *Noblesse Oblige: Charity and Cultural Philanthropy in Chicago, 1849-1929* (Chicago: University of Chicago Press, 1982), 116. Kathryn Kish Sklar discussed the dismissal of overt religious principles by the women of Hull House in the 1920s. Refer to "Religious and Moral Authority as Factors Shaping the Balance of Power for Women's Political Culture in the Twentieth Century," (Paper presented at the 100th anniversary of the founding of Hull House, Rockford, Illinois, October 1989).

26. Hull House Association—Scrapbooks, Ewing Street Church Membership Survey, 1894-1895 (dated February 1895). UIC-Special Collections.

27. Letter, Miss Ella Wilson (clerk) to Rev. M. Smith, August 7, 1894. Hammond Library—Chicago Theological Seminary. The church name was changed to Firman Congregational Church in the early 1900s and later opened its own settlement house.

28. *The Firman Congregational Church and Firman House: A Center*

of Friendliness (Chicago: Chicago City Missionary Society, nd), 2f. Ewing Street Church was one of the meeting places used during the Moody revivals in 1893, further proof of its evangelical spirit. See Rev. H. B. Hartzler, *Moody in Chicago or The World's Fair Gospel Campaign* (New York: Fleming H. Revell Company, 1894), 40.

29. Campbell, "Jane Addams of Hull House, Chicago"; Rev. Theodore Crowl, *The Presbyterian Messenger* (1894), Hull House Scrapbook I, 42. UIC-Special Collections.

30. Hull House Association—Scrapbooks, Ewing Street Membership Survey. The 12th Annual Report of the Chicago City Missionary Society states that Rev. C. W. Barnes was paid $14.58 for his preaching services (1894, p. 52). Graham Taylor also preached at this little church, being paid $100.00 for his supply services of 1894.

31. *Firman News* Vol. 1, No. 2 (Oct 1925); Vol. 1, No. 3 (Nov 1925); and Vol. 1, No. 7 (June 1926), recorded Addams' involvement—from speaking at their fellowship nights to bringing greetings on the ordination of their pastor, to donating a "fine iron bed." Unfortunately, the complete church records of Ewing Street Church/Firman House cannot be located though they are to be stored in the Hammond Library of the Chicago Theological Seminary.

32. Letter, Edward L. Burchard to Ellen Gates Starr, January 16, 1938, Box 11, Folder 107. Sophia Smith Collection.

33. Hull-House Residents and Association—Resident Meetings, Nov. 25, 1893. UIC-Special Collections.

34. Madame Blanc, *The Condition of Woman in the United States: A Traveller's Notes* (Boston: Robert Brothers, 1895), 86.

35. *Hull-House Bulletin* Vol. 1, No. 7 (Dec. 7, 1896).

36. Louise deKoven Bowen, for example, when asked of Addams' faith, said that Addams was Quaker. Refer to *Open Windows: Stories of People and Places* (Chicago: Ralph Fletcher Seymour, 1946), 269.

37. Hull House Scrapbook I, 21. UIC Special Collections.

38. Addams, *The Excellent Becomes the Permanent* (New York: Macmillan Company, 1932), 3. Eulogies include those given for Gordon Dewey (John's young son), Mary Wilmarth, and Sarah Rozet Smith. The book is dedicated to Alice Hamilton "whose wisdom and courage have never failed when we have walked together so many times in the very borderland between life and death."

39. Addams, *Excellent Becomes the Permanent*, 23f.

40. Georgia Harkness, "Jane Addams in Retrospect," *Christian Century* Vol. LXXVII, No. 2 (Jan. 13, 1960): 39.

41. Harkness, "Jane Addams in Retrospect," 40.

42. Edward, *Notable American Women*, s.v. "Starr, Ellen Gates," by Allen F. Davis.

43. Starr, *A Bypath Into the Great Roadway* (Chicago: Ralph Fletcher Seymour, 1926).

44. Starr, *A Bypath*, 3f. While Starr's family was Protestant, her aunt, Eliza Starr, a prominent Chicago artist, had converted to Catholicism in 1850 at the age of twenty-six. Starr therefore had one important non-Protestant role model in her life experience. Refer to EGS, Box 6, Folder 47. Sophia Smith Collection.

45. Starr, *A Bypath*, 4. Starr misspelled Dr. Robert Collyer's name. Collyer was pastor of the Church of the Unity from 1859 until 1879, when he became pastor of Theodore Parker's congregation in Boston.

46. Starr, *A Bypath*, 5.

47. "Notes by Miss Josephine Starr on Ellen Gates Starr" (April 1960), 3. Box 3, Folder 27. Sophia Smith Collection.

48. Starr, *A Bypath*, 5.

49. Charles H. Lippy and Peter W. Williams, eds., *Encyclopedia of the American Religious Experience: Studies of Traditions and Movements* (New York: Charles Scribner's Sons, 1988), s.v."The Anglican Tradition and The Episcopal Church," by David L. Holmes, Vol. 1, 401f. Refer also to David L. Holmes, *A Brief History of the Episcopal Church* (Valley Forge, Pa.: Trinity Press International, 1993), 103-112, 126-131. Vida Scudder, settlement worker in New York City and professor at Wellesley College, was also a member of the Order of the Holy Cross. The spiritual journeys of Starr and Scudder are very similar—and they became close friends. Refer to Vida Scudder, *On Journey* (New York: E. P. Dutton, 1937), and L. DeAne Lagerquist, "Women and the American Religious Pilgrimage: Vida Scudder, Dorothy Day, and Pauli Murray," *New Dimensions in American Religious History*, Jay P. Dolan and James P. Wind, eds. (Grand Rapids: William B. Eerdmans Publishing Company, 1993), 208-228.

50. R. William Franklin and Joseph M. Shaw, *The Case for Christian Humanism* (Grand Rapids: William B. Eerdmans Publishing Co., 1991), 165f.

51. "Settlements and the Church's Duty," No. 28 (Aug. 15, 1896) in *The Church Social Union* (Boston: Office of the Secretary, The Diocesan House), 8.

52. "Settlements and the Church's Duty," 13.

53. Starr, "Art and Labor," in *Hull-House Maps and Papers* (Boston: Thomas Y. Crowell and Co., 1895), Chapter 9.

54. Box 19, Folder 270. Sophia Smith Collection.

55. Starr, "Settlements and the Church's Duty," 7.

56. Box 19, Folder 272. Sophia Smith Collection.

57. Hull House Scrapbook III—Clippings and Publications, 1895-1897, 13. UIC-Special Collections.

58. "Ellen Starr Dies," *New York Times*, Feb. 11, 1940.

59. "Why I Am a Socialist" (nd., *Daily Campaign Edition*), Box 19, Folder 273. Sophia Smith Collection. Starr represents a number of influential nineteenth-century women who were avowedly Christian and Socialist, Frances Willard being one prime example. Refer to Mari Jo Buhle, *Women and American Socialism, 1870-1920* (Urbana: University of Illinois Press, 1981), 108f.

60. Edwards, *Notable American Women* Vol. 3, 352; Anthea Callen, *Women Artists of the Arts and Crafts Movement, 1870-1914* (New York: Pantheon Books, 1979), 198f.

61. Mary Anderson (as told to Mary N. Winslow), *Woman At Work* (Minneapolis: University of Minnesota Press, 1951), 54f.

62. *New York Times*, Feb. 11, 1940.

63. Anderson, *Woman At Work*, 53.

64. Starr, *A Bypath*, 7f.

65. Starr, *A Bypath*, 10f.

66. Starr, *A Bypath*, 26f.

67. Starr, Diary, Box 18. Sophia Smith Collection.

68. Letters, Alice Hamilton to Agnes Hamilton, January 28, 1904 and March 1, 1914 in Barbara Sicherman, *Alice Hamilton: A Life in Letters* (Cambridge: Harvard University Press, 1984), 148, 174.

69. Eleanor Grace Clark, "Ellen Gates Starr, OSB (1859-1940), An Account of the Life of the Co-Foundress of Hull House," *Commonweal* Vol. XXXI (March 15, 1940): 444.

70. "Hull-House: The Realization of an Idea, 1889-1945," Board of Trustees Papers. UIC-Special Collections.

71. Hull House Scrapbook III, Clippings and Publications, 1895-1897, np. UIC Special Collections.

72. Box 11, Folder 143. Sophia Smith Collection.

73. "Notes by Miss Josephine Starr on Ellen Gates Starr," (April 1960), Box 3, Folder 27. Sophia Smith Collection.

74. Jane Reoch to Ellen Gates Starr (Aug. 31, 1909), quoted in Clark, "Ellen Gates Starr."

75. Letter, Victor Yarros to Starr, Feb. 16, 1939, Box 11, Folder 146. Sophia Smith Collection.

76. Letter, Alice Hamilton to EGS, nd [re. 80th birthday, March 19, 1939), Box 11, Folder 146. Sophia Smith Collection.

77. "Social Settlement and the Church's Duty," 15f.

78. Kathryn Kish Sklar, ed. and intro., *The Autobiography of Florence Kelley: Notes of Sixty Years* (Chicago: Charles H. Kerr Publishing Company, 1986), 78.

79. *Twenty Years*, 79.

80. Scrapbook III—Appendix I, Clippings and Publications, 1895-1897. UIC-Special Collections.

81. Sklar, *Autobiography of Florence Kelley*, 78.

82. "Hull-House," in *These Wonderful People*, compiled by Noel Ames (Chicago: Consolidated Press, 1947), 283.

83. "Mary Keyser dies," Hull House Scrapbook III—Clippings and Publications, 1895-1897, 67. UIC-Special Collections.

84. *Hull-House Bulletin* Vol. 1, No. 3 (March 1896), 89.

85. Hull House Scrapbook III—Appendix I, Clippings and Publications, 1895-1897, UIC-Special Collections.

86. Hull House Association—Scrapbooks, February 1895. UIC-Special Collections. The pastor further noted that Keyser was the daughter of Mrs. Henrietta Keyser and the sister of Howard Keyser, both of whom were friendly with the church but did not desire to join it. After the death of Addams' sister Mary, Addams financially supported her orphaned four children. Her remaining sister, Alice, however, did not think Addams was doing her full share. Mary Rozet Smith and Addams became much closer friends during this time of Addams' family stress. Refer to Allen F. Davis, *American Heroine*, 83f.

87. Hull House Account Book, Oct. 1, 1891-1893. UIC-Special Collections.

88. Vol. 1, No. 10 (January 1897): 6.

89. *Chicago Commons* Vol. 1, No. 10 (January 1897), 6.

90. *Feminine Spirituality in America: From Sarah Edwards to Martha Graham* (Philadelphia: Temple University Press, 1980), 169.

91. Madame Catherine Breskovsky, a Russian revolutionary, visited Hull House in 1905, and she and Starr became dear friends. Refer to Alice Stone Blackwell, ed., *The Little Grandmother of the Russian Revolution: Reminiscences and Letters of Catherine Breshkovsy* (Boston: Little, Brown, and Company, 1917). Starr was an ardent letter writer throughout her life. She corresponded regularly with Vida Scudder, Mary Hawes Wilmarth, and Charles Wager. Box 11, Folder 119, 137. Sophia Smith Collection.

92. "The Social Situation: Religious Education and Contemporary Social Conditions," *Religious Education: The Journal of the Religious Education Association* Vol. VI, No. 2 (June 1911): 145f.

Chapter 5

1. List of Residents, March 1, 1894 (in Resident's minutes, 1893). Residents listed (in order): Addams, Starr, Lathrop, Kelley, Keyser, Holbrook, Brockway, West, Benedict, Welsh, Crain, Giles [sic], Zeman; and two men, Barnes and Waldo. Miss Waite is listed as a visitor. The first male resident was Edward Burchard, who became associated with Hull House in 1892. Refer also to Hull-House Scrapbook III—Clippings and Publications, 1895-1897, 471. UIC-Special Collections.

2. Hull-House Residents and Associates—Resident Meetings, March 6, 1894. UIC-Special Collections.

3. Zeman was initially approved as a resident at the March 6, 1894, meeting. Hull-House Residents and Associates—Resident's Meetings, UIC-Special Collections.

4. Refer to Rosabeth Moss Kanter, *Commitment and Community: Communes and Utopias in Sociological Perspective* (Cambridge: Harvard University Press, 1972), for an analysis of mechanisms of group life.

5. "Private Visions, Public Lives: The Hull-House Women in the Progressive Era" (Ph.D. diss., Northwestern University, 1980), 144. Sherrick analyzed seven women of Hull House: Jane Addams, Julia Lathrop, Florence Kelley, Alice Hamilton, Edith and Grace Abbott, and Sophonisba Breckinridge. The Abbott sisters and Breckinridge are not discussed in this project since they came to Hull House in the twentieth century. They were very important to Hull House after its initial decade.

6. Hull-House Association Scrapbooks Miscellany, Inventory of Hull-House Furnishings, 1903. UIC-Special Collections. The value of the contents of the rooms ranged from $44 (Rose Gyles), to $150 (Julia Lathrop). In contrast, the contents of Addams' room were estimated at $850, $500 of which was for an oil painting by Alice Kellogg Tyler. The initials M.R.S. (in parentheses) are noted in the inventory list after the oil painting.

7. Bowen, *Open Windows: Stories of People and Places* (Chicago: Ralph Flectcher Seymour, 1946), 252.

8. Hull-House Scrapbook II (Publications, 1889-1894), np. UIC-Special Collections.

9. *The Grand Domestic Revolution: A History of Feminist Designs for American Homes, Neighborhoods, and Cities* (Cambridge: The MIT Press, 1981), 174.

10. Addams, *Twenty Years at Hull-House* (New York: Signet Classic, 1981 [1910]), 115.

11. "Notes by Miss Josephine Starr on Ellen Gates Starr," Box 3, Folder 27, 5. Sophia Smith Collection.

12. Rose Gyles, for example, became a Hull House resident in the early 1890s and lived there for forty-five years. She was a graduate of Rockford College, in charge of the Hull House gymnasium, and taught at the Chicago Froebel Association. Unfortunately, little other biographical data remains on her.

13. Jane Addams, *My Friend, Julia Lathrop* (New York: Macmillan, 1935), 1f. Refer also to Edward T. James, ed., *Notable American Women: A Biographical Dictionary* Vol. 2 (Cambridge: Belknap Press of Harvard University Press), s.v. "Lathrop, Julia Clifford," by Louise C. Wade.

14. Addams, *My Friend*, 171.

15. Addams, *My Friend*, 23f. Addams noted, however, that William Lathrop did not lead his family in private devotions and prayer.

16. Addams, *My Friend*, 24.

17. *My Friend*, 45.

18. Linn, *Jane Addams: A Biography* (New York: D. Appleton-Century Company, Inc., 1935), 133.

19. *My Friend*, 47.

20. Anna Farnsworth was the first resident to join Addams, Starr, and Keyser. Farnsworth was a woman of independent means and "leisure." She talked with the neighbors, helped them find decent housing, and organized Saturday trips to the park for children of working mothers. Refer to Kathryn Kish Sklar, ed. and introduction, *The Autobiography of Florence Kelley: Notes of Sixty Years* (Chicago: Charles H. Kerr Publishing Company, 1986), 78.

21. "Hull-House: The Realization of An Idea, 1889-1945" (1945?, na), 15. Board of Trustees Papers, UIC-Special Collections.

22. Residents, *Hull-House Maps and Papers* (Boston: Thomas Y. Crowell and Co., 1895), Chapter 8; "Hull-House: The Realization," 15.

23. Refer to Lathrop's publication, *Suggestions for Visitors to County Poorhouses and to Other Public Charitable Institutions* (1905).

24. Letter, Lathrop to Honorable Richard Yates, July 18, 1901. UIC-Special Collections.

25. Edwards, ed., *Notable American Women* Vol. 2, 370.

26. Addams, *My Friend*, 53.

27. *My Friend*, 134.

28. Addams, *My Friend*, 57 and 61.

29. Madeline Parker Grant, *Alice Hamilton; Pioneer Doctor in Industrial Medicine* (London: Abelard-Schuman, 1967), 67; Francis Hackett, *American Rainbow: Early Reminiscences* (New York: Liveright Publishing, 1971), 198.

30. Addams, *My Friend*, 190.

31. Linn, *Jane Addams*, 134.

32. James, *Notable American Women*, Vol. 2, 371.

33. Quoted in Addams, *My Friend*, 227f.

34. Chester McArthur Destler, *Henry Demarest Lloyd and the Empire of Reform* (Philadelphia: University of Pennsylvania Press, 1963), 253.

35. Sklar, ed., *Autobiography of Florence Kelley*, 77. Kathryn Kish Sklar has devoted more than a decade of research to Kelley, and is the expert on her life and work. The first book of a two-volume set is published under the title *Florence Kelley and the Nation's Work: The Rise of Women's Political Culture, 1830–1900* (New Haven: Yale University Press, 1995).

36. *My Friend*, 116.

37. Nicholas Kelley, "Early Days at Hull House," *Social Service Review* Vol. XVIII, No. 4 (Dec. 1954): 426 and 428; *In Memoriam, Jessie Bross Lloyd*, Sept. 27, 1844, to Dec. 29, 1904. UIC-Special Collections.

38. Josephine Goldmark, *Impatient Crusader: Florence Kelley's Life Story* (Urbana: University of Illinois Press, 1953), 35; Nicholas Kelley, "Early Days at Hull House," 429; Frances Perkins, "My Recollections of Florence Kelley," *Social Service Review* Vol. XVIII, No. 1 (March 1954): 14. (Perkins became the first woman cabinet minister in the United States during the tenure of President Franklin Roosevelt.) The Lloyds were likely supportive of Hull House even before its doors opened. Refer to Destler, *Henry Demarest Lloyd*, 252f.

39. Sandra D. Harmon, "Florence Kelley in Illinois," *Journal of the Illinois State Historical Society* Vol. LXXIV, No. 2 (Summer 1981): 165; Kathryn Kish Sklar, "Coming to Terms with Florence Kelley: The Tale of a Reluctant Biographer," in *The Challenge of Feminist Biography: Writing the Lives of Modern American Women*, eds. Sara Alpern, Joyce Antler, Elizabeth Israels Perry, and Ingrid Winther Scobie (Urbana: University of Illinois Press, 1992), 18 and 25.

40. Sklar, ed., *Autobiography of Florence Kelley*, 79.

41. Sklar, ed., *Autobiography of Florence Kelley*, 30f.

42. Sklar, ed., *Autobiography of Florence Kelley*, 31.

43. Sklar, ed., *Autobiography of Florence Kelley*, 37f.

44. Sklar, ed., *Autobiography of Florence Kelley*, 27f.

45. "Early Days at Hull House," 429. For a synopsis of Altgeld's work and life, refer to Alden Whitman, ed. *American Reformers: An H. W. Wilson Biographical Dictionary* (New York: H. W. Wilson Company, 1985), s.v. "Altgeld, John Peter," by James P. Shenton.

46. Allen F. Davis, *American Heroine: The Life and Legend of Jane Addams* (New York: Oxford University Press, 1973), 77f.

47. Amanda Porterfield, *Feminine Spirituality in America: From*

Sarah Edwards to Martha Graham (Philadelphia: Temple University Press, 1980), note 20, 224.

48. Sklar, ed., *Autobiography of Florence Kelley*, 45.

49. Sklar, ed., *Autobiography of Florence Kelley*, 71.

50. Sklar, ed., *Autobiography of Florence Kelley*, 73f.

51. Lillian D. Wald, *Windows on Henry Street* (Boston: Little, Brown, and Company, 1939), 43.

52. Goldmark, *Impatient Crusader*, 17.

53. "Coming to Terms with Florence Kelley: The Tale of a Reluctant Biographer," in *The Challenge of Feminist Biography*, 18.

54. Edward, *Notable American Women* Vol. 2, 317; Goldmark, *Impatient Crusader*, 20. Kelley was always called Mrs. Kelley by her contemporaries.

55. Sklar, ed., *Autobiography of Florence Kelley*, 80f.

56. Edwards, ed., *Notable American Women* Vol. 2, 317. Refer to Kathryn Kish Sklar, "Hull House in the 1890s: A Community of Women Reformers," *Sign: Journal of Women in Culture and Society* Vol. 10, No. 4 (Summer 1984): 658–677, for an analysis of Kelley's role in the 1893 Factory Act.

57. Harmon, "Florence Kelley in Illinois," 167f.

58. Linn, *Jane Addams*, 139f.

59. Madeleine Parker Grant, *Alice Hamilton; Pioneer Doctor in Industrial Medicine* (London: Abelard-Schuman, 1967), 67.

60. Linn, *Jane Addams*, 139.

61. Introduction by Felix Frankfurter in Goldmark, *Impatient Crusader*, ix.

62. Goldmark, *Impatient Crusader*, 57f.

63. Quoted by William L. O'Neill, *Everyone Was Brave: The Rise and Fall of Feminism in America* (Chicago: Quadrangle Books, 1969).

64. Goldmark, *Impatient Crusader*, 77.

65. Perkins, "My Recollections of Florence Kelley," 19.

66. Goldmark, *Impatient Crusader*, 209.

67. Introduction in Goldmark, *Impatient Crusader*.

68. Hamilton, *Exploring the Dangerous Trades* (Boston: Little, Brown and Company, 1943), 60f.

69. Linn, *Jane Addams*, 140.

70. Hamilton, *Exploring*, 64 and 63.

71. Linn, *Jane Addams*, 145.

72. Barbara Sicherman, *Alice Hamilton: A Life in Letters* (Cambridge: Harvard University Press, 1984), 130.

73. Hamilton, *Exploring*, 18.

74. Hamilton, *Exploring*, 31.
75. Hamilton, *Exploring*, 29.
76. Hamilton, *Exploring*, 27f.
77. Hamilton, *Exploring*, 28.
78. Hamilton, *Exploring*, 29.
79. Hamilton, *Exploring*, 35.
80. Hamilton, *Exploring*, 38. Refer to Mary Roth Walsh, *"Doctors Wanted: No Women Need Apply," Sexual Barriers in the Medical Profession, 1835-1975* (New Haven: Yale University Press, 1977) for an overview on women in medicine.
81. Hamilton, *Exploring*, 41.
82. Hamilton, *Exploring*, 42f.
83. Sicherman, *Alice Hamilton*, 90f.; Alice Hamilton, "Edith and Alice Hamilton: Students in Germany," *Atlantic Monthly* Vol. 215, No. 3 (March 1965): 129-132.
84. *Exploring*, 53.
85. Hamilton, *Exploring*, 53f. Hamilton remained in close contact with Agnes, and many of their letters are in Sicherman's collection. Agnes, more evangelical than Alice, eventually became a resident at the Lighthouse Settlement in Philadelphia.
86. Letter, Hamilton to Agnes Hamilton, June 13, 1897. Sicherman, *Alice Hamilton*, 108.
87. Hamilton, *Exploring*, 54f.
88. Letter, Hamilton to Agnes Hamilton, October 13, 1897. Sicherman, *Alice Hamilton*, 115f.
89. Letter, Hamilton to Agnes Hamilton, June 23, 1899. Sicherman, *Alice Hamilton*, 132f.
90. Letter, Hamilton to Agnes Hamilton, June 23, 1899. Sicherman, *Alice Hamilton*, 134.
91. Hamilton, *Exploring*, 75f.
92. Grant, *Alice Hamilton*, 69.
93. Grant, *Alice Hamilton*, 138.
94. Barbara Sicherman and Carol Hurd Green, eds., *Notable American Women, The Modern Period* (Cambridge: Belknap Press of Harvard University, 1980), s.v. "Hamilton, Alice," by Barbara Sicherman, 306.
95. Sicherman, *Alice Hamilton*, 392f.
96. Alice Hamilton, "A Woman of Ninety Looks At Her World," *Atlantic Monthly* Vol. 208, No. 3 (Sept. 1961): 55.
97. Grant, *Alice Hamilton*, 186f.
98. Letter, Hamilton to Katherine Bowditch Codman, January 13, 1959. Sicherman, *Alice Hamilton*, 399.
99. On women as reformers refer to Rosemary Skinner Keller

and Rosemary Radford Ruether, eds., *In Our Own Voices: Four Centuries of American Women's Religious Writing* (San Francisco: HarperCollins, 1995); Carolyn De Swarte Gifford, "Women in Social Reform Movements," in *Women and Religion in America* Vol. 1, eds. Ruether and Keller (San Francisco: Harper and Row, 1981), 294–303.

100. Refer to Barbara Welter, *Dimity Convictions: The American Woman in the Nineteenth Century* (Athens: Ohio University Press, 1976).

101. Refer to Lee Chambers-Schiller, "The Single Woman: Family and Vocation Among Nineteenth-Century Reformers" in *Woman's Being, Woman's Place: Female Identity and Vocation in American History*, ed. Mary Kelley (Boston: G.K. Hall & Co, 1979), 334–350.

102. Refer to Stanton's *The Woman's Bible*, originally published in 1895–98. Numerous reprints are available.

103. Rosemary Skinner Keller, "The Organization of Protestant Laywomen in Institutional Churches," in *In Our Own Voices*, 71.

104. Sklar, ed., *Autobiography of Florence Kelley*, 94f.

105. Refer to Gifford, "Women in Social Reform Movements," 296, for her interpretation on reformers such as Susan B. Anthony, Elizabeth Cady Stanton, and Angelina Grimke: "For many women, reform became their religion, a position of faith as much as a case espoused."

106. For a fascinating analysis of pilgrimage in the lives of three reformers, refer to L. DeAne Lagerquist, "Women and the American Religious Pilgrimage: Vida Scudder, Dorothy Day, and Pauli Murray," in *New Dimensions in American Religious History*, eds. Dolan and Wind (Grand Rapids: William B. Eerdmans Publishing Company, 1993), 208–228.

107. *Writing a Woman's Life* (New York: W.W. Norton & Company, 1988), 22f.

Chapter 6
1. Robert A. Woods and Albert J. Kennedy, eds., *Handbook of Settlements* (New York: The Russell Sage Foundation, 1911), 53.

2. Board of Trustees Minutes, April 1895–July 1919 (Vol. 1). Gertrude Barnum, a Hull House resident, was named assistant treasurer. Refer to Jane Addams' Account Book, 1895–1905, for a complete listing of financial donations and how they were applied to the operating expenses of Hull House. UIC-Special Collections.

3. Anna Morgan, *My Chicago* (Chicago: Ralph Fletcher Seymour, 1918), 140f. Wilmarth was the mother of Anna, who became a social reformer, politician, and writer. In 1911, Anna married Harold Ickes,

a Chicago lawyer who defended Ellen Gates Starr in her labor arrests and who later became Secretary of the Interior.

4. Wilmarth was replaced by Charles L. Hutchinson, wealthy banker and key supporter of the Art Institute of Chicago.

5. Edward T. James, ed., *Notable American Women: A Biographical Dictionary* (Cambridge: Belknap Press of Harvard University, 1971), s.v. "Ickes, Anna Wilmarth Thompson," by J. Leonard Bates, Vol. 2, 251f; Ellen Gates Starr—Box 3, Folder 27, "Notes," and Box 11, Folder 143, "Mary Hawes Wilmarth to Ellen Gates Starr," Sophia Smith Collection.

6. Hull House Scrapbook III, 96; Board of Trustees Minutes—April 1895-July 1919 (Vol. 1). UIC-Special Collections. Dewey is sometimes remembered as an original trustee, an easy enough mistake since Colvin served only for the first year. Refer to Paul U. Kellogg, "Twice Twenty Years at Hull-House," *The Survey* Vol. LXIV, No. 6 (June 15, 1930): 265.

7. Kellogg, "Twice Twenty Years at Hull-House," 266.

8. Alzina Parsons Stevens, "Life in a Social Settlement—Hull-House, Chicago," *Self Culture* Vol. IX, No. 1 (March 1899): 45, 48f. Stevens provides insight into the life and activities of Hull House, but unfortunately, mentions no one by name except for Addams. An article such as this contributed to the perception that the only Hull House person worthy of note was Addams.

9. Herma Clark, *The Elegant Eighties, When Chicago Was Young* (Chicago: A. C. McClurg, 1917), 231. Clark's work, while a fictitious account of Chicago life, was based on her memories and was an attempt to "capture accurately life in the 80s." Refer also to Hull-House Quit-Claim Deed which shows Hull's personal property worth approximately $100,000 and real estate worth approximately $900,000, 32. UIC-Special Collections.

10. Clark, *Elegant Eighties*, 233; Kathleen D. McCarthy, *Noblesse Oblige: Charity and Cultural Philanthropy in Chicago, 1849-1929* (Chicago: University of Chicago, 1982), 154f.

11. Thomas W. Goodspeed, *Helen Culver*, reprinted from *The University Record* Vol. IX, No. 1 (January 1923), 1f. Refer also to Goodspeed, *The University of Chicago Biographical Sketches* Vol. II (Chicago: University of Chicago Press, 1925), 76-99. [Volume I contains a discussion of Charles Jerald Hull's life, 123-145.]

12. *Culver*, 8f.

13. *Elegant Eighties*, 231.

14. Goodspeed, *Culver*, 10.

15. Goodspeed, *Culver*, 11f.

16. Goodspeed, *Culver*, 10f.

17. *Culver*, 13.

18. In 1895, Culver also donated one million dollars worth of property to the University of Chicago, and in 1905 financed the City Club of Chicago. Goodspeed, *Culver*, 16 and 18.

19. Goodspeed, *Culver*, 16f.

20. Quoted in Goodspeed, *Culver*, 14.

21. Goodspeed, *The University of Chicago Biographical Sketches* Vol. I (Chicago: University of Chicago Press, 1922), 141f; Charles Hull, *Reflections from a Busy Life*.

22. Goodspeed notes that Dr. Robert Collyer was Culver's "old pastor", *Culver*, 16; 17, 23.

23. Quoted in McCarthy, *Noblesse Oblige*, 155, from Thomas Wakefield Goodspeed, *The University of Chicago Biographical Sketches* Vol. II (Chicago: University of Chicago Press, 1925), 97.

24. For a short overview of philanthropic ideology, refer to Peter Dobkin Hall, "The History of Religious Philanthropy in America," in *Faith and Philanthropy in America: Exploring the Role of Religion in America's Voluntary Sector*, eds. Robert Withnow and Virginia A. Hodgkinson (San Francisco: Jossey-Bass Publishers, 1990), 38–62.

25. Alice Hamilton, *Exploring the Dangerous Trades* (Boston: Little, Brown and Company, 1943), 67.

26. James Weber Linn, *Jane Addams: A Biography* (New York: D. Appleton-Century Company, Inc., 1935), 147.

27. *Hull-House: The Realization of An Idea, 1889–1945* (nd [1945?], na), 20. Board of Trustees Papers, UIC-Special Collections.

28. Louise deKoven Bowen, *Open Windows: Stories of People and Places* (Chicago: Ralph Fletcher Seymour, 1946), 245f.

29. Eleanor and Mary were not related. *Service to honor the memory of Eleanor Smith*, Founder of Hull-House Music School (June 15, 1858, to June 30, 1942), Hull House, Oct. 3, 1942, 8 and 14. UIC-Special Collections.

30. Jane Addams, *The Excellent Becomes the Permanent* (New York: Macmillan Company, 1932), 29f.; Gale Zona, "Great Ladies of Chicago," *The Survey Graphic* Vol. LXVIII, No. 9 (Feb. 1, 1932): 482.

31. Linn, *Jane Addams*, 147.

32. Robyn Muncy, *Creating A Female Dominion in American Reform, 1890–1935* (New York: Oxford University Press, 1991), 16.

33. Bowen, *Open Windows*, 227.

34. Minutes from January 7, 1895, Residents' meeting. Hull House Residents and Associates, UIC-Special Collections.

35. Allen F. Davis, *American Heroine: The Life and Legend of Jane Addams* (New York: Oxford University Press, 1973), 85f.

36. Blanche Wiesen Cook, "Female Support Networks and Political Activism: Lillian Wald, Crystal Eastman, Emma Goldman," in *A Heritage of Their Own: Toward a New Social History of American Women*, eds. Nancy F. Cott and Elizabeth H. Pleck (New York: Simon and Schuster, 1979), 419. I have found no evidence to support Cook's claim.

37. Bowen, *Open Windows*, 263f.

38. Letter, Alice Hamilton to Edith Hamilton, Feb. 23, 1934, in Barbara Sicherman, *Alice Hamilton: A Life in Letters* (Cambridge: Harvard University Press, 1984), 346f.

39. John Drury, "Old Chicago Houses," *Chicago Daily News*, Sept. 27, 1940, in "Mrs. Joseph T. Bowen, Hull House, 1939-1940," Scrapbook. UIC-Special Collections.

40. Linn, *Jane Addams*, 148. The letters from Addams to Smith provide the basis of the Jane Addams Papers of the Swarthmore College Peace Collection.

41. Linn, *Jane Addams*, 149f.

42. Davis, *American Heroine*, 91.

43. Davis, *American Heroine*, 306, note 45; Sicherman, *Alice Hamilton*.

44. Carroll Smith-Rosenberg, "The Female World of Love and Ritual: Relations Between Women in Nineteenth-Century America," in *A Heritage of Their Own*, eds. Cott and Pleck, 311-342 (also printed in Smith-Rosenberg's book, *Disorderly Conduct*); Martha Vicinus, *Independent Woman: Work and Community for Single Women, 1850-1920* (Chicago: University of Chicago Press, 1985), 158f.

45. For an overview on understandings of female Victorian sexuality, refer to Nancy F. Cott, "Passionlessness: An Interpretation of Victorian Sexual Ideology, 1790-1850," in *A Heritage of Her Own: Toward A New Social History of American Women* eds. Nancy F. Cott and Elizabeth H. Pleck (New York: Simon and Schuster, 1979), 162-181. For overviews on changing sexual mores and the emergence of dualistic heterosexual/homosexual categories, refer to Lillian Faderman, *Surpassing The Love of Men: Romantic Friendship and Love Between Women From the Renaissance to the Present* (New York: William Morrow and Co., Inc., 1981), esp. 147f.; and John D'Emilio and Estelle B. Freedman, *Intimate Matters: A History of Sexuality in America* (New York: Harper and Row, 1988), esp. 190f. For a contemporary study on romantic but asexual lesbian relationships, refer to Esther D. Rothblum and Kathleen A. Brehony, eds., *Boston Marriages: Romantic But Asexual Relationships Among Contemporary Lesbians* (Boston: University of Massachusetts Press, 1993).

46. Cook, "Female Support Networks," 418.

47. Faderman, *Surpassing The Love of Men*, 17. In contemporary North American culture it seems that lesbianism is often a label of self-definition occurring within a lesbian/gay subculture still largely hidden from dominant society.

48. For an example of a recent publication arguing for the lesbian identity of some select historical persons, including Smith and Addams, refer to Dell Richards, *Superstars: Twelve Lesbians Who Changed the World* (Carroll and Graf, 1993). For a general source on lesbian/gay history, refer to Martin Bauml Duberman, Martha Vicinus, and George Chauncey, Jr., eds., *Hidden From History: Reclaiming the Gay and Lesbian Past* (New York: New American Library Books, 1989).

49. Barbara Sicherman and Carol Hurd Green, eds. *Notable American Women, The Modern Period* (Cambridge: Belknap Press of Harvard University, 1980), s.v. "Bowen, Louise deKoven," by Mary Lynn McCree.

50. Bowen, *Growing Up*, 6.

51. Bowen, *Growing Up*, 19.

52. Rima Lunin Schultz, "Woman's Work and Woman's Calling in the Episcopal Church: Chicago, 1880-1989," in *Episcopal Women: Gender, Spirituality, and Commitment in an American Mainline Denomination*, ed. Catherine M. Prelinger (New York: Oxford University Press, 1992), 21.

53. Bowen, *Growing Up*, 46f.

54. Bowen, *Growing Up*, 49.

55. Bowen, *Growing Up*, 45f.

56. Bowen, *Growing Up*, 85.

57. Schultz, "Woman's Work and Woman's Calling," 29.

58. Bowen, *Growing Up*, 51.

59. Bowen, *Open Windows*, 215; *Growing Up*, 86.

60. Bowen, *Growing Up*, 87f.

61. Bowen, *Growing Up*, 88.

62. Linn, *Jane Addams*, 143.

63. Refer to "How to Prevent Delinquency," *The Welfare of Children*, Proceedings of the Two-Hundred and Twenty-Second Regular Meeting of The Commercial Club of Chicago, January 13, 1912: 3-20; *The Colored People of Chicago* (Chicago: Juvenile Protective Association, 1913; *Fighting to Make Chicago Safe for Children* (Chicago: Juvenile Protective Association, 1920).

64. Milton S. Mayer, "First Citizen of Chicago," *Chicago Daily News*, February 20, 1940; Carleton Kent, "Honor First Lady of Hull-House," *Sunday Times*, February 25, 1940. Mrs. Joseph T. Bowen, Hull House 1939-1940—Scrapbook, UIC-Special Collections.

65. Bowen, *Growing Up*, 101.

66. Bowen, *Open Windows*, 203.

67. "Mrs. Joseph T. Bowen, Hull House 1939-1940," Scrapbook. UIC-Special Collections; Louise deKoven Bowen, *Baymeath* (Chicago: privately printed, 1945).

68. Bowen, *Growing Up*, 92f.

69. Hamilton, *Exploring the Dangerous Trades*, 67f.

70. Bowen, *Growing Up*, 94f.

71. Biographical information on Stevens is limited. Refer to Edwards, ed., *Notable American Women* Vol. 3, s.v. "Stevens, Alzina Parsons," by Allen F. Davis; Alden Whitman, ed., *American Reformers: An H. W. Wilson Biographical Dictionary* (New York: The H. W. Wilson Company, 1985), 762; Frances E. Willard and Mary A. Libermore, eds., *A Woman of the Century, Fourteen Hundred-Seventy Biographical Sketches* (Chicago: Charles Wells Moulton, 1893), 684f.

72. Ray Ginger, *Altgeld's America: The Lincoln Deal versus Changing Realities* (New York: Funk and Wagnalls Company, 1958), 134f.

73. Alice Hamilton, *Exploring the Dangerous Trades* (Boston: Little, Brown and Company, 1943), 87f, 63.

74. "Hull-House: The Realization of an Idea, 1889-1945," (nd [1945?], na). Board of Trustees Papers. UIC-Special Collections. The lines referred to were crossed out of the original, apparently not making it into the final published copy; Bowen, *Open Windows*, 145.

75. Rice was an 1891 graduate of the Medical College of New York Infirmary. She likely came to Chicago shortly after graduation, since she was first listed in the *McDonald's Cook County Medical Directory* in 1893. She is listed as an "independent resident" in minutes from a resident's meeting of November 1894. Like Starr, she received a monthly fellowship for at least part of her Hull House residency. An 1895 newspaper article stated that she was a "young colored woman of excellent ability" who was the house physcian and had a private practice (Hull-House Scrapbook III—Clippings and Publications, 1895-1897, 11 and 12. UIC-Special Collections).

A conflict of some kind occurred between Rice and the women of Hull House. In a letter written from Addams to Smith in 1895, Addams stated that Rice "has not the settlement spirit" and that Rice refused to "do anything for the sick neighbors." Addams continued, "I am constantly perplexed about her—JL [Julia Lathrop] promised to talk to her of her race, but never had been one to do so very vigorously" (February 3, 1895, Peace Collection). Rice apparently failed at establishing a private practice and became resident doctor at the Chicago Maternity Hospital before moving to a research position at Columbia Hospital in New York City. Rice wrote to Addams from Boston in 1928:

> I wrote once to dear Miss Mary, but she never answered. So I suppose she did not like it because I told her the absolute truth; or, because she had really believed that I was not strictly honest, or something. Anyway, I had once hoped sometime to see her again before I died; and I always felt it was only fair for her to know that I did not leave H.H. just for fun! (December 7, 1928, Peace Collection)

In a final letter written to Smith in 1933, Rice was in an emotional and financial depression. She lamented her lack of friends and recognition for her life work (June 12, 1933, Peace Collection).

Rice's experience reflected the obverse of historian Bettina Aptheker's analysis that black women doctors who persevered in the late nineteenth and early twentieth centuries were "[s]upported by their communities, inspired by the optimism born of the knowledge that no matter how rough it was, nothing could be worse than slavery" ("Quest for Dignity: Black Women in the Profession, 1865–1900," in her *Woman's Legacy: Essays on Race, Sex and Class in American History* [Amherst: University of Massachusetts Press, 1982], 102f.). Why Rice did not thrive at Hull House is unknown. Unconscious racism and unrealistic demands on the part of white residents, combined with the difficulties associated with a black woman doctor's attempting to establish a private practice, are likely contributing factors.

76. Bowen, "Colored People of Chicago," np.

77. Refer to Elisabeth Lasch-Quinn, *Black Neighbors: Race and the Limits of Reform in the American Settlement House Movement, 1890–1945* (Chapel Hill: University of North Carolina Press, 1993); Bettina Aptheker, intro. and ed., *Lynching and Rape: An Exchange of Views, by Jane Addams and Ida B. Wells* (New York: American Institute for Marxist Studies, Inc., Occasional Paper No. 25, 1977); Emily Townes, *Womanist Justice, Womanist Hope*, American Academy of Religion Academic Series, No. 79 (Atlanta: Scholar's Press, 1993).

78. "Mrs. Joseph T. Bowen Reviews City Cavalcade," 2/20/39, Bowen Scrapbook. UIC-Special Collections.

79. Linn, *Jane Addams*, 142.

80. Bowen, Speech, February 27, 1939. "Mrs. Joseph T. Bowen, Hull House 1930–1940," Scrapbook. UIC-Special Collections.

81. *Baymeath*, 9.

82. Bowen, *Growing Up*, 92.

83. Raymond, *A Passion for Friends: Toward a Philosophy of Female Affection* (Boston: Beacon Press, 1986), 152f.

84. Refer to Michael Pakaluk, ed., *Other Selves: Philosophers on Friendship* (Indianapolis: Hackett Publishing Company, Inc., 1991), 28f.

Conclusion

1. Refer to William R. Hutchison, ed., *American Protestant Thought in The Liberal Era* (Lanham Md.: University Press of America, 1968). Compare to the argument by Eugen Rosenstock-Huessy, *The Christian Future: Or the Modern Mind Outrun* (New York: Harper Torchbooks, 1966), 43f, who argued that "pragmatic" John Dewey forgot—or was silent about—the heritage of his Christian faith and thereby "erected a complete system of agnostic ethics and morality" (p. 44).

2. Hunt, *Fierce Tenderness: A Feminist Theology of Friendship* (New York: New York, 1991), 146.

Select Bibliography

Manuscript Collections

Jane Addams Memorial Collection, University of Illinois at Chicago Circle (UIC-Special Collections).

Jane Addams Papers, Swarthmore College Peace Collection, Series 1. (Peace Collection)

Ellen Gates Starr Papers, Sophia Smith Collection, Smith Collection (Smith Collection).

Works by Hull House Women

Addams, Jane. "A Function of the Social Settlement." ANNALS of the American Academy of Political and Social Science (AAPSS). Vol. 13 (May 1899): 323-345.

———. *Democracy and Social Ethics.* Cambridge: Belknap Press of Harvard University, 1964 (1902).

———. "Social Settlements in Illinois," *An Illinois Reader,* ed. Clyde C. Walton. DeKalb: Northern Illinois University Press, 1970, 323-335. (Originally published in *Transactions of the Illinois State Historical Society,* 1906, 162-171.)

————. "Hull-House, 1889-1909." Chicago: Privately printed, 1909?.

————. "The Reaction of Modern Life Upon Religious Education." *Religious Education*, Vol. IV (April 1909): 23-29.

————. *Twenty Years at Hull-House.* New York: Signet Classic, 1981 (1910).

————. "The Social Situation: Religious Education and Contemporary Social Conditions." *Religious Education*, Vol. VI (June 1911): 145-152.

————. *The Excellent Becomes the Permanent.* New York: Macmillan Company, 1932.

————. *My Friend, Julia Lathrop.* New York: Macmillan Company, 1935.

Addams, Jane and Ellen Gates Starr. "Hull House: A Social Settlement." Printed in pamphlet form on February 1, 1894, revised January 1, 1895. Chicago: Privately printed.

Bowen, Mrs. Joseph T. "How to Prevent Delinquency." *The Welfare of Children*, Proceedings of the Two-Hundred and Twenty-Second Regular Meeting of The Commercial Club of Chicago, January 13, 1912: 3-20.

Bowen, Louise De Koven. *The Colored People of Chicago.* Chicago: Juvenile Protective Association, 1913.

————. *Fighting to Make Chicago Safe for Children.* Chicago: Juvenile Protective Association, 1920.

————. *Growing Up With A City.* New York: Macmillan Company, 1926.

————. *Baymeath.* Chicago: Privately printed, 1945.

————. *Open Windows: Stories of People and Places.* Chicago: Ralph Fletcher Seymour, 1946.

Hamilton, Alice. *Exploring the Dangerous Trades.* Boston: Little, Brown and Company, 1943.

————. "A Woman of Ninety Looks At Her World." *Atlantic Monthly*, Vol. 208, No. 3 (Sept. 1961): 51-55.

————. "Edith and Alice Hamilton: Students in Germany." *Atlantic Monthly*, Vol. 215, No. 3 (March 1965): 129-132.

Hull House Residents. *Hull-House Maps and Papers.* Boston: Thomas Y. Crowell and Co., 1895.

Lathrop, Julia. "What the Settlement Work Stands For." National Conference of Charities and Correction Proceedings, 1896, 106-110. (Reprinted in Pacey, Lorene M., *Readings in the Development of Settlement Work.* New York: Association Press, 1950.)

Sicherman, Barbara, editor. *Alice Hamilton: A Life in Letters.* Cambridge: Harvard University Press, 1984.

Sklar, Kathryn Kish, ed. and introduction. *The Autobiography of Florence*

Kelley: Notes of Sixty Years. Chicago: Charles H. Kerr Publishing Company, 1986.

Starr, Ellen Gates. "Settlements and the Church's Duty." *The Church Social Union* (Boston: Office of the Secretary, The Diocesan House), No. 28 (Aug. 15, 1896).

———. *A Bypath Into the Great Roadway*. (Reprinted from the *Catholic World*, May and June, 1924.) Chicago: Ralph Fletcher Seymour, 1926.

Stevens, Alzina Parsons. "Life in a Social Settlement—Hull-House, Chicago," *Self Culture*, Vol. IX, No. 1 (March 1899): 42-51.

Dissertations/Theses

Barry, David W. "The Relationship of the Social Gospel to the 'settlement idea.'" B.Div. diss., Chicago Theological Seminary, 1941.

Berreth, Edwin Oscar. "Settlement Ideas for the Church." B.Div. diss., Chicago Theological Seminary, 1945.

Cederborg, Hazel Paris. "The Early History of Rockford College." M.A. thesis, Wellesley College, 1929.

Lane, Lionel Charles. "Jane Addams as Social Worker, The Early Years at Hull House." D.S.W. diss., University of Pennsylvania, 1963.

Reep, Samuel Nicholas. "The Organization of the Ecclesiastical Institutions of a Metropolitan Community." Diss., Graduate Divinity School of the University of Chicago, 1910.

Sherrick, Rebecca L. "Private Visions, Public Lives: The Hull-House Women in the Progressive Era." Ph.D. diss., Northwestern University, 1980.

Walsh, John Patrick. "The Catholic Church in Chicago and Problems of an Urban Society: 1893-1915." Ph.D. diss., University of Chicago, 1948.

Articles/Periodicals

Antler, Joyce. "'After College, What?': New Graduates and The Family Claim." *American Quarterly*, Vol. 32, No. 4 (Fall 1980): 409-434.

Barnett, Samuel A. "The Ways of 'Settlements' and of 'Missions.'" *Nineteenth Century* 42 (Dec. 1897): 975-984.

Brown, Joanne Carlson. "Protestant Women and Social Reform." In *In Our Own Voices: Four Centuries of American Women's Religious Writing*, eds. Rosemary Skinner Keller and Rosemary Radford Ruether, 249-260. San Francisco: HarperCollins, 1995.

Campbell, Helen. "Jane Addams of Hull House, Chicago: Her Personality and Philosophy of Life." *The Congregationalist* (*Christian World*), May 4, 1901.

Chambers-Schiller, Lee. "The Single Woman: Family and Vocation Among Nineteenth-Century Reformers." In *Woman's Being, Woman's Place: Female Identity and Vocation in American History*. Boston: G.K. Hall and Company, 1979.

Chicago Commons, 1894 to 1911.

Christopher, Louise. "Henry Whitehead, Circuit Rider." *Chicago History*, Vol. 5, No. 1 (Spring 1976): 2-11.

Clark, Eleanor Grace. "Ellen Gates Starr, OSB (1859-1940), An Account of the Life of the Co-Foundress of HH." *Commonweal*, Vol. XXXI (March 15, 1940): 444-447.

Cleary, James F. "Catholic Participation in the World's Parliament of Religions, Chicago, 1893." *The Catholic Historical Review*, Vol. 55, No. 4 (January 1970): 585-609.

Conway, Jill. "Jane Addams: An American Heroine." *Daedalus*. Vol. 93, No. 2, (Spring 1964): 761-780.

———. "Women Reformers and American Culture, 1870-1930." *Journal of Social History*. Vol. 5, No. 2 (Winter 1971-1972): 166-177.

Davis, Ozora Stearns. "Mansfield House University Settlement." *Hartford Seminary Record*, Vol. IV, No. 2 (Dec 1893): 64-74.

Elshtain, Jean Bethke. "A Return to Hull House: Reflections on Jane Addams." *Cross Currents*, Vol. XXXVIII, No. 3 (Fall 1988): 257-267.

Fish, Virginia Kemp. "The Hull House Circle: Women's Friendships and Achievements." In *Gender, Ideology, and Action*, ed. Janet Sharistanian, 185-227. New York: Greenwood Press, 1986.

Freedman, Estelle. "Separatism as Strategy: Female Institution Building and American Feminism, 1870-1930." *Feminist Studies*, Vol. 5, No. 3 (Fall 1979): 512-529.

Gale, Zona. "Great Ladies of Chicago." *The Survey Graphic*, Vol. LXVIII, No. 9 (Feb. 1, 1932): 479-482.

Gifford, Carolyn De Swarte. "Women in Social Reform Movements." In *Women and Religion in America*, Vol. 1., eds. Rosemary Radford Ruether and Rosemary Skinner Keller, 294-303. San Francisco: Harper and Row, 1981.

Hall, Peter Dobkin. "The History of Religious Philanthropy in America." In *Faith and Philanthropy in America: Exploring the Role of Religion in America's Voluntary Sector*, eds. Robert Withnow and

Virginia A. Hodgkinson, 38-62. San Francisco: Jossey-Bass Publishers, 1990.

Harkness, Georgia. "Jane Addams in Retrospect." *Christian Century*, Vol. LXXVII, No. 2 (January 13, 1960): 39-41.

Harmon, Sandra D. "Florence Kelley in Illinois." *Journal of the Illinois State Historical Society*, Vol. LXXIV, No. 2 (Summer 1981): 163-178.

Hegner, Herman. "Scientific Value of the Social Settlements." *American Journal of Sociology*, Vol. 111, No. 2 (Sept 1897): 171-182.

Hodges, Dean George. "Religion in the Settlement." In *National Conference of Charities and Correction Proceedings*, 1896: 150-153.

Hull-House Bulletin, 1896-1906.

Juliani, Richard N. "The Settlement House and the Italian Family." In *Italian Immigrant Women of North America*, eds. Betty Boyd Caroli, Robert F. Harvey, and Lydio F. Tomasi, 103-123. Ontario: Multicultural Historical Society of Ontario, 1978.

Kalberg, Stephen. "The Commitment to Career Reform: The Settlement Movement Leaders." *Social Service Review*, Vol. 49, No. 4 (December 1975): 608-628.

Keller, Rosemary Skinner. "The Deaconess: 'New Woman' of Late Nineteenth Century Methodism." *Explor: A Journal of Theology*, Vol. 5, No. 1 (Spring 1979): 33-41.

―――. "The Organization of Protestant Laywomen in Institutional Churches." In *In Our Own Voices: Four Centuries of American Women's Religious Writing*, 64-80. San Francisco: HarperCollins, 1995.

Kelley, Nicholas. "Early Days at Hull House." *Social Service Review*, Vol. XXVIII, No. 4 (Dec. 1954): 424-429.

Kellogg, Paul U. "Twice Twenty Years at Hull-House." *The Survey*, Vol. LXIV, No. 6 (June 15, 1930): 265-267.

Kerber, Linda K. "Separate Spheres, Female Worlds, Woman's Place: The Rhetoric of Women's History." *Journal of American History*, Vol. 75, No. 1 (June 1988): 9-39.

Kinceloe, Samuel C. "City Missions, Institutional Churches and Neighborhood Houses." In *The Place of the Church in a Century of Progress, 1833-1933*, 20-23. Chicago: Chicago Church Federation, nd (1933?).

Lagerquist, L. DeAne. "Women and the American Religious Pilgrimage: Vida Scudder, Dorothy Day, and Pauli Murray." In *New Dimensions in American Religious History*, eds. Jay P. Dolan and James P. Wind, 208-228. Grand Rapids: William B. Eerdmans Publishing Company, 1993.

Landes, Joan B. "Women and The Public Sphere: A Modern Perspective." *Social Analysis*, No. 15 (August 1984): 20-31.

Lerner, Gerda. "Placing Women in History: Definitions and Challenges." *Feminist Studies*, Vol. 3, No 1/2 (Fall 1975): 5-14.

McCree, Mary Lynn. "The First Year of Hull-House, 1889-1890, In Letters by Jane Addams and Ellen Gates Starr." *Chicago History* (Fall 1970): 100-114.

Mathews, Shailer. "The Significance of the Church to the Social Movement." *American Journal of Sociology*, Vol. IV, No. 5 (March 1899): 603-620.

———. "The Christian Church and Social Unity." *American Journal of Sociology*, Vol. V, No. 4 (Jan 1900): 456-469.

Mink, Gwendolyn. "The Lady and the Tramp: Gender, Race, and the Origins of the American Welfare State." In *Women, The State, and Welfare*, ed. Linda Gordon, 92-122. Madison: University of Wisconsin Press, 1990.

Perkins, Frances. "My Recollections of Florence Kelley." *Social Service Review*, Vol. XXVIII, No. 1 (March 1954): 12-19.

Rauschenbusch, Walter. "The Stake of the Church in the Social Movement." *American Journal of Sociology*, Vol. III, No. 1 (July 1897): 18-30.

Renner, Richard Wilson. "In a Perfect Ferment: Chicago, the Know-Nothings, and the Riot for Lager Beer." *Chicago History*, Vol. 5, No. 3 (Fall 1976): 161-170.

Rousmaniere, John P. "Cultural Hybrid in the Slums: The College Woman and the Settlement House, 1889-1914." *American Quarterly*, Vol. 22 (1970): 45-66.

Ruether, Rosemary Radford. "Catholic Women in North America." In *In Our Own Voices: Four Centuries of American Women's Religious Writing*, 19-60. San Francisco: HarperCollins, 1995.

Sandburg, Carl. "Chicago." *Chicago Poems*. Urbana: University of Illinois Press, 1992.

Schultz, Rima Lunin. "Woman's Work and Woman's Calling in the Episcopal Church: Chicago, 1880-1989." In *Episcopal Women: Gender, Spirituality, and Commitment in an American Mainline Denomination*, ed. Catherine M. Prelinger, 19-71. New York: Oxford University Press, 1992.

Shapiro, Edward D. "Robert A. Woods and the Settlement House Impulse." *Social Service Review*, Vol. 52, No. 2 (June 1978): 215-226.

Simkhovitch, Mary Kingsbury. "Settlements' Relation to Religion." *AAAPSS*, Vol. XXX, No. 3 (Nov 1907): 490-495.

Sklar, Kathryn Kish. "Hull House in the 1890s: A Community of

Women Reformers." *Signs: Journal of Women in Culture and Society,* Vol. 10, No. 4 (Summer 1985): 658-677.

———. "Religious and Moral Authority as Factors Shaping the Balance of Power for Women's Political Culture in the Twentieth Century." Unpublished paper presented at the 100th anniversary of the founding of Hull House, Rockford, Illinois. October, 1989.

———. "Coming to Terms with Florence Kelley: The Tale of a Reluctant Biographer." In *The Challenge of Feminist Biography: Writing the Lives of Modern American Women,* eds. Sara Alpern, Joyce Antler, Elizabeth Israels Perry, and Ingrid Winther Scobie, 17-33. Urbana: University of llinois Press, 1992.

Szuberla, Guy. "Three Chicago Settlements: Their Architectural Form and Social Meaning." *Journal of the Illinois State Historical Society,* Vol. LXX, No. 2 (May 1977): 114-129.

Taylor, Graham. "The Social Settlement Religion and the Church." In *Christianity and Social Adventuring,* ed. Jerome Davis, 165-176. New York: Century Co., 1927.

U.S. Census Report. 1860 and 1926.

Wade, Louise C. "The Social Gospel Impulse and Chicago Settlement-House Founders." *Chicago Theological Seminary Register,* Vol. LV, No. 8 (April 1965), 1-12.

Welter, Barbara. "The Cult of True Womanhood, 1820-1860." *American Quarterly,* Vol. 18 (Summer 1966): 151-174.

Wise, Winifred E. "Hull-House." In *These Wonderful People,* compiled by Noel Ames, 280-297. Chicago: Consolidated Press, 1947.

Wortman, Marlene Stein. "Domesticating the Nineteenth-Century American City." *PROSPECTS: An Annual of American Cultural Studies,* ed. Jack Salzman, Vol. 13: 531-572. New York: Burt Franklin and Company Inc.

Books

Adams, Henry C., ed. *Philanthropy and Social Progress, Seven Essays.* New York: Thomas Y. Crowell and Company, 1893.

Anderson, Mary, as told to Mary N. Winslow. *Woman At Work.* Minneapolis: University of Minnesota Press, 1951.

Appelbaum, Stanley, text. *Chicago World's Fair of 1893: A Photographic Record.* New York: Dover Publications, Inc., 1980.

Aptheker, Bettina, intro. and ed., *Lynching and Rape: An Exchange of Views, by Jane Addams and Ida B. Wells.* New York: American Insti-tute for Marxist Studies, Inc., Occasional Paper No. 25, 1977.

————. *Woman's Legacy: Essays on Race, Sex and Class in American History.* Amherst: University of Massachusetts Press, 1982.

Barnett, Samuel A. *The Service of God: Sermons, Essays, and Addresses.* London: Longmans, Green, and Co., 1897.

Barnett, Henrietta O. *Canon Barnett: His Life, Work, and Friends.* Two vols. Boston: Houghton Mifflin, 1919.

Beadle, Muriel, and the Centennial History Committee. *The Fortnightly of Chicago, The City and Its Women: 1873–1973.* Chicago: Henry Regnery Company, 1973.

Bellah, Robert N. *et al., Habits of the Heart.* Berkeley: University of California Press, 1985.

————. *The Good Society.* New York: Alfred A. Knopf, 1991.

Blackwell, Alice Stone, ed. *The Little Grandmother of the Russian Revolution: Reminiscences and Letters of Catherine Breshkovsky.* Boston: Little, Brown, and Company, 1917.

Blair, Karen J. *Clubwoman as Feminist: True Womanhood Redefined, 1868–1914.* New York: Holmes and Meier, 1980.

Blanc, Madame. *The Condition of Woman in the United States: A Traveller's Notes.* Boston: Robert Brothers, 1895.

Bliss, W. D. P., ed. *The New Encyclopedia of Social Reform.* New York: Funk & Wagnalls Company, 1908.

Blumberg, Dorothy Rose. *Florence Kelley: The Making of a Social Pioneer.* New York: Augustus M. Kelley, 1966.

Bowie, Fiona, ed. and introduction. *Beguine Spirituality: Mystical Writings of Mechthild of Magdeburg, Beatrice of Nazareth, and Hadewijch of Brabant.* New York: Crossroad, 1990.

Briggs, Asa, and Anna McCartney. *Toynbee Hall: The First Hundred Years.* London: Routledge, Chapman and Hall, 1984.

Buhle, Mari Jo. *Women and American Socialism, 1870–1920.* Urbana: University of Illinois Press, 1981.

Callen, Anthea. *Women Artists of the Arts and Crafts Movement, 1870–1914.* New York: Pantheon Books, 1979.

Carmody, Denise Lardner, and John Tully Carmody, *The Republic of Many Mansions: Foundations of American Religious Thought.* New York: Paragon House, 1990.

Carson, Mina. *Settlement Folk: Social Thought and the American Settlement Movement, 1885–1930.* Chicago: University of Chicago Press, 1990.

Chalvet, S. *Social Settlements in France.* Paris: Centre D'Informations Documentaires, 1936.

Chambers, Clarke. *Seedtime of Reform: American Social Service and Social Action, 1918–1933.* Minneapolis: University of Minnesota Press, 1963.

Christiano, Kevin J. *Religious Diversity and Social Change: American Cities, 1890–1906.* Cambridge: Cambridge University Press, 1987.

Clark, Herma. *The Elegant Eighties, When Chicago Was Young.* Chicago: A. C. McClurg, 1917.

Cole, William. *Motives and Results of the Social Settlement Movement.* Publications of the Department of Social Ethics in Harvard University, No. 2. Cambridge: Harvard University, 1908.

Cott, Nancy. *The Bonds of Womanhood: "Women's Sphere" in New England, 1780–1835.* New Haven: Yale University Press, 1977.

Cott, Nancy F., and Elizabeth H. Pleck, eds. *A Heritage of Her Own: Toward A New Social History of American Women.* New York: Simon and Schuster, 1979.

Cronon, William. *Nature's Metropolis: Chicago and the Great West.* New York: W. W. Norton and Company, 1991.

Curtis, Susan. *A Consuming Faith: The Social Gospel and Modern American Culture.* Baltimore: Johns Hopkins University Press, 1991.

Davis, Allen F. *Spearhead for Reform: The Social Settlements and the Progressive Movement, 1890–1914.* New York: Oxford University Press, 1967.

———. *American Heroine: The Life and Legend of Jane Addams.* New York: Oxford University Press, 1973.

Davis, Allen F., and Mary Lynn McCree, eds. *Eighty Years at Hull-House.* Chicago: Quadrangle Books, 1969.

Deegan, Mary Jo. *Jane Addams and The Men of the Chicago School, 1892–1918.* New Brunswick, N.J.: Transaction, Inc., 1988.

Degler, Carl N. *At Odds: Women and The Family in America From the Revolution to the Present.* New York: Oxford University Press, 1980.

D'Emilio, John, and Estelle B. Freedman. *Intimate Matters: A History of Sexuality in America.* New York: Harper and Row, 1988.

Destler, Chester McArthur. *Henry Demarest Lloyd and the Empire of Reform.* Philadelphia: University of Pennsylvania Press, 1963.

Divers, Vivia H. *The 'Black Hole' or The Missionary Experience of a Girl in the Slums of Chicago, 1891–1892.* Chicago: Privately published, 1893.

Dolan, Jay P. *The American Catholic Experience: A History from Colonial Times to the Present.* Notre Dame: University of Notre Dame Press, 1992.

Donovan, Josephine. *Feminist Theory: The Intellectual Traditions of American Feminism.* New York: Continuum Publishing Company, 1985.

Duberman, Martin Bauml, Martha Vicinus, and George Chauncey, Jr., eds. *Hidden From History: Reclaiming the Gay and Lesbian Past.* New York: New American Library Books, 1989.

Earp, Edwin L. *Social Aspects of Religious Institutions.* New York: Eaton and Mains, 1908.

Ely, Richard. *Social Aspects of Christianity and Other Essays.* New and enlarged edition. New York: Thomas Y. Crowell and Company, 1889.

Faderman, Lillian. *Surpassing The Love of Men: Romantic Friendship and Love Between Women From the Renaissance to the Present.* New York: William Morrow and Co., Inc., 1981.

Farrell, John C. *Beloved Lady: A History of Jane Addams' Ideas on Reform and Peace.* Baltimore: Johns Hopkins Press, 1967.

Frank, Henriette Greenbaum, and Amalie Hofer Jerome, compilers. *Annals of the Chicago Woman's Club for the First Forty Years of its Organization, 1876–1916.* Chicago: Chicago Woman's Club, 1916.

Franklin, R. William, and Joseph M. Shaw. *The Case for Christian Humanism.* Grand Rapids: William B. Eerdmens Publishing Co., 1991.

Gilbert, James. *Perfect Cities: Chicago's Utopias of 1893.* Chicago: University of Chicago Press, 1991.

Ginger, Ray. *Altgeld's America: The Lincoln Deal versus Changing Realities.* New York: Funk and Wagnalls Company, 1958.

Goldmark, Josephine. *Impatient Crusader: Florence Kelley's Life Story.* Urbana: University of Illinois Press, 1953.

Goodspeed, Thomas Wakefield. *A History of The University of Chicago.* Chicago: University of Chicago Press, 1916.

———. *The University of Chicago Biographical Sketches,* Two vols. Chicago: University of Chicago Press, 1922 and 1925.

———. *Helen Culver.* Reprinted from *The University Record,* Vol. IX, No. 1 (January 1923).

Grant, Madeleine Parker. *Alice Hamilton: Pioneer Doctor in Industrial Medicine.* New York: Abelard-Schuman, 1967.

Grossman, James R. *Land of Hope: Chicago, Black Southerners and the Great Migration.* Chicago: University of Chicago Press, 1989.

Hackett, Francis. *American Rainbow: Early Reminiscences.* New York: Liveright Publishing, 1971.

Halper, Albert, ed. *This is Chicago: An Anthology.* New York: Henry Holt and Company, 1952.

Handy, Robert T. *Undermined Establishment: Church-State Relations in America, 1880–1920.* Princeton: Princeton University Press, 1991.

Hayden, Dolores. *The Grand Domestic Revolution: A History of Feminist Designs for American Homes, Neighborhoods, and Cities.* Cambridge: The MIT Press, 1981.

Hartzler, Rev. H. B. *Moody in Chicago or the World's Fair Gospel Campaign, Account of Six Months' Evangelical Work in the City of Chicago and Vicinity During the Time of the World's Columbian Exposition, Conducted by Dwight L. Moody and His Associates.* New York: Fleming H. Revell Company, 1894.

Heilbrun, Carolyn G. *Writing a Woman's Life.* New York: W.W. Norton and Company, 1988.

Henderson, Charles R. *The Social Spirit in America.* Freeport, N.Y.: Books for Libraries Press, 1972 (1897).

————. *Social Settlements.* New York: Lentilhon and Company, 1899.

————. *Social Duties from the Christian Point of View.* Chicago: University of Chicago Press, 1909.

Hill, Mary A. *Charlotte Perkins Gilman: The Making of a Radical Feminist, 1860-1896.* Philadelphia: Temple University Press, 1980.

Hofstadter, Richard. *The Age of Reform.* New York: Alfred A. Knopf, 1955.

Hogan, David John. *Class and Reform: School and Society in Chicago, 1880-1930.* Philadelphia: University of Pennsylvania Press, 1985.

Holli, Melvin G., and Peter D'A. Jones, eds. *Ethnic Chicago*, revised and expanded edition. Grand Rapids: William B. Eerdmans Publishing Company, 1984.

Holmes, David L. *A Brief History of the Episcopal Church.* Valley Forge: Trinity Press International, 1993.

Horowitz, Helen Lefkowitz, *Culture and the City: Cultural Philanthropy in Chicago from the 1880s to 1917.* Lexington: University Press of Kentucky, 1976.

————. *Alma Mater: Design and Experience in the Women's Colleges From Their 19th-Century Beginnings to the 1930s.* New York: Alfred A. Knopf, 1984.

Huggins, Nathan Irvin. *Protestants Against Poverty: Boston Charities, 1870-1900.* Westport: Greenwood Publishing Corporation, 1971.

Hughey, Michael W. *Civil Religion and Moral Order: Theoretical and Historical Dimensions.* Westport: Greenwood Press, 1983.

Hull, Charles. *Reflections from a Busy Life.* Chicago: Knight and Leonard, 1881.

Hunt, Mary E. *Fierce Tenderness: A Feminist Theology of Friendship.* New York: Crossroad, 1991.

Hutchison, William R., ed. *American Protestant Thought in The Liberal Era.* Lanham, Md.: University Press of America, 1968.

Jacobs, Leo. *Three Types of Practical Ethical Movements of the Past Half Century.* New York: MacMillan Company, 1922.

James, Edward T., ed. *Notable American Women, 1607-1950: A Biographical Dictionary.* Three vols. Cambridge: The Belknap Press of Harvard University Press, 1971.

Johnson, Mary Ann, ed. *The Many Faces of Hull-House: The Photographs of Wallace Kirkland.* Urbana: University of Illinois Press, 1989.

Kanter, Rosabeth Moss. *Commitment and Community: Communes and Utopias in Sociological Perspective.* Cambridge: Harvard University Press, 1972.

Keller, Rosemary Skinner, ed. *Spirituality and Social Responsibility: Vocational Vision of Women in The United Methodist Tradition.* Nashville: Abingdon Press, 1993.

Kuzmack, Linda Gordon. *Woman's Cause: The Jewish Woman's Movement in England and The United States, 1881-1933.* Columbus: Ohio State University Press, 1990.

Lasch, Christopher, ed. *The Social Thought of Jane Addams.* Indianapolis: Bobbs-Merrill Company, Inc., 1965.

———. *The New Radicalism in America, 1889-1963.* New York: Alfred A. Knopf, 1965.

Lasch-Quinn, Elisabeth. *Black Neighbors: Race and the Limits of Reform in the American Settlement House Movement, 1890-1945.* Chapel Hill: University of North Carolina Press, 1993.

Lerner, Gerda. *The Majority Finds Its Past: Placing Women in History.* New York: Oxford University Press, 1979.

Levine, Daniel. *Jane Addams and The Liberal Tradition.* Madison: State Historical Society of Wisconsin, 1971.

Linn, James Weber. *Jane Addams: A Biography.* New York: D. Appleton-Century Company, Inc., 1935.

Lippy, Charles H., and Peter W. Williams, eds. *Encyclopedia of the American Religious Experience: Studies of Traditions and Movements.* New York: Charles Scribner's Sons, 1988.

Lissak, Rivka Shpak. *Pluralism and Progressives: Hull House and the New Immigrants, 1890-1919.* Chicago: University of Chicago Press, 1989.

Luker, Ralph E. *The Social Gospel in Black and White: American Racial Reform, 1885-1912.* Chapel Hill: University of North Carolina Press, 1991.

Magnuson, Norris. *Salvation in the Slums: Evangelical Social Work, 1865-1920.* Metuchen, N.J.: Scarecrow Press and The American Theological Library Association, 1977.

Marty, Martin. *Modern American Religion: The Irony of It All, 1893-1919.* Chicago: University of Chicago Press, 1986.

McCarthy, Kathleen D. *Noblesse Oblige: Charity and Cultural Philanthropy in Chicago, 1849–1929.* Chicago: University of Chicago Press, 1982.

Meacham, Standish. *Toynbee Hall and Social Reform.* New Haven: Yale University Press, 1987.

Mead, Rev. George Whitefield. *Modern Methods in Church Work; The Gospel Renaissance.* New York: Dodd, Mead and Company, 1897.

Meigs, Cornelia. *Jane Addams: Pioneer for Social Justice.* Boston: Little, Brown and Company, 1970.

Morgan, Anna. *My Chicago.* Chicago: Ralph Fletcher Seymour, 1918.

Muncy, Robyn. *A Female Dominion in American Reform, 1890–1935.* New York: Oxford University Press, 1991.

Noll, Mark A. *A History of Christianity in the United States and Canada.* Grand Rapids: William B. Eerdmans Publishing Co., 1992.

Ochs, Carol. *Women and Spirituality.* Totowa, N.J.: Rowman and Allanheld, 1983.

O'Neill, William L. *Everyone Was Brave: The Rise and Fall of Feminism in America.* Chicago: Quadrangle Books, 1969.

Pakaluk, Michael, ed. *Other Selves: Philosophers on Friendship.* Indianapolis: Hackett Publishing Company, Inc., 1991.

Phillips, George S. *Chicago and Her Churches.* Chicago: E. B. Myers and Chandler, 1868.

Philpott, Thomas Lee. *The Slum and The Ghetto: Immigrants, Blacks, and Reformers in Chicago, 1880–1930.* Belmont, Cal.: Wadsworth Publishing Company, 1991.

Picht, Werner. *Toynbee Hall and the English Settlements.* London: G. Bell and Sons Ltd., 1914.

Pierce, Bessie Louise, compiler and ed. *As Others See Chicago: Impressions of Visitors, 1673–1933.* Chicago: University of Chicago Press, 1933.

———. *A History of Chicago,* 3 vols. Chicago: University of Chicago Press, 1937–1957.

Pimlott, J. A. R. *Toynbee Hall: Fifty Years of Social Progress, 1884–1934.* London: J.M. Dent, 1935.

Polacheck, Hilda Satt. *I Came A Stranger: The Story of a Hull-House Girl.* Urbana: University of Chicago Press, 1989.

Porterfield, Amanda. *Feminine Spirituality in America: From Sarah Edwards to Martha Graham.* Philadelphia: Temple University Press, 1980.

Raymond, Janice G. *A Passion for Friends: Toward a Philosophy of Female Affection.* Boston: Beacon Press, 1986.

Riley, Thomas James. *The Higher Life of Chicago.* Chicago: University of Chicago Press, 1905.

Robertson, Darrel M. *The Chicago Revival, 1876: Society and Revivalism in a Nineteenth-Century City*. Studies in Evangelicalism, No. 9. Metuchen, N.J.: Scarecrow Press, Inc., 1989.

Rosenstock-Huessy, Eugen. *The Christian Future, Or the Modern Mind Outrun*. New York: Harper Torchbooks, 1966.

Rothblum, Esther D., and Kathleen A. Brehony, eds. *Boston Marriages: Romantic But Asexual Relationships Among Contemporary Lesbians*. Boston: University of Massachusetts Press, 1993.

Sandburg, Carl. *Chicago Poems*. Urbana: University of Illinois Press, 1992 (1916).

Scott, Anne Firor. *Making The Invisible Woman Visible*. Urbana: University of Illinois Press, 1984.

Scudder, Vida. *On Journey*. New York: E. P. Dutton, 1937.

Seager, Richard Hughes, ed. *The Dawn of Religious Pluralism: Voices from the World's Parliment of Religions*. LaSalle, Ill.: Open Court, 1993.

Sheldon, Charles. *In His Steps*. Chicago: Advance Publishing Co., 1897.

Sicherman, Barbara, and Carol Hurd Green, eds. *Notable American Women, The Modern Period*. Cambridge: Belknap Press of Harvard University, 1980.

Smith, Timothy L. *Revivalism and Social Reform in Mid-Nineteenth-Century America*. New York: Abingdon Press, 1957.

Smith, T. V., and Leonard D. White. *Chicago: An Experiment in Social Science Research*. Chicago: University of Chicago Press, 1929.

Smith-Rosenberg, Carroll. *Disorderly Conduct: Visions of Gender in Victorian America*. New York: Oxford University Press, 1985.

Soloman, Barbara Miller. *In The Company of Educated Women: A History of Women and Higher Education in America*. New Haven: Yale University Press, 1985.

Soloman, Hannah G. *Fabric of My Life*. New York: Bloch Publishing Company, 1946.

Spear, Allan H. *Black Chicago: The Making of a Negro Ghetto, 1890–1920*. Chicago: University of Chicago Press, 1969.

Stackhouse, Perry J. *Chicago and the Baptists: A Century of Progress*. Chicago: University of Chicago Press, 1933.

Stead, William T. *If Christ Came to Chicago: A Plea for the Union of All Who Love in the Service of All Who Suffer*. Evanston: Chicago Historical Bookworks, 1990 (1894).

Stelzle, Charles. *Christianity's Storm Centre: A Study of the Modern City*. New York: Fleming H. Revell Company, 1907.

———, et al. *The Social Application of Religion*. The Merrick Lectures for 1907–1908. Cincinnati: Jennings and Graham, 1908.

Thompson, Warren E. *Building a Christian Chicago: A History of the Chicago Congregational Union, 1882–1932*. np., 1932.

Tims, Margaret. *Jane Addams of Hull-House: 1860-1935.* London: George Allen and Unwin Ltd., 1961.

Townes, Emily M. *Womanist Justice, Womanist Hope.* American Academy of Religion Academic Series, No. 79. Atlanta: Scholars Press, 1993.

Trolander, Judith Ann. *Professionalism and Social Change: From the Settlement House Movement to Neighborhood Centers, 1886 to Present.* New York: Columbia University Press, 1987.

Tucker, Cynthia Grant. *Prophetic Sisterhood: Liberal Women Ministers on the Frontier.* Boston: Beacon Press, 1990.

Vicinus, Martha. *Independent Women: Work and Community for Single Women, 1850-1920.* Chicago: University of Chicago Press, 1985.

Wade, Louise C. *Graham Taylor: Pioneer for Social Justice, 1851-1938.* Chicago: University of Chicago Press, 1964.

Wagenknecht, Edward. *Chicago.* Norman: University of Oklahoma Press, 1964.

Wald, Lillian D. *Windows on Henry Street.* Boston: Little, Brown, and Company, 1939.

Walsh, Mary Roth. *"Doctors Wanted: No Women Need Apply," Sexual Barriers in the Medical Profession, 1835-1975.* New Haven: Yale University Press, 1977.

Warner, Amos Griswold, et al. *American Charities and Social Work.* 4th ed. New York: Thomas Y. Crowell Company, 1930.

Weimann, Jeanne Madeline. *The Fair Women: The Story of the Woman's Building, World's Columbian Exposition, Chicago 1893.* Chicago: Academy Press, 1981.

White, Jr., Ronald C., and C. Howard Hopkins. *The Social Gospel: Religion and Reform in Changing America.* Philadelphia: Temple University Press, 1976.

Whitman, Alden, ed. *American Reformers: An H. W. Wilson Biographical Dictionary.* New York: H. W. Wilson Company, 1985.

Willard, Frances E. *How I Learned to Ride the Bicycle: Reflections of an Influential 19th Century Woman,* introduction by Edith Mayo, edited by Carol O'Hare. Sunnyvale, Cal.: Fair Oaks Publishing, 1991.

Wilson, Christine. *Thirty Neighborhood Houses: A Survey of Thirty Presbyterian Neighborhood Houses.* New York: Board of National Missions of the Presbyterians Church in the U.S.A., Department of City, Immigrant and Industrial Work, 1925.

Woodroofe, Kathleen. *From Charity to Social Work: In England and the United States.* London: Routledge and Kegan Paul, 1968.

Woods, Robert A., and Albert J. Kennedy, eds. *Handbook of Settlements.* New York: Russell Sage Foundation, 1911.

————, eds. *The Settlement Horizon: A National Estimate.* New York: Russell Sage Foundation, 1922.

Zorbaugh, Harvey Warren. *The Gold Coast and the Slum: A Sociological Study of Chicago's Near North Side.* Chicago: University of Chicago Press, 1929.

Appendix

List of residents who have been at Hull House for six months or longer (from Appendix, *Hull-House Maps and Papers*, 1895).

Jane Addams
Ellen Starr
Julia Lathrop
Florence Kelley
Mary A. Keyser
* Anna M. Farnsworth
Agnes Sinclair Holbrook
Josephine Milligan, MD
Wilfreda Brockway
Rose M. Gyles
Gertrude Barnum
Ella Raymond Waite

Annie Fryar
Josefa Humpal Zeman
Margaret M. West
* Jeannette C. Welch
Enella Benedict
* Clifford W. Barnes
* Alex A. Bruce
* Edward L. Burchard
* Henry B. Learned
* Chas C. Arnold
John Adams Linn
Edwin A. Waldo

*No longer in residence

As of January 1, 1895, twenty residents lived at Hull House, including those who had not yet resided for six months.

Residents and Resident Workers

(From "Hull-House: A Social Settlement," January 15, 1895. Pamphlet originally published on February 1, 1894)

Living at Hull-House: Miss Addams, Miss Starr, Mrs. Kelley,
    Miss Keyser, Miss Barnum, Miss West, Miss Benedict,
    Miss Crain, Miss Gyles, Miss Waite, Miss Fryer,
    Madam Conovor, Miss Warner, Mrs Zeman
Living at 247 Polk Street: Mr. Waldo, Mr. Linn, Mr. Pierson
Living at 245 Polk Street: Mr. Sikes
Living at 247 Ewing Street: Dr. Rice
Living at 186 Polk Street: Mr. and Mrs. Valocio
Living at 253 Ewing Street: Jane Club (50 members)
Living at 245 Polk Street: Phalanx Club (10 members)

Index

Boldface numerals indicate photograph